REWRITING SHAKESPEARE, REWRITING OURSELVES

REWRITING SHAKESPEARE, REWRITING OURSELVES

PETER ERICKSON

University of California Press

Berkeley · Los Angeles · Oxford

University of California Press
Berkeley and Los Angeles, California

University of California Press, Ltd.
Oxford, England

© 1991 by
The Regents of the University of California

Library of Congress Cataloging-in-Publication Data

Erickson, Peter.
  Rewriting Shakespeare, rewriting ourselves / Peter
Erickson.
    p. cm.
  Includes bibliographical references and index.
  ISBN 0-520-07445-9 (cloth)
    1. Shakespeare, William, 1564–1616—Criticism and
interpretation—History—20th century. 2. Shakespeare,
William, 1564–1616—Appreciation—United States. 3.
Feminism and literature—United States—History—20th
century. 4. Women and literature—United States—His-
tory—20th century. 5. Shakespeare, William, 1564–
1616—Characters—Women. 6. Sex role in literature.
7. Women in literature.   I. Title.
  PR2971.U6E75 1991
  822.3′3—dc20   91-28856
                                                    CIP

Printed in the United States of America
9 8 7 6 5 4 3 2 1

The paper used in this publication meets the minimum
requirements of American National Standard for
Information Sciences—Permanence of Paper for Printed
Library Materials, ANSI Z39.48-1984. ♾

For my parents,
Elinor Brown Erickson
and
Irving Peter Erickson

Contents

Acknowledgments

I am grateful to Harry Berger and Doris Kretschmer for valuable support. The scholars whose work and conversation I have had most in mind while writing this book are Jean Howard, Louis Montrose, and Carol Neely. I thank my wife, Tay Erickson, whose art work provides an inspiring standard, and my children, Andrew, Ingrid, and Benjamin, who have given me more energy than I thought possible.

For citations to Shakespeare's works, I have used throughout the New Arden editions. An abridged version of chapter 8 appeared in *Women's Re-Visions of Shakespeare*, ed. Marianne Novy (Urbana: University of Illinois Press, 1990).

In a sense the very power of the expanded
Marxist tradition can supply a reason for
renouncing what still seems to me the
necessary engagement with the established
English culture. Why do I discuss a minor
18th-century poet in more detail than I do
Marx? Because this is where a really
reactionary social consciousness is being
continually reproduced, and to till your own
alternative garden to it is not enough. In fact,
it would be a trap for me.

Raymond Williams,
Politics and Letters (1979)

It may be that we must see the continuous
centring of Shakespeare as the cultural token
which must be appropriated as itself tending
to reproduce the existing order: that however
the plays are presented they will exercise a
relatively conservative drag, that any radical
influence can hardly extend beyond the
educated middle class, that in practice
conservative institutions are bound to
dominate the production of such a national
symbol, and that for one cultural phenomenon
to have so much authority must be a
hindrance to radical innovation.

Alan Sinfield,
Political Shakespeare (1985)

INTRODUCTION:
CRITICAL LOCATIONS

This project takes off from two quite distinct areas of literary study: first, the new historicism as practiced in English Renaissance scholarship; second, contemporary feminist criticism as exemplified by Adrienne Rich. My interest is in points of intersection between the two modes.

One common denominator is the effort to locate the critic in his or her own historical moment. In new historicism this concern is expressed in the latest work of Louis Adrian Montrose and Leah S. Marcus. As Montrose notes, "Not only the poet but also the critic exists in history."[1] Marcus comments: "'Localization' is an idea we need to apply to ourselves as readers as well as to what we read."[2] This emphasis on the critic's historical location can be linked to recent developments in the feminist criticism of Adrienne Rich. "Notes toward a Politics of Location (1984)," the title of the final essay in Rich's collection *Blood, Bread, and Poetry*, signals the volume's focus on location.

The link between new historicist and feminist articulations of this issue is reinforced by what can be called the historicist turn in Rich's work. Rich renounces her earlier tendency to use the terms *patriarchy* and *women* as monolithic entities and adopts a more multifaceted and historically differentiated account. Acknowledging the danger of abstraction when "the concept of patriarchy" becomes "a backstop in which all the foul balls of history end up," Rich stresses instead that "patriarchy has no pure and simple existence," "patriarchy exists nowhere in a pure state."[3] Correspondingly, Rich places greater stress on differences among women.

1

Yet the juxtaposition of passages from Montrose and Marcus on one hand and from Rich on the other also reveals striking contrasts. Compared to the specificity and detail of Rich's analysis of the critic's location, new historicist statements appear abstract, brief, and peripheral. Moreover, Rich's treatment of location strikes a more consistently strong, explicit political note. Montrose's revision of his earlier work—to invoke the spirit of Rich's use of the term[4]—goes some distance toward closing the gap between new historicist and feminist dispositions. His title, "Professing the Renaissance: The Poetics and Politics of Culture," makes the political a more visible, central category. However, while Montrose's essay touches on most of the issues discussed in this book, his often highly condensed formulations need elaboration. In particular, I want to pursue conjunctions between new historicism and feminist criticism in order to clarify and extend the scope of the terms *historical* and *political*.

The organization of this study is designed to foster an exploration of these terms. The movement between Part 1, with its focus on Shakespeare's work in its Renaissance cultural context, and Part 2, with its shift to twentieth-century literature, enlarges and highlights the interactions between past and present that we construct and negotiate. The collocation of Parts 1 and 2 raises the issue of the critic's location by preventing a one-way historicism that sheds the present to enter the past. The format manifests a two-directional concept of the relationship between past and present.

In any critical endeavor we may be dimly aware of an uncanny double resonance, as though we were writing two histories at once: the history of the period from which the literature comes and the history of our own period.[5] This dual context is sometimes easier to see when we reconstruct the history of criticism in an earlier era. This phenomenon applies whether the focus of the criticism is on Renaissance or on twentieth-century literature. To be sure, in the first case the periods of author and critic are separate, whereas in the second they coincide. But in both, critical activities are conducted from the same historical location in the present; both are marked by their context in our own moment. Because no study of the past is totally separated from, or uninformed by, the present, the historical distinction between past and present is relative rather than absolute. Thus both phrases in the title of this book, *Rewriting Shakespeare, Rewriting Ourselves*, apply equally to both parts of the study. In both sections the figure criticism makes is twofold: it is the figure of the critic as well as of the artist.

Because the two parts of this study together raise questions about the formation and reformulation of the literary canon, the book's organization calls attention to the term *political* as a distinct category. The term *historical* is not enough. It is not self-sufficient; nor should it encompass and subsume the political. Although my immediate reference point for the political as an analytic concept is the canon question, I want to comment more generally on this component of my criticism. I use the term not only to bring out the political implications of the literature under study but also to indicate the values, choices, and commitments involved in our own critical writing. I reject the automatic equation of the political with the reductive: political analysis and intellectual complexity are not mutually exclusive. One does not cease to be scholarly when one starts to be political. For example, the political element in feminist criticism refers to a set of issues to be explored, not to a set of fixed positions to which one must subscribe. As with any ongoing scholarly investigation, the issues develop and change and, at any given point, feminist critics may and do sharply disagree. The field of feminist inquiry includes the disagreements. At the same time, this disagreement does not preclude active commitment, within one's criticism, to social change.

Literary criticism has recently taken on a more overt political cast partly because the barriers that normally separate and isolate academic work from public discourse have suddenly become permeable. The emergence of the literary canon as a public policy issue worthy of notice at the level of national politics has given scholarly study a symbolic impact outside the boundaries of professional discourse.[6] Whether this impact proves a constraint or an opportunity (or both) depends on how its cultural symbolism is interpreted—on whose terms, in the struggle over interpretive control, gain the widest resonance, the fullest power to convince. It is important not to characterize the struggle itself as merely the product of conservative Republican resistance. The unease that a changing canon generates is far more pervasive, cutting across traditional political lines.

Taking an example from liberal journalism as a case in point, consider the feature article on "The Battle of the Books" that appeared in the Sunday *New York Times Magazine* for June 5, 1988. Of particular interest is the way that visual images, starting with Edward Sorel's vivid cover illustration, frame the debate. In Sorel's image, angry classical authors are massed in protest against a perceived threat to their cultural standing. Shakespeare is given a visual prominence befitting his instantly recognizable status as preeminent symbol of the established tradition. Shakespeare stands out not only because he literally rises above the crowd but also because of the singular determination of his protest: unlike the surrounding figures, who bear placards, Shakespeare brandishes a sword. Gentle Shakespeare's aggressive display and potential violence are evidently justified because he is the last line of defense in the protection of a cultural ideal.

Sorel's illustration counterpoints a photograph inside the magazine, at the beginning of the article, showing black students at Stanford demonstrating against the standard course in western civilization in favor of a new, modified version. How is Shakespeare's name being used here? The arrangement of visual images (which James Atlas's text does next to nothing to disrupt) polarizes our response: either we are for Shakespeare or we are for black students. But the question is loaded, settled in advance, because the overall framework is weighted toward Shakespeare. Who could be against Shakespeare? is the self-evident message of this visual medium. The smooth operation of this one-sided dichotomy is promoted by the conspicuous absence of black faculty from both visual and textual representation. The article's title page pairs the black student demonstrators with the larger-than-life, full-color image of a white male academic.[7] The back pages include pictures of three white female faculty, but the layout awards the central power position of mediating between black students and Shakespeare to the white male, whose self-preoccupied expression combines toughness with latent weariness and anguish. I want to suggest the narrowness of the visual frame by noting how a different sense of power relations and of intellectual possibilities might be communicated by giving prominence instead to a black scholar.

The basic assumption sustaining this oversimplified version of Shakespearean/minority tension is that, since Shakespeare is a fixed, unchanging point, then all change can be portrayed as challenges coming from outside, from external, somehow alien forces. In this view, so long as Shakespeare's position is kept secure, his mere presence induces order as a magnet organizes iron filings. But this image of Shakespeare neglects or denies the reformulation of the canon from inside through the reinterpretation of canonical figures, including Shakespeare. Within current Shakespeare studies, new historicists and feminist critics agree that Shakespeare's work cannot be treated as aesthetically autonomous or historically transcendent. Like a protective mantle shorn of its magical efficacy, the assertion of Shakespeare's special universality, which seemed hitherto to exempt his works from critical questions concerning gender, class, race, and national identity, no longer convinces. The result is a complicated reassessment of Shakespeare that contributes to the larger projects of rewriting the Renaissance and of revaluating the entire literary tradition.

The debate is not about Shakespeare's elimination from the canon but rather about the terms on which his work is to be included. The first step toward a more accurate approach is to acknowledge that Shakespeare is not a static icon, to be defended by any means necessary, but part of the change. This is only a first step, however. For when we move from a simple either/or split to a conception that includes both sides, the difficulties begin: what exactly are the ramifications of "opening up" and "expanding" the canon when we view the overall effort as a whole rather than as the piecemeal operations of compartmentalized subsections?

The inclusionist model does not in itself resolve matters because it can be understood according to two different principles—one of addition, the other of transformation. The logic of addition implies an incremental process of admission by which only individual authors make the grade and only the truly great need apply. The additive method suggests that the concept of the canon remains intact and need not come under scrutiny. The alternative principle of transformation means a fundamental change in the conventions by which we understand and organize canons. This latter view, which is the one I shall adopt here, leads, I think, to a more productive formulation of questions about the interrelationships among works in an expanded literary tradition.

My position can be summarized as follows. Part 1 of this study demonstrates that I continue to be a committed Shakespearean; Part 2 shows that I have an equally strong commitment to contemporary minority literatures and that Shakespeare in no way justifies a canonical status quo. These two activities are not mutually exclusive professional options between which one must choose. Bringing them together within the framework of a single book makes possible a sustained examination of the relationship between the two, especially as it bears on the question of conflict. The aim of my procedure is not to eliminate conflict but rather to provide a different, more sophisticated basis for considering it. The sense of tension between established and emergent traditions is expressed in the specific questions that motivate my study: What effect does a revised canon have on Shakespeare's position? How does our relationship to Shakespeare's work change in the new context?

At the outset, however, I want to acknowledge a possible problem with my inquiry, since the very form of my leading questions, with their focus on Shakespeare, may signify a built-in constraint. Does the attempt to read contemporary literature in relation to Shakespeare actually privilege Shakespeare and thus reinstate the standard canonical measure I am purportedly revising?[8] It is not my purpose to convict others of ideological difficulties while claiming exoneration for myself. But if I am naming my own ideological bind here, I want to clarify its outlines in order to avoid misconception. There are two ways to read the epigraphs at the beginning of this book. In a positive view, the two passages from Raymond Williams and Alan Sinfield can be read as a sequence that defines the book's double commitment: Williams's remarks justify the continuing need to study Shakespeare, while Sinfield's suggest the importance of finding alternate literary resources so as not to be confined to Shakespeare. Also possible, however, is a more negative construction that sees the passages not as two phases of a coordinated effort but rather as two sides in a disagreement; from this vantage, Williams's dedication is sharply undercut by Sinfield's acidly corrosive skepticism.

Sinfield's comments occur in "Reproductions, Interventions," his introduction to the second half of *Political Shakespeare*, which examines how contemporary institutions process Shakespeare's work. Sinfield's pessimism about the political efficacy of such investigation comes close to shutting down the whole project before it starts: since the power of hegemonic Shakespearean reproduction is so total, the prospects for an intervention that could change this course seem nil. Although the two-part structure of this book resembles the organization of *Political Shakespeare*, there is an important difference in their respective second parts. Whereas *Political Shakespeare* focuses on representations of Shakespeare in contemporary theatrical performance and pedagogy, my study turns to the distinctly different cultural site of contemporary literature, which has relatively more room for imaginative free play and for the development of an independent perspective. How is Shakespeare represented *here*? What interventions are possible in this particular cultural space? This shift reopens the question of Shakespeare's position in determining the overall orientation of the canon and makes it possible to avoid Sinfield's dispirited anticipation of a foregone conservative conclusion.

I

This study bears, in various ways, the marks of its historical moment; the best way to establish my own ideological situation is to trace the book's immediate context in critical developments through the 1980s. During the past ten years, four major lines of criticism—psychoanalytic, feminist, new historicist, and cultural materialist—have emerged and coalesced. Symbolic markers for these critical trends are, respectively, *Representing Shakespeare: New Psychoanalytic Essays* (1980); *The Woman's Part: Feminist Criticism of Shakespeare* (1980); *Renaissance Self-Fashioning: From More to Shakespeare* (1980); and *Political Shakespeare: New Essays in Cultural Materialism* (1985).[9] The convergence of these forces is very strong; it is as though all four were trying to occupy the same space in different ways. The present book locates itself in, and is located by, the highly turbulent confluence of the four critical currents.

Several ways of coping with the tensions among the four modes suggest themselves. The most attractive is reconciliation through synthesis. In my experience this approach does not survive close examination. The chief impediment is the crucial issue of whose terminology, assumptions, and overall framework will implicitly direct and incorporate the others. In an attempt to avoid the basic dilemma of which critical mode should have precedence, we may entertain other options. We can envision a purely tactical collaboration by appealing to the idea of a united front that draws attention to external opponents and that emphasizes common interests by muting or glossing over internal differences. We can settle for a disengagement whereby competing modes try to go their separate ways. We can say that the labels themselves are the problem and make them disappear by proposing a moratorium.

There is much to be said against labels. Given the constant flux and rapid change in current critical theories, the predictive reliability of labels diminishes and it seems only prudent to steer clear of them. Labels are too crude to keep pace with subtle intellectual shifts. Moreover, they can encourage artificial divisiveness and intellectual oversimplification when they function solely as paltry counters in professional networking and rivalry. Yet critical labels do have intellectual value because they encode our history and point to genuine differences of approach. It is an escapist fantasy to assume that we can declare all labels null and void, start over again with a clean slate, and go back to being plain Shakespeareans without fancy modifiers.

Labels are not immutable; neither are they disposable. At the beginning of his admirable analysis of London's topography, for example, Steven Mullaney advocates dropping the term *new historicism* in favor of Raymond Williams's *cultural materialism*.[10] I find this move unconvincing because Mullaney speaks as though it could be accomplished by the act of renaming; he neither acknowledges nor works through the significant philosophical differences between the two modes. In Mullaney's highly selective use of Williams, the aspect conspicuously missing is the contemporary political commitment that so strongly accented and enhanced Williams's scholarship. The presence or lack of political spirit is a principal distinguishing mark between cultural materialism and most new historicism. Although Mullaney adopts the cultural materialist name, the absence of its spirit means that he remains substantially a new historicist in practice.

My own proposal concerning the terms *psychoanalytic, feminist, new historicist,* and *cultural materialist* is that we should focus on rather than elide the differences and conflicts among them. We must squarely face the paradox that these differences are too important to ignore but also too intractable to lend themselves to easily harmonious collaboration. I believe this exploration of critical difference can be a constructive process—if also admittedly a stressful one—because the potential for intellectual breakthrough at the intersection of our differences is so great. The critical labels present both a historical burden and a historical opportunity; it is a major part of the critical labor of our period to sort through the difficulties specific to the relations among psychoanalytic, feminist, new historicist, and cultural materialist variants. For me, the discussion of our internal differences is where the main hope for progress lies. The exploration of the interrelations among the four modes is not the monopoly of one group but must be undertaken from different points of view, each of which frankly declares its priorities. In my case, a feminist perspective organizes the use of the other three elements in the critical mix.[11] I now turn to a more personal account of this perspective in order to define the terms of this particular study. I do not mean to present myself as a totally free agent single-handedly inventing a new critical world but rather as one responding to, and shaped by, a process larger than any one individual. My particular feminist-centered orientation is only one approach, one part of a collective generational project; other approaches are needed for a full picture.

My first book was written largely within the tradition of American feminist psychoanalytic criticism of Shakespeare as it existed at the end of the 1970s. The development of which this book is a record can be summarized as a shift away from psychoanalytic criticism toward an intensive engagement with new historicism and cultural materialism for the purpose of strengthening feminist criticism by expanding its bases. Feminist criticism remains my primary commitment; the overall goal of the interaction with other modes is to make my work more feminist, not less, in the spirit of Adrienne Rich's "Toward a More Feminist Criticism."[12]

It is too early to speak of a second wave of feminist criticism of Shakespeare, but the first wave, having made its contribution, has lost much of its momentum as a sharply defined entity. The original core group of feminist Shakespeare critics has to some extent dispersed; other critics who do not belong to this group and do not share its purview have decisively entered the field. The result is that the disagreements within the original group no longer set and control the agenda. Were a sequel to *The Woman's Part* to be published

ten years later, its introduction would be very different from
that of the first: the various strands are much more heterogeneous and consequently more difficult to coordinate. Such
a development is to be expected as part of what Carol Neely
calls "Feminist Criticism in Motion."[13]

In order to delineate my critical locations more precisely, I
shall undertake a brief survey of the benefits and drawbacks
of psychoanalytic, new historicist, and cultural materialist approaches, as seen from my particular feminist standpoint.
The value of psychoanalytic criticism lies for me in its focus
on family politics and especially in its emphasis on the way
definitions of gender are refracted and shaped by family
roles. More generally, I find attention to psychological states
and fantasies an indispensable component of cultural analysis. In my view, the principal difficulty is that psychoanalytic approaches tend to constitute an inclusive explanatory
system that encourages reliance on a self-enclosed, self-validating world view. Even when no conflict is seen in principle,
psychoanalytic critical practice leaves out historical and social
analysis. In particular, gender and sexual politics cannot be
treated as exclusively psychological concepts. Categories of
gender and sexuality within a Freudian tradition, even as
perceptively revised, for example, by Nancy Chodorow, are
too fixed and encumbered to serve as an adequate basis for
the full critical exploration required by feminist criticism. A
much wider range of reference is needed, for which one must
in part look elsewhere.

These reservations have led me to reassess the close connections between psychoanalytic and feminist criticism in
American Shakespeare studies and to want to loosen, if not
altogether break, this tie. The historical links between the two
modes at the inception of feminist Shakespeare criticism in
the United States do not entail a necessary, intrinsic connection. I think it is important now to construct an independent
feminist criticism capable both of critically evaluating psychoanalytic frameworks and of ranging widely outside their
boundaries. In this effort, I am not repudiating my own genealogy or trying to get psychoanalysis completely "out of

my system," as one critic put it.[14] Rather, I am aiming for a shift in the relative weight assigned to the various resources in the critical repertoire; this realignment involves a de-emphasis on, rather than abandonment of, psychoanalytic criticism, upon which I continue to draw.

One reason for this shift of emphasis has been the impact of new historicism, with its focus on historical, culture-specific contexts. I accept the new historicist argument as compelling at this level and, in particular, my commentary on Queen Elizabeth in this book has been inspired by new historicist work. As I see it, the problems with new historicism have been its avoidance of gender issues, its one-sided preoccupation with containment, and its silence about contemporary political implications.[15] Louis Montrose has always been an exception to these generalizations, and his new essay, "Professing the Renaissance: The Poetics and Politics of Culture," is exemplary in this regard. Nevertheless, Montrose's explicit acknowledgment of the value of feminist interpretation is not the same as making theoretical provision for the full scope of feminist investigation within a new historicist program. The question is one not of symbolism but of intellectual control. For Montrose, new historicism is understandably the center around which everything else is arrayed; to place feminist criticism under this new historicist rubric is to risk less outright neglect or absorption than the danger of having feminist concerns factored in as tangential or secondary considerations.

In several respects, British cultural materialism offers useful alternatives to the treatment prevalent in American new historicism. Cultural materialism provides a more balanced account of the containment / subversion issue, with greater allowance for the prospects of resistance and opposition; places more stress on class divisions and on their relation to national identity; and manifests a political stance that has palpable designs on the present.[16] Given different cultural conditions in England and the United States, a key question is whether and how the cultural materialist political profile can be applied in an American context. In this connection

Shakespeare Reproduced: The Text in History and Ideology (1987) is an important landmark. Though its contributions were not exclusively American, the collection's main immediate application was to the United States; adapting the model of *Political Shakespeare*, *Shakespeare Reproduced* showed that ideological criticism could be initiated in an American context. While British cultural materialism cannot be mechanically imported, neither is its transfer automatically blocked by a permanent cultural divide. As with new historicism, however, it is necessary to ask what status is accorded to specifically feminist issues within cultural materialism.

The conclusion of this review is that psychoanalytic criticism, new historicism, and cultural materialism all offer significant resources but that none can be fully hospitable to feminist criticism because each has other priorities and criteria that interfere with a strong feminist emphasis. I am committed to using psychoanalytic, new historicist, and cultural materialist elements in my work because I value their accomplishments and because feminist criticism without them is less rich and complex than it could be. But I need both to mine the insights of these other critical modes and to examine them. While valuable, they also in their different ways inhibit—actively impede—the full development of a feminist perspective.

II

The missing ingredient in the preceding overview of critical modes is new criticism. There is a tendency, amounting to a consensus, to assume that new criticism has been superseded and to shun it accordingly. I want to reintroduce new criticism, understood as close reading, as a valid element in the current situation. I pursue this methodological issue through the cogent interchange between Louis Montrose and Harry Berger in *Revisionary Play: Studies in the Spenserian Dynamics*,[17] and I examine the terms of debate in detail because of their close bearing on my own concerns here.

The ostensible subject of Montrose's account of Berger's

work is Berger's relation to new historicism; but the real agenda involves the status of new criticism. Montrose's attempt to construct a new historicist lineage deriving from Berger oscillates between citing Berger as forerunner and criticizing him for falling short of new historicist principles. In the end Montrose has to concede that Berger is not "a fellow traveler of the 'New Historicism'" (p. 15); Berger's iconoclasm is too wayward to fit this telescoped view. In particular, Berger explicitly uses new criticism to assert his difference from new historicism: "The idea behind these projects was not to leave close reading behind" (p. 453); "I wanted to see whether new orientations defining and integrating themselves into a kind of movement by taking a stand against New Criticism could help me improve and reconstruct a practice I still thought of as a version of New Criticism" (p. 458). The name *new historicism* amalgamates and cancels two earlier terms, *old historicism* and *new criticism*, but Berger's ongoing commitment to new criticism undoes this cancellation.

Forced to address Berger's preferred terms, Montrose makes a telling criticism of Berger's new critical formulation of the author's position:

> An axiom of Berger's interpretive practice here is that he is not engaged in deconstructing Spenser's text but merely in explicating its own strategies of deconstruction; the claim is that the poem already constitutes a reflexive critique of its own sources, genre, and content. . . .
> . . . At the same time that Berger's analysis of the text places the autonomous and unified speaking subject into question at the level of character, Berger tacitly recuperates such a subject in the person of the poet who has "created" the text and/or in the person of the critic who interprets it. . . . By adapting to his present purposes a strict New-Critical distinction between the writer and his characters, Berger's essays strongly imply that such linguistic slippages are not so much a general condition of discourse as manifestations of the author's ironic mastery that the critic expounds and thereby shares.
>
> (pp. 14–16)

Berger has modified and complicated his approach: the concept of "conspicuous allusion" cited by Montrose (pp. 5, 10) has given way to a new emphasis on "conspicuous ambivalence" (p. 467). The latter term implies a less stable and predictable authorial stance, greater potential for gaps in the author's control. Nevertheless, the ambivalence does not entail genuinely uncertain self-division; the qualifier *conspicuous* still tips the balance in favor of a priori awareness and self-conscious control. On one hand, "the poem does not always maintain its critical distance"; on the other hand, "for such a complex and ambivalent enactment to succeed, the poem must in some manner persuade readers both to embrace the kidnapped discourses and to reestablish the critical distance" (p. 469). By this logic, authorial complicity can never, by definition, be uncritical; the author's critical perspicacity is a guaranteed hierarchical priority. By the application of the prefix *meta*, as in *metadiscursivity* (pp. 463, 467), the author's perspective can always be "raised to a higher power" (p. 466) and thereby rescued.

In Berger's final sentence—"By showing us how not to read *The Faerie Queene*, he opens up another way to read it" (p. 473)—"he" refers to the narrator, "another way" is Spenser's. The same stroke that neatly separates narrator and author, implicating the former and exculpating the latter, also brings together author and critic in a reciprocal, circular bond that protects both. Once the absolute separation of character and author is disallowed, the identification of critic with author is broken up: not only the author's but also the critic's position becomes vulnerable.[18] There is no point at which immersion in ideology stops: one cannot draw an ideological circle around the author outside of which the critic stands immune. With admirable consistency, Montrose's discussion encompasses critic as well as author: "The interpretive activity of the critic of Renaissance literature is, like its object, a production of ideology" (p. 7).

To summarize, Montrose's salient critique makes, from my point of view, two important gains. First, it places the author within rather than above the ideological fray. I would therefore replace Berger's notion of "conspicuous ambivalence" with a concept of ideological ambivalence. I accept Berger's distinction between narrator and author but interpret it as a sign of the author's higher-level ambivalence rather than of total insight and control. Second, Montrose's attention to the critic has the added benefit of opening up the question of our contemporary locations and of our own involvement in ideological processes. However, despite these invaluable contributions, Montrose does not have the final word. In particular, he neither answers nor disproves Berger's claims for new criticism in the sense of close reading.

Close reading is by no means a single practice; though I differ from Berger in my redefinition of close reading as ideological analysis, I agree with his insistence on the continuing validity of a reconstructed close reading and think that new historicism in particular has been prone to underestimate its value. By contrast, Jonathan Dollimore includes "textual analysis" as one of four components comprising cultural materialism: "Textual analysis locates the critique of traditional approaches where it cannot be ignored" (*Political Shakespeare*, p. vii).

One objection to turning close reading in the direction of the ideological analysis I propose is that such a move results in cursory interpretation. If ideology is defined as official doctrine and received ideas, then literary meanings can be seen as inevitably too subtle to be captured by the crude forms of ideology. But the problem is not the danger of surface reading but the superficial definition of ideology. As I use the term here, *ideology* refers to a far more ingrained and finely graded interplay of cultural forces whose presence in literary works can be examined only with the help of in-depth, nuanced close reading. An adequate formulation requires that we understand the operation and pull of ideology at more deep-seated levels of individual and institutional psyches. It is in the emotional charge and psychological investment involved in the engagement with a set of issues that we may locate an ideological stance in its full, particularized complexity. With regard to Shakespeare's representation of gender and class, for example, ideology marks an area of stressfulness in which values and expectations are placed under an intense dramatic pressure not completely under the control of authorial intention. Ideology is thus lived out, not merely crafted and manipulated for maximum artistic impact. The spatial imagery of text and context creates a misleading figure of inside and outside. This image makes context appear an alien import from outside that displaces the purely literary qualities inside the text. Against this false separation of intrinsic literary and extrinsic cultural effects, I suggest that ideology is "in" the text and that close reading helps to bring it out. Ideological analysis thus does not bypass but requires the textual inwardness associated with close reading.

Once the linked concepts of the autonomous work of art and the autonomous author are rejected, it becomes a pressing concern to formulate a theory of limited autonomy convincing enough to withstand the slide toward the other extreme of the complete denial of agency. This is a dilemma to which new historicism has seemed particularly susceptible; if, for example, Harry Berger attributes too much freedom to the author (and, by implication, to the critic), then Louis Montrose can be seen as confronting the reverse problem of too little. The concept of ideology plays a crucial role here because it so acutely raises the question of what degree, if any, of individual agency is consistent with a rigorous understanding of identity formation as an ideological process. The next chapter deals with specific ideological conditions pertaining to Elizabethan England; I conclude the present chapter with a brief general account of ideology.

III

Critics sometimes write as though there were only two basic treatments of ideology from which to choose—either the French example of Louis Althusser or the English counterinstance of E. P. Thompson's *The Poverty of Theory* (1978). Given these two options, it is perhaps not surprising that Althusser continues to be a favored reference point for the definition of ideology. However, the work of Stuart Hall provides a third alternative because he deconstructs the simple opposition between Althusser on the one hand and Thompson and Raymond Williams on the other. In the process, Hall criticizes limitations on both sides and attempts to combine their respective strengths.[19] My discussion highlights Hall's departures from these writers, but it needs to be said that Hall is clear throughout about his dependence on them. Hall has responded specifically to Thompson's *Poverty of Theory*.[20] But more important is the larger framework of Hall's "Cultural Studies: Two Paradigms" because it encompasses the work of Raymond Williams as well. Hall's critique focuses on the split in Williams's usage between the two terms *ideology* and *experience*, a split whereby Williams tends to elevate the latter while conceptually devaluing the former.[21] In contrasting the structuralist approaches of Lévi-Strauss and Althusser with the culturalist approaches of Williams and Thompson, Hall places special emphasis on ideology: "Whereas the 'culturalist' paradigm can be defined without requiring a conceptual reference to the term 'ideology' (the *word*, of course, does appear, but it is not a key concept), the 'structuralist' interventions have been largely articulated around the concept of 'ideology.'" In particular, Hall notes the "strength which structuralism exhibits . . . in its decentering of 'experience' and its seminal work in elaborating the neglected category of 'ideology.'"[22] The result is to remove the barrier between the two terms.

However, Hall is equally critical of some of the particular formulations by which Althusser links ideology and experience. I single out here only one aspect of Hall's response to Althusser, his objection to a functionalist tendency in Althusser's mode of argument. If, in Hall's view, Williams gives too little emphasis to structure, Althusser's version of ideology is too simply structured, with insufficient attention to ideological conflict and to the specific balance of forces in particular situations. According to Hall,

> two fundamentally different processes are being described. The first (Althusser's "Ideological State Apparatuses" essay) is the use of existing apparatuses to reproduce the already given ruling ideology; the second (mine) is the struggle and contes-

tation for the space in which to construct an ideological hegemony. . . .

It is Althusser's functionalism that drives him to give an overintegrative account of ideological reproduction and to collapse the state/civil society distinction as if it were without real or pertinent effects. Everything suggests that we must conceptualize the process by which the dominant ideology reproduces itself as a contradictory and contested one. Indeed, the term "reproduction," with its strong functionalist associations, carries quite the wrong connotations.[23]

While acknowledging Althusser's modifications of his position, Hall finds them too minor to alter the preponderant functionalist cast.[24]

Hall develops a more fully dynamic model with greater emphasis on the ideological struggle involved both in constructing and sustaining a particular hegemony and in opposing and attempting to change it. The element I should like especially to note is Hall's description of the articulation, disarticulation, and rearticulation of ideological meanings:

The notion of *the* dominant ideology and *the* subordinated ideology is an inadequate way of representing the complex interplay of different ideological discourses in any modern developed society. Nor is the terrain of ideology constituted as a field of mutually exclusive and internally self-sustaining discursive chains. They contest one another, often drawing on a common, shared repertoire of concepts, rearticulating and disarticulating them within different systems of difference or equivalence. . . .

. . . A particular ideological chain becomes a site of struggle, not only when people try to displace, rupture or contest it by supplanting it with some wholly new alternative set of terms, but also when they interrupt the ideological field and try to transform its meaning by changing or re-articulating its associations, for example, from the negative to the positive. Often, ideological struggle actually consists of attempting to win some new set of meanings for an existing term or category, of dis-articulating it from its place in a signifying structure.[25]

To apply this formulation to my own work, I want to connect the term *rewriting* in my title with the process of disarticulating and rearticulating some of the discursive chains within the specific ideological field designated as Shakespearean. Part 2 of this book examines challenges and limits to the power of the term *Shakespearean* to reach into our twentieth-century culture and to maintain its generative hold so that contemporary literature is produced in its image. Part 1, to which I now turn, focuses on selected Shakespearean works from the last decade of Elizabeth's forty-five-year reign, especially as this work sets up crosscurrents and tensions that place it tacitly at variance with the queen's cultural authority. Chapter 1 presents a general outline of this potential conflict, while chapters 2 through 4 pursue this motif through detailed interpretation of individual works.

PART ONE

SHAKESPEARE'S
REPRESENTATIONS OF WOMEN

Her [Elizabeth's] presence as a female, capable
of acting in public, continues to remain a
shock to the patriarchal system; it is constantly
in need of recuperation through the
ideological functioning of what we call
Elizabethan literature. . . .
. . . What she may have found funny about a
Falstaff, enhorned and mocked by a society of
women, may have been different from what
the male political nation found comic in
Braggadocchio or Faunus. But we all know
what a relief it is to laugh at our terrors. If
Queen Elizabeth could laugh at the kind of
fears that became all too real with the
braggadocio of an Essex, Spenser's readers
could laugh at the power that was real
enough, finally, to cut off the Earl's head.

Maureen Quilligan,
"The Comedy of Female Authority
in *The Faerie Queene*" (1987)

1

Female Rule, Patriarchal Ideology

The study of patriarchal ideology in Shakespeare's work is chiefly a matter of identifying stress points, not of explicating fixed doctrine. Patriarchal conventions that promote male power are significant because they cannot, in Shakespeare's work, be taken for granted as an automatic, settled norm. Instead, patriarchal control must constantly be renegotiated, with the outcome variable and uncertain. Patriarchy is not monolithic but multivalent; even within a single historical period it has multiple versions rather than one—versions that range from the crude and blatant to the intricate and subtle. Ideology is not restricted to the former: a contrast between the simple and the complex should not underwrite a division into the ideological and the nonideological. My definition of ideology extends the concept to everyone and to the most complicated aspects of experience. Patriarchal conventions have relative degrees of sophistication, but all involve an ideological stance. Attainment of a sufficient degree of complexity does not mean that Shakespeare thereby escapes from ideology into the nonideological or converts from the patriarchal into the antipatriarchal.[1]

In *The Taming of the Shrew* Shakespeare creates a rudimentary distinction he later refines between two modes of patriarchy: a crude, violent form based on force and a benevolent form based on persuasion, the latter reflected in the need for Kate's consent as well as in the concern for her welfare and happiness. The distinction between these two models is, however, too slight for comfort. Kate discovers what is good for her only when it is imposed on her by the indefatigable male suitor. Yet even when subsequently refined, the mode of persuasion retains a subtly patriarchal character; an element of cultural and psychological coercion persists that rules out male-female equality.[2]

But the two options of violent and benign patriarchy do not exhaust the range of possibilities, for in some Shakespearean works male control cannot be achieved by either mode. These exceptions offer vivid evidence that the conclusion is not guaranteed in advance and that we are witnesses to genuine exploration and struggle rather than to the unfolding of doctrine. Two of the works chosen for detailed analysis contain female characters who are less susceptible to patriarchal containment, whose perseverance blocks their ready adaptability to the protocols of male power. Though their assertiveness is by no means ideal in twentieth-century feminist terms, Venus and Helena display a capacity to dominate and to challenge that significantly disrupts the social systems of which they are part. One cannot assume, however, that the upsetting of smoothly operating patriarchal endings by persistent female strength expresses protofeminist insight or support. The attitude toward the female character often consists not of unreserved sympathy but of mixed, equivocal emotions. Shakespearean works with strong women may still have a patriarchal accent; the tone shifts from resolute patriarchal control to patriarchal anxiety and dismay.

The presence of strong women in Shakespeare's work from the Elizabethan period can be read as oblique glances at the cultural presence of Queen Elizabeth I. In *The Merry Wives of Windsor* "our radiant Queen" is explicitly invoked. However, my study deals not with direct allusions or exact analogues but with particular cultural resonances, the case for the resonance being argued in each instance. The study of Shakespeare's representations of Elizabeth has been marked out and exemplified by Louis Montrose's work on *A Midsummer Night's Dream* and by Leah Marcus's and Gabriele Bernhard Jackson's work on *1 Henry VI.*[3] My aim is to contribute to this field by considering the issues it raises in relation to other Shakespearean works.

If Elizabeth did not exist, we would have to invent her: so runs the skeptical line. But Elizabeth is not simply an all-too-convenient means for historicizing the topic of gender; her existence also presents enormous interpretive difficulties. The crucial question concerns her status as a female ruler in a patriarchal culture. At one level there is no conflict. Elizabeth did not set out to challenge patriarchal assumptions; to the contrary, her conservatism led her to adapt herself to them and to mute as far as possible any sense of incongruity between the traditionally male position she occupied and her female sex. This strategy was implemented through the institutionalization of a "cult of Elizabeth."[4] The point here is not to argue that Elizabeth either could have or should have more aggressively opposed patriarchal constraints and used her authority to empower other women but rather, in the interests of precise cultural analysis, to make explicit the historical conditions under which she operated.[5]

The cult of Elizabeth was not a perfect solution that completely eliminated all difficulty. The very need for the calculated fashioning of Elizabeth's gender identity acknowledged the existence of a potential problem and thus suggested, even as it mitigated, an underlying cultural dissonance. This latent tension was compounded by differences in the degree of royal control of various cultural media. Whereas the production of portraits of Elizabeth was subject to close official regulation, as Roy Strong documents,[6] commercial public theater, despite royal patronage and censorship, was more responsive to heterogeneous cultural influences. The theatrical medium opened up a space for an interplay between Elizabeth's self-fashionings and their Shakespearean representations. Elizabeth constructed, Shakespeare reconstructed: an element of uncertainty is introduced about whether the two actions are identical in cultural effect.

One critical formulation that forecloses this gap before it can be examined is the image of cultural likeness between Elizabeth and Shakespeare. Their successes are seen as analogues of each other, thus assimilating one to the other. Elizabeth is celebrated as "a rare bird like Shakespeare": "A skeptical despot, unlike her bigoted sister but suggesting 'Laodicean' Shakespeare, the Queen got on without opinions, not believing in much except herself and England's greatness."[7] Elizabeth and Shakespeare are presented as two of a kind, their common bond being an adroit avoidance of fixed positions, a nonideological canniness. This image, positing a felicitous continuity and alignment, makes it all but impossible to get beyond a sentimental identification of the two figures.

I propose a more complicated three-point historical model that allows for the possibility of their divergence, even their disparity. The three points are Elizabeth, Essex, and Shakespeare, where these names refer not just to individuals but primarily to institutional sites—the female monarchy, the aristocratic faction led by Essex, and the public theater. My discussion of Shakespeare's symbolic representations of these sites within his work does not imply any assumption about his direct personal contact with Elizabeth or Essex. Rather, I focus on theatrical responses to the larger cultural forces embodied in these figures.[8]

The cult of Elizabeth positioned the queen and her male courtiers in gender roles that facilitated and enforced their subordination to her. This system did not exclude conflict but channeled it into predictable and manageable forms in an attempt to contain it. This built-in conflict is not defined merely by gender, nor is gender the ultimate cause or explanation. Conflicting international and national security policies were crucial in shaping the differences between Elizabeth and courtiers motivated by a Protestant vision, the queen opting for restraint as against their more interventionist approach. Nevertheless, gender was a significant component because in moments when disagreements reached the flash point, they were likely to be expressed in gendered form. In particular, conflicts in military policy frequently registered as gender-inflected tension. Nor was this phenomenon peculiar to Essex. Leicester's Netherlands campaign in 1586, for instance, exhibited a familiar cyclical pattern of discord: the queen's monitoring of her military commander's conduct, her recall and rebuke of him, and their eventual reconciliation. The Essex subculture through the 1590s intensified and exacerbated a preexisting pattern.

Seen as the third point in a triangular situation, the institution of the theater is at one remove from the direct conflict between Elizabeth and Essex. The question is: what is the nature of that remove? Recent work on the relation of the public theater to royal and aristocratic networks of power has emphasized the theater's relative independence.[9] External control measures are not adequate to ensure that theatrical productions express an orthodox royal point of view. The problem is to account for both the theater's independence and its interdependence, to avoid the notion of the theater as a completely insulated, free-standing institutional site. When one considers the interaction of the three symbolic locations from the vantage point of the theater, two approaches are possible. In the first, Shakespeare's use of the theater favors neither Elizabeth's nor Essex's cultural position, but instead deliberately plays the two sides off against each other to achieve a fully independent theatrical perspective. In the second, Shakespeare's distinctive position is constituted as much by ambivalence toward each of the other two as by conscious criticism of them. The issue turns on the degree to which Shakespeare's use of the theater structures, or is structured by, ideological ambivalence. The latter emphasis preserves the idea of Shakespeare's implication in the cultural forms he represents, and I adopt this second approach as the working hypothesis to be tested and clarified in the specific case studies that follow.

I would like to acknowledge at the outset the limited scope of a cultural analysis with Elizabeth, Essex, and Shakespeare as the three focal points. Jean Howard has pointed out the dangers of a concentration on the figure of the monarch, even if female, while Carol Neely has similarly commented on a preoccupation with aristocratic males.[10] I would argue that the study of Elizabeth in its current phase is still a developing, productive area that can make a valuable contribution to our understanding of gender in the Renaissance. I would also argue that the Essex subculture is not merely an isolated aberration. Despite the narrow social basis of the coterie surrounding Essex, its gender tension has a wider cultural resonance; its symbolic ramifications connect with the larger context Howard describes as "a sex-gender system under pressure."[11] Nevertheless, I agree that the Elizabeth-Essex-Shakespeare triangulation explored here cannot be treated as a microcosm for the system as a whole but must be seen as one element in the overall cultural picture; a much wider social framework is necessary for a comprehensive account. Elizabeth did not set the whole tone of power relations, nor did the interaction between Elizabeth and Essex and its reverberations in Shakespeare's theater generate all the culture's assumptions about gender. These are not the only places where gender was defined; elsewhere in the culture gender may have been defined differently.

New work on the representations of gender by Renaissance women writers from diverse social situations provides a case in point.[12] Essays by François Rigolot and Ann Rosalind Jones in *Rewriting the Renaissance* emphasize distance from the court as an important factor in making women's writing possible, and both essays indicate that gender difference, when combined with class difference, can produce a significantly different angle of vision.[13] The overall effect of this new field is to construct a previously unavailable vantage point from which to reassess Shakespeare's cultural position. I want to suggest a relationship between my approach to Shakespeare and the study of Renaissance women writers, and to do so in two ways.

First, in my view, we cannot equate Shakespeare's work with Renaissance culture. However capacious his vision and however varied its theatrical performance, his work is not coextensive with the culture as a whole but is instead a subsection of it; his work does not contain every point of view but represents a set of positions within the culture. Once we stop magnifying Shakespeare into the all-inclusive master voice of the Renaissance, his particular configurations and limitations become accessible to criticism. In earlier work, I emphasized the patriarchal effects of male bonding in Shakespeare's drama not in order to erase or to silence his women characters but rather to develop a critique of Shakespeare that enables us to revise his status. I believe this approach is consistent with the attempt to rewrite the Renaissance by focusing on actual women as opposed to Shakespeare's female characterizations. It cannot be assumed that Shakespeare necessarily assimilated and expressed all the possible political stances open to women.[14] Studies of Renaissance women, including women writers, may provide a comparative perspective that allows us to see how Shakespeare's works narrow the range of options actually available and produce their own restricted view of women.

Second, though the study of Renaissance women writers will contribute to the reformulation of our image of Shakespeare, such study may in turn have its own built-in historical limits. Part 2 of this book makes a related attempt to gain perspective on Shakespeare's work by placing it in a larger context, but with the difference that I have chosen to use twentieth-century rather than Renaissance women authors. While related, these two efforts are not simple extensions of each other, as Kathleen McLuskie's distinction between "feminist history" and "a history of feminism" makes clear: "For history which concerns itself with the analysis of women's struggle within social contradictions must be called feminist. It is, however, different from a history of feminism which seeks to identify the point at which unruliness and disobedience on the part of individual women become a political movement presenting a more concerted challenge to patriarchal power."[15] Twentieth-century women writers have access to a full-scale feminist politics that Renaissance women writers lacked; we cannot blur this difference if we are to avoid overstating the power of Renaissance women writers and underestimating that of women writers in our own historical moment.

I turn now to the specific studies that form Part 1. The next three chapters bring to bear on individual texts the model sketched here. Chapters 2 and 3 regard Adonis in *Venus and Adonis* and Bertram in *All's Well That Ends Well* as manifestations of the Essex subculture's frustration with Elizabeth's military caution and female authority. Hamlet, considered in chapter 4, presents a more complicated but related figure of the blocked, striving male. Hamlet is denied even the circumscribed military outlet allowed to Bertram; yet, though Hamlet's military potential remains unfulfilled, thwarted, and canceled from the very beginning, the final representation of this potential—the military image Hamlet gains in death—is far more magnificent than anything achieved by Bertram's limited exploits.

Refracted Images of Queen Elizabeth in *Venus and Adonis* and *The Rape of Lucrece*

The thematic shift from the eroticism of *Venus and Adonis* to the chastity of *The Rape of Lucrece* can be taken as testimony not only to Shakespeare's sheer diversity but also to his inviolable disinterestedness. He moves freely from subject to subject, even from one extreme to the other; he can take on any situation but never fixes on one theme or position. Thus, for instance, Dover Wilson celebrates Shakespeare's aesthetic virtuosity and philosophical versatility as evidence of "his large-hearted tolerance and universal sympathy":

> He never commits himself deeply to a cause or to a point of view, whatever his affection or admiration for those who held it might be, because Life itself in all its infinite variety is far more interesting than any opinions, doctrines, or points of view about it. No sooner, for example, had he captured London by *Venus and Adonis* than he turns to the "graver labour" of *The Rape of Lucrece*, as if to say "You thought I was that kind of man, but you are mistaken: I can sing the praises of Chastity with the best of them. Or rather, I am not to be labelled with moral labels at all: I am a poet, who chooses to make a study of Desire one day and of Chastity the next." Like his royal mistress, he went forward by keeping his balance.[1]

I shall call this view of Shakespeare the "negative capability" argument, after Keats, whom Wilson cites in the sentence immediately preceding the passage I have quoted. Against this romantic view, I shall argue that the Shakespearean perspective, for all its complexity, is neither infinitely variable and impartial nor entirely compatible with Queen Elizabeth's.

My aim in this chapter is to see *Venus and Adonis* and *The Rape of Lucrece* as a connected pair that enacts the metamorphosis of Venus into Lucrece.[2] The cultural significance of this transformation is brought out by considering the two poems' female figures as fractured images of Queen Elizabeth. Elkin Calhoun Wilson describes the political efficacy of the cult of Elizabeth in mythological terms: "Elizabeth wrought her spell over the loyalties of her Renaissance knights because she played at serving Venus all the while that she abode in fealty to Diana."[3] The two poems encompass the mythological range implied by Elizabeth's combination of qualities associated with Venus and Diana, but the overall effect of the poems is to undo Elizabeth's complex synthesis. The poetic equivalents are not exact but distorted, fragmentary analogues of the queen. Venus evokes the erotic flirtation in Elizabeth's practice of courtship, but the queen conspicuously shares neither Venus's dedication to procreation nor her lack of finesse. Lucrece connects with Elizabeth's ethic of female purity, but the queen's purity is a sign of royal independence that contrasts sharply with Lucrece's vulnerability. Taken together, the two poems decompose the queen's unified image into separate elements, which can then be subjected to a process of reworking and dispersal. This fragmentation makes possible an ideological counteraction that attempts to neutralize, if not negate, the queen's power.

I

One of the most obvious features that *Venus and Adonis* and *The Rape of Lucrece* have in common is the dedicatory letters addressed to Southampton. I shall argue that the letters are fundamental to an account of the poetry because the poems are attuned to deep needs of the patron, whose presence the letters make an explicit part of the poetic transaction.

A major attempt to make analytic use of the dedications to Southampton is G. P. V. Akrigg's study *Shakespeare and the Earl of Southampton.*[4] However, Akrigg's appeal to the Southampton connection is topical in a fashion that is too literal and particularized. Muriel Bradbrook's commentary is more promising because its larger frame of reference establishes a general cultural, rather than narrowly biographical, context.

In Bradbrook's view, a particular literary form is also a specific cultural institution. Because of the "gulf that lay between popular playwriting and courtly poetry," Shakespeare's decision to turn to the latter in *Venus and Adonis* represents an attempt "to make a second reputation for himself"—one distinctly different from the reputation he had already achieved in the former.[5] As F. T. Prince puts it, "The two narrative poems have nevertheless a unique distinction: they were the only works Shakespeare published in which he claims the status of a professional poet. The poems are given signed dedications to a noble patron, and presented with as much care as Spenser gave to his books."[6] The social status of patron and poet is thus linked: not only is courtly poetry appropriate to Southampton's aristocratic position but also it serves as a vehicle for Shakespeare's own social aspiration. In Bradbrook's words, *"Venus and Adonis* furnishes a literary equivalent of the application to Herald's College for a coat of arms" (p. 62). Despite the self-effacing tone of his address to Southampton, Shakespeare's ambition is directly expressed in the two-line quotation from Ovid incorporated into the dedication. In this dedicatory context, the Ovidian language conveys an authorial elevation whose claim is at once artistic and social.

The Rape of Lucrece intensifies this motif of advancement both by the profession in the new dedication of greater confidence in the tie with the patron and by the offering of a more ostentatious product: *"The Rape of Lucrece* is an ambitious poem. It is more than a third as long again as *Venus and Adonis,* and while *Venus and Adonis* was put out in an unimpressive little quarto, *The Rape of Lucrece* is a handsome and much more costly piece of book-production."[7] A further meaning of the "graver labour" presented by the second poem lies in its status as tragedy: the new poem moves up the generic hierarchy, which carries overtones of a class hierarchy. Ultimately my goal will be to explore the resonance between Shakespeare's turn to this more noble literary form and his announcement of a more confident relation with his noble patron. First, however, it is necessary to consider a methodological problem concerning the relation between a poem's external context and its internal content.

Despite the suggestiveness of the social context Bradbrook constructs for *Venus and Adonis* and *The Rape of Lucrece*, its bearing on the interpretation of the poems remains indistinct and undeveloped. A detailed analysis showing why these particular poems with these particular configurations is lacking. The question—is their content arbitrary and random, or are the external circumstances registered as specific internal pressures within the poems?—is not sufficiently addressed. As a result, the interpretive value of the cultural context is limited by a critical model that treats such material as ancillary background. One talks about the culture and then one talks about the poem, but these are to a large extent separate conversations. In order to realize the interpretive potential of Shakespeare's letters of dedication, we must not only analyze the deep structures of the court system and of Southampton's milieu but also demonstrate their interconnections with the deep structures of the poems.

Toward this end, the remainder of this chapter is organized as three steps: first, an elaboration of Elizabeth's status as a female ruler in a patriarchal culture; second, a brief account of Southampton's relation to the Elizabethan court system; and finally, an assessment of the poems as responses to Southampton's situation. The reason for beginning with Elizabeth is that Shakespeare's dedications participate in a larger network of patronage of which she is the head.[8] As courtier, Shakespeare's patron Southampton is himself dependent on the ultimate patron, the queen.

Sheila ffolliott's study "Catherine de' Medici as Artemisia: Figuring the Powerful Widow" provides a fine comparative perspective for assessing Elizabeth's self-presentation as a female ruler.[9] Catherine differs from Elizabeth in having literal access to two acceptably conventional roles, wife and mother, through which to represent and to pursue her power. As widow, she derives power from her husband, to whose legacy she remains loyal by continuing it; as regent for her son, she maternally oversees the preparation for his resumption of the male line of royal authority. This contrast makes Elizabeth's independence—her ability, despite pressure, to assert and preserve her unmarried status—all the more striking. The visual images of Catherine in the Artemisia drawings place her at the side of the composition, whereas portraits of Elizabeth dispense with this obliqueness. The iconography of Elizabeth displays her image as central, frontal, and dominating.

Yet Elizabeth's power is, in turn, limited and relative—and for reasons of gender. Her independence of the traditional images of wife and mother is not total since she adapted them metaphorically to describe and justify her rule. In aligning her authority with this solicitous, reassuring imagery, Elizabeth accepted actual constraints on her power because she thereby not only manipulated but also reaffirmed traditional gender expectations. Allison Heisch has shown how Elizabeth's uniqueness isolated her from other women and left largely intact the patriarchal system with which she cooperated.[10] Nor is Heisch's analysis the product of an illicit procedure in which the critical connotations of our contemporary notion of the "token woman" are extrapolated to an earlier period for which they are inappropriate; for the concept of the exception was explicitly developed to designate Elizabeth's status in her own time.

Elizabeth's accession to power in 1558, following Mary's reign, again made the theoretical question of the legitimacy of female rule a policy matter of immediate practical concern. As James E. Phillips's "The Background of Spenser's Attitude toward Women Rulers" shows, the new regime consistently refused the overtures of John Knox, even though his *First Blast of the Trumpet Against the Monstrous Regiment of Women* (1558) originated in opposition to the Catholic rule of Mary of England and Mary of Scotland and even though Knox belatedly struggled to make an exception for the Protestant Elizabeth.[11] But Calvin's appeals also failed, despite his attempt to distinguish Knox's intemperate views from his own more moderate position. Elizabeth's government required more decisive expressions of allegiance, such as the formal repudiation forced on Christopher Goodman, whose *How Svperior Powers Oght to be Obeyd* (1558) had allied him with Knox's stance in *The Monstrous Regiment:*

> And not withstanding the which book so by me written, I do protest and confess, that good and godly women may lawfully govern whole realms and nations; and do from the bottom of my heart allow the queen's majesty's most lawful government, and daily pray for the long continuance of the same.
>
> (quoted in Phillips, p. 23)

Finally, John Aylmer's response to Knox, *An Harborowe for Faithfvll Trewe Subiectes, agaynst the late blowne Blast, concerninge the Gouernment of Wemen* (1559), earned his pardon, and he was rewarded by a place in the English Church (Phillips, p. 15, n. 39).

The withholding and granting of favor as a means of shaping a debate vital to the queen's interests is not surprising. More significant is the inadequacy of Aylmer's "answer": "John Aylmer's response the next year can hardly be called a defense; while arguing for woman's God-given right to rule, he simultaneously insists upon her basic weakness and inferiority to man."[12] Gordon J. Schochet observes that "monarchist authors during the reign of Queen Elizabeth failed to come to grips with Knox's inherent patriarchalism."[13] The reasons for this failure are instructive. Though the queen could intervene to influence the outcome of the debate, her political authority encounters an obstacle that is not completely susceptible to government control. She cannot rewrite the terms of the debate to eliminate deep-seated cultural conventions about gender; instead, these conventions appear not only in the work of those designated as her enemies but also in that of the spokesmen appointed to defend her. The queen could exclude Knox, but she could not entirely suppress the assumptions on which he drew.

The existence of prejudice against women within Elizabeth's government can be suggested by the case of Sir Thomas Smith, whose career, while not spectacularly successful, nevertheless culminated in service as Elizabeth's Principal

Secretary in the 1570s. The first part of R. W. K. Hinton's essay "Husbands, Fathers and Conquerors" counterpoints the English Smith, whose "voluntaristic spirit" expresses the principle of government by "mutual consent," with the French Bodin, who is "a true patriarchalist" because he conceives of rule as "absolute mastery."[14] However, Hinton construes the term *patriarchalist* too narrowly, as can be seen in his summary of chapters 11–13 in Book I of *De Republica Anglorum*, which Smith wrote from 1562 to 1565, during his ambassadorship to France:

> No work of political theory describes marriage more charmingly: it is a partnership. "The man stern, strong, bold, adventurous, negligent of his beauty, and spending: the woman weak, fearful, fair, curious of her beauty, and saving"; the man going out to work to earn money, the woman tarrying at home to distribute it among the family; for nature has forged men and women with complementary qualities so that each excels the other in things belonging to their office; . . . "each obeyeth and commandeth other and they two together rule the house". . . . And when Smith glides from the family as metaphor to the family as a point of origin he continues to emphasize the same two elements of consent and cooperation. The first grandfather, he says, was a monarch because the sons and grandsons had no thought of striving against the one from whom they had received life and being: that is, because they obeyed him willingly. When the grandfather died his sons and nephews agreed to rule by consultation among themselves: that is, they originated aristocracy by mutual consent.
>
> (Hinton, pp. 292–93)

However valid the relative contrast with Bodin, there is certainly a "logic of patriarchalism" at the heart of Smith's thinking. First, the complementarity of husband and wife is grounded in the imagery of inequality that gives the husband decisive superiority; their ostensibly shared rule presupposes gender hierarchy. Second, when Smith turns to the origin of state government, the woman drops out altogether. The female body disappears from a body politic in which males trace their origins exclusively to the first male: as Smith puts it, "For he loved them as his owne children and nephewes, cared for them as members of his owne body. . . . They againe honoured him as their father of whose bodie they came."[15] The cooperative government instituted after the grandfather's death is a cooperation among males.

Smith's patriarchal bias is confirmed in the discussion of the female ruler, which Hinton leaves out of his account. While Smith allows for rule by the queen, he does so only to assure stability in the transmission of power, as his use of the word *except* signals:

> And in this consideration also we do reject women, as those whom nature hath made to keep home and to nourish their familie and children, and not to medle with matters abroad, nor to beare office in a citie or common wealth no more than children or infantes: except it be in such cases as the authoritie is annexed to the bloud and progenie. . . . for there the blood is respected, not the age or the sexe.
>
> (p. 64)

His negative attitude toward women remains plainly in view through the parallel construction of female and underage rule and through the insistence on the male counsel to compensate for female deficiency:

> For the right and honour of the blood, and the quietness and suertie of the realme, is more to be considered, than either the base age as yet impotent to rule, or the sexe not accustomed (otherwise) to intermeddle with publicke affaires, being by common intendment understood, that such personages never do lacke the counsell of such grave and discreete men as be able to supplie all other defaultes.
>
> (p. 65)

Smith's negative attitude in the treatise is reinforced by the account provided by Mary Dewar's biography, in which she offers this blunt summary: "He thoroughly disliked the Queen. He looked at the throne and was neither dazzled by Gloriana nor bewitched by Eliza. He never even saw the point of behaving as if he were"; "He could never cope with Elizabeth. All through his letters the one genuine feeling about her which emerges unmistakably is sheer irritation."[16] One can take Smith's irritation as evidence of Elizabeth's triumph;

his lack of adroitness with the queen frequently casts him, in Dewar's portrait, in the role of a comically ineffectual figure. However, because his frustration registers entrenched feelings that had wide cultural resonance and that Elizabeth had to countenance and to accommodate, it cannot be dismissed as inconsequential.

Edmund Spenser, the recipient of modest government patronage, more subtly articulates male distancing from Elizabeth. In Book V of *The Faerie Queene,* Spenser ostentatiously circumscribes Elizabeth's status as an exception—"But vertuous women wisely understand, / That they were borne to base humilitie, / Unless the heavens lift them to lawfull soveraintie" (5.5.25)—and starkly reaffirms male privilege through Britomart's ultimate subordination to Artegall. This moment offers a focal point for a critical perspective on the term *exception* as applied to Elizabeth:

> Because she was always uniquely herself, Elizabeth's rule was not intended to undermine the male hegemony of her culture. Indeed, the emphasis upon her *difference* from all other women may have helped to reinforce it. . . . The royal exception could prove the patriarchal rule in society at large.

> Elizabeth, then, like Britomart, is the exception who proves the rule of women's "base humilitie"; the patriarchal basis of legitimate authority is restored.[17]

In the figure of Britomart, Spenser pays Elizabeth a backhanded compliment. As David Norbrook notes in his chapter "'The Faerie Queene' and Elizabethan Politics," the Britomart-Elizabeth equation breaks down when, after defeating Radigund's female power, Britomart herself is made to submit to the male authority she has restored, and her submission takes the form of marriage.[18] Either Elizabeth is implicitly criticized for her failure to comply with marital expectations or she is further isolated as an exception to emphatically reimposed patriarchal norms. The purpose of such analysis is not to deny the substantial power that Elizabeth successfully held, but rather to suggest that her power was refracted through a patriarchal cultural medium that constricted as well as shaped its actual use.

How does this Elizabethan courtly situation apply specifically to Southampton? The history of Southampton's troubled
relations with the queen illustrates the gender-inflected antagonism to which interaction between male courtier and female sovereign could lead. Southampton first incurred the
queen's anger over his involvement with and eventual marriage to one of her maids of honor and a cousin of Essex.[19]
Tension between Elizabeth and Southampton culminated
during Essex's Irish expedition and its aftermath: she over-
ruled Essex, denying his appointment of Southampton as
General of the Horse; she refused to approve the governor-
ship awarded to him by Mountjoy; Southampton actively participated in Essex's rebellion against Elizabeth, earning im-
prisonment in the Tower and loss of his earldom for the
remainder of her reign. The cultural significance of these
events lies less in Southampton's individual biography than
in the wider ramifications of his close ties with Essex. The
emergence of Essex as a potential successor from the younger
generation to replace Leicester as the queen's principal courtier creates a new situation in the 1590s; for Essex's faction was
not only a political but also a cultural grouping, centered
emphatically on the male ethic of military honor.[20] For the
courtiers around Essex this cult of heroic masculinity constituted an alternative source of energy and meaning to the cult
of Elizabeth, which was already contradicted by the queen's
increasing age at this late point in her rule.

Shakespeare's poems of 1593 and 1594 of course predate
the open conflict between the cults of Elizabeth and Essex. So
far as Southampton is concerned, the only conflict with the
Elizabethan power structure by the time of Shakespeare's
dedications was his unyielding resistance to Burghley's plans
for the arranged marriage of his ward to Elizabeth Vere. Nor
should the poems be read as predictions of the Essex rebellion. Shifting from the topical to a cultural approach allows us
to reframe the question: what cultural forces are activated and
released in Shakespeare's art by the patronage transaction
with Southampton? My answer is that the poems are attuned
to Southampton in his courtly environment through their re-

sponsiveness to the latent gender tension involved in male reaction to female rule.

In *Venus and Adonis* Venus's domination evokes Elizabeth's control,[21] and this undercurrent helps to account for the poem's unstable tonal mixture of defensive jocularity and genuine alarm. In *The Rape of Lucrece*, Lucrece's chastity overlaps with the mythologically enhanced cult of Elizabeth as the virgin queen. The poem condemns the assault on female virtue in advance, but it nonetheless dramatizes an elaborately drawn-out violation, thereby converting the royal image of powerful virginity into helpless vulnerability. The poem's representation of violent male temptation overriding a taboo deploys the same cultural symbolism as Essex's action of reaching for his sword in anger against Elizabeth in 1598, though of course the poem is not a literal anticipation of the later moment.[22] When the two poems are placed in this specifically Elizabethan context, the gender conflicts the poems put into play enact versions of the tension between Elizabeth and her male courtiers. These poetic renditions of court politics may involve fantasies, but they are culturally significant fantasies.

The primary wish fulfilled by the overall progression of the two poems is the elimination of the threat of Elizabeth's power. The first poem highlights that threat in the form of a self-pitying fantasy of a young man driven to destruction by an overbearing woman, with whom he is belatedly reunited; the second poem·conveys an aggressive counter-fantasy of male violation of a woman, followed by a political action carried out by men that purifies the male body politic. Insofar as *The Rape of Lucrece* performs what the first dedicatory letter calls its "graver labour" by appealing to the higher genre of tragedy, the poem uses tragic conventions to facilitate the displacement of women, including Elizabeth, and to promote the final emphasis on male heroism. The function of Shakespeare's dedications to Southampton can now be formulated by assuming a correlation between the male alliance led by Brutus inside the poem with the male alliance celebrated outside the poem in the second letter to Southampton. The change in the poems—the transition from female control to the realization of a male republic—is accompanied by the change in the letters—greater confidence in the male bond between patron and poet. The strengthening of the male tie in the letters thus mirrors, and is mirrored by, increased male confidence within the poems.

Evidence that the Shakespeare-Southampton tie and the poems this tie makes possible are directed against the central figure of Elizabeth as female monarch includes the political cast implied by the liberation at the end of *The Rape of Lucrece.* Not only is Tarquin banished but also the form of government is changed from a monarchy to a republic. Shakespeare is on delicate ground here and employs the utmost circumspection, but the implications for the English monarch are present nevertheless: the poem cannot help conveying a brief sensation of questioning the philosophical ground of Elizabeth's authority.[23] Shakespeare's affinity with Southampton is based, however, less on formal opposition to monarchy in general than on a shared uneasiness about the specific effects of female rule.

II

Rather than a sign of Shakespeare's unlimited freedom, the differences between *Venus and Adonis* and *The Rape of Lucrece* provide points of connection between the two poems: the second poem responds to the first by a logic of reaction and revision. What organizes the differences into a significant relationship is the major common denominator the two poems share. In each case, the counterpoint between two worlds or sets of activities provides the poem's overall framework. The opposition between love and the hunt in *Venus and Adonis* is matched by a similar contrast between domestic love and the war scene at "besieged Ardea" (1) in *The Rape of Lucrece.* In each case, gender is a salient category for the poem and for critical analysis because hunting and warfare are portrayed as separate, exclusively male spheres and because the love is deeply troubled by this cultural division.

The social situation of the later poem is far more detailed. *Venus and Adonis* has no equivalent to the context provided by the opening "Argument" of *The Rape of Lucrece*. In theory, Adonis's hunt is not a solitary activity, as his allusions to his (male) friends (588, 718) and the sound of their holla (973) and horns (1025) indicate. But since they never actually appear, they are for practical purposes nonexistent. As a result, *Venus and Adonis* is sharply restricted to the two named figures, creating a foreshortened, claustrophobic atmosphere and an effect of isolation. By contrast, *The Rape of Lucrece* fills in the picture of male cultural patterns by stressing Tarquin's friendship with Collatine—"my dear friend" (234, 237) has referential authority—and by providing additional male characters in old Lucretius and in Brutus, whose "deep policy" (1815) directs the poem's final action. Moreover, Venus's generalized philosophical meditation is replaced by Lucrece's more specific focus on kingship, and this excursion into political theory is given point by the poem's attention to actual change in Rome's governmental structure. Nevertheless, despite the absence of a fully realized social and political environment in *Venus and Adonis*, Adonis's stance—"Hunting he lov'd, but love he laugh'd to scorn" (4)—is a recognizable male gesture that has the same cultural force as Bertram's "I shall prove / A lover of thy [Mars's] drum, hater of love" in *All's Well That Ends Well* (3.3.10–11). The link between the role of the hunt in the first poem and of war in the second is reinforced by Venus's use of the love/war topos in the earlier poem (97–114).

Against the poems' common background, their differences may appear less random and more coordinated. What stands out as the most striking element in the transition from the first poem to the second a year later is the reversal of gender roles: from the drama of female aggressor against male victim to that of male aggressor against female victim. According to the negative capability argument, this change can be represented as further evidence of authorial evenhandedness. *The Rape of Lucrece* is balanced by the "rape of Adonis," showing that Shakespeare could see both sides, all sides. However, I would argue that sequence is important here. If we see the second poem as a response to the first, then the female threat symbolized by Venus is followed by the restoration of orthodox female subordination in Lucrece, whose "mortal stars as bright as heaven's beauties / With pure aspects did him [her husband] peculiar duties" (13–14). After witnessing the deception of Venus's "cunning love" (471), we are assured thus early in the second poem both of Lucrece's purity ("pure aspects") and of her devotion ("duties"), and both remain constant: we are never in the course of the poem given cause to doubt these qualities.

A more active rendering of the negative capability argument asserts, however, that the two poems demonstrate that Shakespeare had a positive interest in and sympathy for women because the woman is featured as the central character in each poem and in this sense both women dominate. While it is true that, relative to their opposite male numbers, Venus and Lucrece are more fully developed and given the primary focus, this account, if unqualified, leaves out a crucial further element in the overall narrative situation: the controlling male perspective. One small textual indication of this narrative framing is the reference to "Their gentle sex" in *The Rape of Lucrece* (1237), which implies a male poet addressing a male audience. Much as they seem to dominate, Venus and Lucrece do not possess the shaping imaginations of their respective poems. Instead, however weak individual male characters within the poems may be, Venus and Lucrece are seen from an external male point of view that, under pressure, favors its own interests at the expense of Dover Wilson's "universal sympathy." In this view, both poems are preoccupied with male problems and anxieties and are related as two sides or faces of the same overall male psychological bind, one that alternates between uncomfortable, finally intolerable, vulnerability on the one hand and defensive violence on the other.

In the transition from *Venus and Adonis* to *The Rape of Lucrece*, the reversal of gender is accompanied by and intertwined with a reversal of genre: "*Venus and Adonis* treats sexual desire in the spirit of romantic comedy; *Lucrece* does so in the spirit of tragedy."[24] This description of the generic shift will serve as a useful starting point, though it must be immediately qualified with the further comment that these respective generic emphases occur in poems each of which possesses its own tragi-comic mixture. Putting it schematically, we might distinguish the two generic blends by saying that *Venus and Adonis* presents comic women and tragic men, while *The Rape of Lucrece* treats tragic women and comic men. In the latter, there is a faintly ridiculous air attaching to the melodramatic character of Tarquin, despite the seriousness of his action; and the absurdly drawn-out competition between Lucrece's husband and her father conveys a comical deflation that borders on farce.

By contrast, in *Venus and Adonis* the comic element is directed mainly at Venus. Initially she provokes uncomplicated laughter, which, however, is increasingly arrested by an uncomfortable feeling. This uneasiness is largely associated with Adonis, for it is when we turn from Venus and focus on Adonis's perspective that a tragic undertone begins to emerge. The crux of the discomfort is less Adonis's resistance than his helplessness, male defiance represented as humiliation. In the dynamic of Adonis's "aw'd resistance" (69), evocations of embarrassment—"blush'd" (33), "red for shame" (36), "bashful shame" (49), "Pure shame" (69), "crimson shame" (76)—far outweigh the reference to his "anger ashy pale" (76). The best he can do with his anger is hide it under the bonnet which Venus teasingly removes (339, 351). The depth of the emotional charge is too great for us to dismiss this embarrassment merely as comic fun, a dilemma the poem recognizes and tries to ease by its later maudlin shift toward a quasi-tragic key.[25]

This mitigation is not sufficiently secured within the terms of *Venus and Adonis* and is hence deferred to *The Rape of Lucrece*, where a more fundamental rearrangement of psychological and gender elements becomes possible. The nature of our discomfort is substantially altered when, across poems, vulnerability is transferred from Adonis to Lucrece. The shamefaced aspect previously associated with Adonis changes to a positive quality of modesty when transplanted in Lucrece: "When virtue bragg'd, beauty would blush to shame; / When beauty boasted blushes, in despite / Virtue would stain that o'er with silver white" (54–56). Such demureness is becoming for Lucrece as it is not for Adonis because Lucrece's behavior conforms to standard gender expectations. Lucrece has all of Adonis's innocence and inexperience, but these are less profoundly disturbing in her because they can be regarded as "normal" and "natural." Lucrece is set up in a loaded situation that will extract an enormous price, but we are on secure ground in that we are able to recognize in advance the dynamics of her sacrifice:

> For unstain'd thoughts do seldom dream on evil,
> Birds never lim'd no secret bushes fear:
> So guiltless she securely gives good cheer
>   And reverend welcome to her princely guest,
>   Whose inward ill no outward harm express'd.
>   (87–91)

Familiar conventions of gender and genre combine to identify Lucrece's female innocence as inherently predisposed to tragedy and to help us accept this process as a paradoxically unfortunate but necessary confirmation and vindication of the female virtue that contributes to her demise.

With regard to these two poems, I would reverse F. T. Prince's assertion that "Comedy was the easier, safer, form for Shakespeare" (p. xxxviii). To the contrary, the comic tendency of *Venus and Adonis* is problematic, whereas the "Black stage for tragedies" (766) provided by *The Rape of Lucrece* is deeply satisfying. *The Rape of Lucrece* is upsetting in predictable and containable—and therefore "safer"—ways, but the comic touch in *Venus and Adonis* exposes an anxiety in Adonis that remains obscure and unresolved. The poem early on hints that Venus's desire is amenable to a gender order that reinstates male initiative: "Backward she push'd him, as she would be thrust" (41). But when Venus later appears to relinquish the position of "women on top"[26]—"He on her belly falls, she on her back. / Now is she in the very lists of love, / Her champion mounted for the hot encounter" (594–96)—Adonis remains unresponsive: "He will not manage her" (598). Though Venus maintains this posture for over two hundred lines (594–811), she concedes failure: "The warm effects which she in him finds missing" (605). The narrator's direct intervention enforces this point: "good queen, it will not be" (607).

The humor in this moment is particularly destabilizing, moving in several directions at once. Adonis's refusal to cooperate registers a wry, if pathetic, protest against female dominance by setting a strict limit to Venus's ability to enforce her desires. The joke is not only on Venus, however. Adonis's refusal can be read as heterosexual impotence that implies a homosexual motive, toward whose fulfillment the poem expresses reservations as strong as its restiveness about female power. As C. L. Barber notes, Adonis's encounter with the boar is presented in negative, destructive terms as a figure of "homosexual rape."[27] Adonis is placed in a no-win situation: if Venus's importunity is unacceptable, so is the alternative of homosexual attraction. The implied Shakespearean perspective here cannot be construed as one-sided identification with Southampton; if he can sympathetically address Southampton's resentment of Elizabeth's authority as female monarch, he also conveys ambivalence about Southampton in the role of Adonis-like courtier. Whether or not the rumors of Southampton's homosexual activity are accurate,[28] *Venus and Adonis* allows for this possibility in a manner so equivocal that it undermines any prospect of a unitary male perspective. By contrast, *The Rape of Lucrece* works to establish a form of male bonding that avoids or sublimates the specifically homoerotic potential.

III

The Rape of Lucrece affords a "solution" to the intractable difficulties of *Venus and Adonis* in that the male indignity of the first poem is answered by the female dignity of the second. The tragic decorum which is instrumental in shaping Lucrece's dignity is not only an aesthetic but also a political issue because this generic decorum becomes a means of reasserting gender decorum. According to the politics of genre which I shall elaborate here, the tragic motif of *The Rape of Lucrece* enables both the control of woman and the representation of this control to be seen as benign. In Lucrece, Shakespeare has reinvented an acceptable woman; she provides a positive portrait of a woman who can be accorded full, unreserved sympathy because her image is favorable to a patriarchal order.

Lucrece's acceptance of female subordination is evident throughout in her deferential attitude toward her husband. To this intrinsic submissiveness the poem's cruel redundancy adds a second in the form of the submission Tarquin enforces on her: as though the poem is taking no chances, she is thus doubly put in her place as a woman. Shakespeare, far from endorsing Tarquin's aggression, supports Lucrece through a generalized critique of male inhumanity: "Since men prove beasts . . ." (1148). The poem unequivocally condemns Tarquin, "this devil" (85), as unredeemable and, in the final line that gives the poem its neat closure, dismisses him to unhappiness: "The Romans plausibly did give consent / To Tarquin's everlasting banishment" (1854–55). But it is also evident that the male banishers themselves need reform: the poem squarely places the responsibility for Lucrece's violation on her husband's competitive boasting about her virtue (10–11, 15–21, 33–35). The "high proud rate" (19) of Collatine's self-aggrandizing boast is enough to associate him with Tarquin's tyrant father: "for his excessive pride surnamed Superbus" ("Argument"). The whole network of male culture is thus contaminated, as Shakespeare underlines through the repetition of Collatine's participation in the competition of male self-pity near the poem's end (1751–1806). This male degradation is relieved only by the purification of the male body politic which Lucrece's suicide makes possible—a purgation symbolized by literal governmental reform but connoting male psychological regeneration as well.

What makes this critique of male behavior possible, however, is the nonthreatening nature of the woman associated with it. Lucrece's grief may rise to a curse: "And let mild women to him lose their mildness, / Wilder to him than tigers in their wildness" (979–80). But we are assured that, in her own person, she will not lose her mildness nor challenge male prerogative. Suicide is a form of action that preserves her mildness because it calls men to their duty without usurping their authority. The poem praises and values the female spirit while at the same time restrictively defining it and requiring its elimination.

The equivocal, double-edged nature of the sympathy extended to Lucrece is exemplified by the conspicuously set off, three-stanza narrative apostrophe (1240–60) following Lucrece's encounter with her maid after the rape (1214–39). The maid's intuitive, spontaneous compassion and the two women's shared weeping epitomize the quality of sympathy: "Her circled eyne, enforc'd by sympathy" (1229). Yet this capacity is portrayed with some condescension as a specifically female attribute: "Their gentle sex to weep are often willing, / Grieving themselves to guess at others' smarts, / And then they drown their eyes or break their hearts" (1237–39). The narrator then interrupts the narrative line to launch a lengthy defense of women and critique of men, but the defense hurts as much as it helps because the appeal is based on women's inherent weakness and need for responsible male leadership:

> For men have marble, women waxen, minds,
> And therefore are they form'd as marble will;
> The weak oppress'd, th' impression of strange kinds
> Is form'd in them by force, by fraud, or skill.
> Then call them not the authors of their ill,
>   No more than wax shall be accounted evil . . .
>   (1240–45)

There is perhaps a slight inconsistency in describing Lucrece's mind as waxen immediately after she has become marble constant in her commitment to the "plot of death" (1212). But this is not a conscious irony that permits us to distinguish the narrator from the omniscient author who undercuts him as though the former worked to build up stereotypical gender differences that Shakespeare busily deconstructed. Rather, the Shakespeare of this poem invests himself in these gender platitudes.

This view is confirmed by Brutus's intervention at the end of the poem. Particularly striking is the way his objection to the men's "relenting dew of lamentations" (1829) takes the form of sharp criticism of Lucrece: "Such childish humor from weak minds proceeds; / Thy wretched wife mistook the matter so, / To slay herself that should have slain her foe" (1825–27). Brutus's remark does not suggest that the poem seriously proposes that Lucrece could or should have directed her violence against Tarquin instead of herself. Rather, the function of Brutus's comment is twofold: to assert that women's behavior cannot be a model for men and, by ingratitude if need be, to place limits on men's indebtedness to Lucrece's action. The phrase "weak minds" (1825) in Brutus's unkind reference to Lucrece echoes the narrator's expostulation about the waxen minds of "weak-made women" (1260). Brutus's role clarifies the gender distinctions that Collatine's tears, overriding "manly shame" (1777), are in danger of blurring. Unimpeded by a personal connection with Lucrece, Brutus can transform and complete her action by giving it a masculine turn: "This said, he strook his hand upon his breast, / And kiss'd the fatal knife to end his vow" (1842–43). Male unity, validated by this erotic touch, rescues "Rome herself" (1833). Lucrece's "bleeding body" (1851) does the state some service, but only when bequeathed to male hands directed by Brutus.

The conversion of male grief to manly revenge is a cliché, but one which the poem finds it necessary to stress as antidote to male dependence on women.[29] The male self-pity that suffuses and paralyzes *Venus and Adonis* is reenacted in the self-pitying displays of father and husband that threaten to overwhelm *The Rape of Lucrece*. What allows the later poem to escape is the generic politics by which pity, now authorized as tragic decorum, is redirected with a vengeance toward a female victim. The disrespect that tinges and narrows this pity is suggested by the unpleasant image of dumping when Brutus makes his move: "Began to clothe his wit in state and pride, / Burying in Lucrece' wound his folly's show" (1809–10).[30]

Taken as a sequence, *Venus and Adonis* and *The Rape of Lucrece* can be seen as successive explorations in managing the emotion of sympathy which is associated with women. In this regard, there is a convergence between Venus and Lucrece since both play the designated female role of lamenter. What makes Venus relatively less oppressive, more palatable, in the second half of the poem is her shift from seduction to lamentation. Whereas earlier she has advanced her sovereignty over Mars, now she submits to the higher power of Death, "Imperious supreme of all mortal things" (996), the "invisible commander" (1004) with whom "she humbly doth insinuate" (1012). Moreover, the generalizing quality of her lament gives it a wider appeal because it displaces the special pleading associated with the pursuit of her particular self-interest, making her now seem "th' impartial gazer" (748). Finally, having abandoned her assault, Venus seems touched by genuine concern for Adonis; her mourning can be seen as working in his behalf instead of against it.

This stance is reinforced by the maternal aspect of Venus's newly gratifying solicitude, an aspect conveyed in part by the breast imagery that helps to structure the poem's symbolic action.[31] Adonis flees Venus's "pleasant fountains" (234) as erotic objects only to be united with them after the fountains have been refigured as nurturant: "Like a milch doe, whose swelling dugs do ache, / Hasting to feed her fawn" (875–76). The metaphorical shift from "pleasant fountains" to "swelling dugs" begins at the midway point when jealous apprehension of her rival death turns her focus to a prolonged mourning in advance: "Within my bosom, whereon thou dost lie, / My boding heart pants, beats, and takes no rest, / But like an earthquake, shakes thee on my breast" (646–48). This ungainly "shaking" anticipates the more blissful "rocking" of the conclusion. The image of separation—"And wakes the morning, from whose silver breast / The sun ariseth in his majesty" (855–56)—is transformed through Adonis's disembodied flowery form after death from deprivation into fulfillment:

> Here was thy father's bed, here in my breast;
> Thou art the next of blood, and 'tis thy right.
> Lo in this hollow cradle take thy rest;
> My throbbing heart shall rock thee day and night
> (1183–86)

One problem with this happy ending is that it is too transparent to be comfortable. The image awakens the fears it seeks to soothe and allay because the escape from unwanted sexual attention is accomplished through a desired maternal solace that produces further anxiety about male dependence on women. The cloying decorative surface arouses as much as it placates these anxieties. Unlike Prospero's dramatic gesture excluding Venus in *The Tempest* (4.1.86–101), the poem's final stanza announcing Venus's withdrawal provides insufficient protection.

The Rape of Lucrece draws on the same female images as *Venus and Adonis*. This version of weeping, for instance, might be readily transposed to Lucrece:

> Here overcome, as one full of despair,
> She vail'd her eyelids, who like sluices stopp'd
> The crystal tide that from her two cheeks fair
> In the sweet channel of her bosom dropp'd
> (955–58)

The second poem develops the association of profuse tears and compassion with the nurturant breast, but in doing so, it builds safeguards against male exposure to the full force of women's capacity for sympathy. Tarquin's attack focuses on Lucrece's breasts (407–13, 437–41, 463–69); Lucrece's remedy for "clear[ing]" the "poisoned fountain" (1707) which this violation makes her is also directed at the breast (1723):

> And from the purple fountain Brutus drew
>   The murd'rous knife, and as it left the place,
>   Her blood in poor revenge held it in chase.
> And bubbling from her breast, it doth divide
> In two slow rivers . . .
> (1734–38)[32]

The blood, as though literally pouring forth the female virtue that will sustain and fortify her husband, proves her integrity: "Some of her blood still pure and red remain'd" (1742). Though grotesque, this icon is made plausible by Lucrece's schooling in the great epic tradition that provides material for tragedy (1366–1582). In particular, she learns her affinity with the maternal Hecuba (1443–65)—"I'll tune thy woes with my lamenting tongue." This consolation builds her resolve, enabling her to submit to the role required of her as the vehicle of tragic pity. At the same time, male distance and agency are imposed by Brutus's actions in removing the knife from Lucrece's breast and in redefining the knife's significance. The gesture of pounding his own male breast completes the neutralization of Lucrece's energy. Her female identity is depersonalized as it is transferred and absorbed into the metaphorical abstraction of female Rome, a political ideal shaped and protected by male initiative.

The poem's final effect is to construct a male catharsis without vulnerability to compassion, to make it possible to receive steady sympathy while being relieved of the obligation to return it to the same degree. This gender asymmetry reverses the relationship between Elizabeth and her male courtiers. In his study of Ralegh's interactions with Elizabeth, for example, Stephen Greenblatt shows that the logic of courtship imposed by the cult of Elizabeth implied different degrees of commitment: "Elizabeth manages both to play the game of poetic love and to remain aloof from it, to indulge herself without commitment and to participate without danger. Ralegh, however, must assert his total involvement."[33] In relation to this situation, *The Rape of Lucrece* transmutes the power of female chastity to make it serve rather as the basis for the creation of a purified male state.

IV

Shakespeare's two narrative poems engage the culture's prevailing symbolic economy so as to redirect the royal iconography into more palatable forms. No general formula can be drawn from this particular instance, however. The fashioning of the containment of female authority is not settled once and for all and is not easy to maintain; rather, such containment has to be continually reenacted and cannot always be successfully achieved. The fantasy of the displacement of female power bodied forth in *The Rape of Lucrece* depends on the omission of the actual state of female rule. The emergence of strong women in other Shakespearean works can be seen as a cultural process of the return of the repressed: what is suppressed in *The Rape of Lucrece* reappears elsewhere in less tractable versions of powerful women. The legacy of Venus, canceled by *The Rape of Lucrece*, is continued in such dominant female characters as the Princess in *Love's Labour's Lost*, Portia in *The Merchant of Venice*, Helena in *All's Well That Ends Well*, and the title characters in *The Merry Wives of Windsor*.

The demythologizing trend from goddess to women increases female power because this power can no longer be explained as an attribute of divinity. The trend is accentuated by a downward shift in class status. The Princess of *Love's Labour's Lost* and Portia of *The Merchant of Venice* inhabit aristocratic pastoral environments. Helena and the wives, by contrast, are controlling women who are more down-to-earth because their social standing is explicitly nonaristocratic. They therefore pose to patriarchal ideological control a double threat of gender and of class.[34] In particular, the exercise of overwhelming power by ordinary women erodes the special category of exceptionality reserved for Elizabeth. The cultural strategies for managing the queen's power by isolating it as a unique instance begin to break down if other women routinely exercise extraordinary power. This is not to propose that cross-class female coalitions were an actual political possibility, but rather to suggest that the imaginary conjunction of female gender and nonaristocratic status creates a potential disruption of ideological categories that is not easy to control.

Class is not used here in the sense of modern class structure and class consciousness. The term is nevertheless necessary to describe the period's "incipient class dimension."[35]

The traditional vocabulary of rank was inadequate for new economic developments:

> The contemporary commentators, most of whom were of gentle or bourgeois origin, tended to present a conservative, legalistic view of the world. Their major difficulty, which still cannot be satisfactorily resolved, lay in trying to describe a society whose legal system and status system were based on possession of land at a time when non-landed skills, wealth and power were increasingly significant.[36]

As a particular instance of "non-landed skills, wealth and power," London commercial theaters provided an especially sensitive focal point for questions about social categorization:

> Drama was a thriving if unseemly business enterprise in early modern England, theaters sites of exchange, players regarded with the same ambivalence as merchants for their protean capacities to cross or violate the class boundaries and cultural hierarchies. Merchants and players were homologous figures in the moral imagination of the period, each representing a degree of social mobility that threatened to produce a state of social alchemy. . . . If merchants changed place with gentlemen, the player's range was more extensive, subjecting all social classes and categories, from peasant to monarch, to a theatrical system of exchange and thereby inculcating in the audience a potent sense of social mobility and of the protean capacity of the self.[37]

The uncertain social standing of upwardly mobile actors created a built-in instability: "However aristocratic the explicit message of a play, the conditions of its production introduced alternative effects." Because of "the subversion of aristocratic and clerical superstructure by artisanal substructure," "the total theatrical process meant more than, and something different from, what the dramatic text itself meant."[38]

The importance of *All's Well That Ends Well*, to be considered in the next chapter, comes from the way it reproduces the general condition of the theater as institutional site in its specific content through the dramatization of Helena's social mobility. Or, vice versa, the reverberations of the play's content—Helena's ascendancy—are reinforced by the theatrical environment. Hence the significance of the difference in media between the court poetry of *Venus and Adonis* and the public theater of *All's Well That Ends Well:* the wider social base of the latter makes its implications potentially more volatile and unpredictable.

3

The Political Effects of Gender and Class in *All's Well That Ends Well*

One of the most striking features of *All's Well That Ends Well* is its full rendering of specifically male frustration in the person of Bertram, a besieged and recalcitrant Adonis writ large.[1] But the problem of Bertram cannot be adequately discussed at the level of individual character, as though our response hinged exclusively on the question of his personal defects and of his capacity to overcome them in the end. The analysis must rather be extended to the larger cultural forces operating on, and embodied in, Bertram. This latter approach can be opened up by noting the cultural overlap between Bertram's situation and that of the Essex-Southampton group: in both cases an emphatically military definition of masculinity is placed under intense pressure and ultimately frustrated. Yet the equation of Bertram with Southampton in G. P. V. Akrigg's reading of *All's Well That Ends Well* constitutes a methodological obstacle to this interpretation.[2] Treated as literal topical allusions, such connections are impossible to prove and are readily dismissed by a stringently factual account such as Samuel Schoenbaum's: "Shakespeare did not again dedicate one of his writings to a noble lord. Southampton now departs from the biographical record."[3] However, by responding at the same level as the critics he rejects, Schoenbaum remains within the framework of a limited historical mode now challenged by new historicists, among others.

For a cultural analysis of *All's Well That Ends Well*, Mervyn James's essay "At a Crossroads of the Political Culture: The Essex Revolt, 1601" provides a more promising and substantial starting point than Akrigg's narrowly conceived work.[4] Two elements in James's study of the cultural formation of the Essex-Southampton group have a strong resonance with Bertram's predicament. First, this historically specific male identity had its source in a military subculture, creating a concept of manhood that was potentially volatile, destabilizing, and anachronistic.

> But what gave the Essex connection its special tone, and many of its cultural characteristics, was its strongly military orientation. . . . Moreover, the military relationship had been given a special aura, of a traditionalist and chivalric kind, by the lavish way in which Essex, in spite of the queen's protests, had used his military prerogative to confer the honour of knighthood on those who distinguished themselves under him on the field. . . . To those who received it [as Southampton did], knighthood implied a special relationship with Essex himself.
>
> (pp. 427–28)

As the clause "in spite of the queen's protests" suggests, this male bonding and solidarity is defensive—a defiant assertion of threatened male privilege:

> Yet the sense of ancestry, in the Essexian context, strikes a special note: often self-confidently arrogant, but marked by a nostalgia for past glories, and a sense of being, as it were, under siege. . . . The sense of political frustration, of being unjustly slighted and so their honour defaced, was an experience shared with the leader by many courtier Essexians also, including such peers as . . . the earl of Southampton.
>
> (pp. 433–34)

Second, the gendered quality of this thwarted masculinity was accentuated by the mutually suspicious relationship between the cult of male military honor and the cult of Elizabeth. The latter appeared to place men in a double bind because the queen both stimulated chivalric heroism and curbed it—a bind which made graphically clear the queen's female rule and against which Essex bridled in sexual terms:

> Yet his relationship to the queen nevertheless became progressively charged with a tension which contained the seeds of

violence. The tension, rooted in political failure and exclusion, was related to his view of their respective sexual roles. . . . Essex never wavered in the conviction that, when important decisions had to be made, the weaknesses of the queen's femininity must be overwhelmed by a rough masculine initiative. . . . The so-called "great Quarrel" of July 1598, the point of no return in relations between Essex and the queen, generated so much bitterness precisely because of the earl's assessment of their respective sexual roles in terms of honour. For by striking him in the course of a Council meeting at which he had rudely turned his back on her, the queen had shown an unnatural male aggressiveness, and had thus submitted Essex to the unbearable dishonour which a publicly administered woman's blow involved. . . . He himself replied with a violent gesture, clapping his hand to his sword, and equally violent words, till the other councillors separated them.

(pp. 443–45)

Even before Helena's action has transformed the king into a vehicle for her power, Bertram has already figured the obstruction of his military drive as female:

> I shall stay here the forehorse to a smock,
> Creaking my shoes on the plain masonry,
> Till honour be brought up, and no sword worn
> But to dance with.
>
> (2.1.30–33)

The contrast with *Henry V* is instructive. The military aspirations of Hal as Henry V are given wide scope. The new king's qualms of conscience may create residual complications, but there are no external impediments to stop the forward movement of his nationalist enterprise.[5] Bertram's heroic ambition is sharply circumscribed, his military adventure accorded only abbreviated and truncated dramatization. Military achievement is discounted and devalued in advance by being presented as a delaying action, an escapist diversion from the central issue—Helena's strongly registered claim: "his sword can never win / The honour that he loses" (3.2.93–94); "The great dignity that his valour hath here acquired for him shall at home be encount'red with a shame as ample" (4.3.65–67).

Like Essex, Bertram uses military service as a cultural escape route that enables him to establish a field of male action in a remote location whose distance from the female-dominated central court temporarily affords a measure of protection. But Helena invades this space, thus intensifying the conflict between male prerogative and female rule. While Helena may not match the queen's "unnatural male aggressiveness" as experienced by Essex, her determined pursuit of Bertram is nevertheless sufficiently forceful and relentless to constitute aggression.[6] *All's Well That Ends Well* thus hits a sensitive cultural nerve, and the open question announced in the title is less one of aesthetics than of sexual politics: can all end well if female power undercuts male heroism?

Mervyn James, citing the Chorus that begins act five of *Henry V* (5.Cho.29–35), attributes to Shakespeare a strictly orthodox attitude supporting the queen's position with regard to Essex: "So Shakespeare had seen. . . . It was as 'the general of our gracious empress' that the earl's heroic image as the embodiment of lineage, arms and honour acquired validity" (p. 452).[7] However, in the larger context of *Henry V*, the effect of this circumspect, correct statement of Essex's subordination to Elizabeth is complicated and counteracted by the appeal of Henry V's male prowess, which runs roughshod over Queen Isabel and Princess Kate in the final scene. In order to make the parallel with Elizabeth-Essex work, Henry V has to occupy both positions: he is both chivalric warrior and monarch, and his dual role displaces Elizabeth as a specifically female ruler. This effect is confirmed by the way subsequent dramatic events assert male domination in Henry V's high-handed appropriation of Katherine: Henry V in the most decisive manner reverses Essex's subordinate position. The uneasy coexistence of two quite different models of male-female relations—the Choric acknowledgment of female authorization of male chivalry and the dramatization of male self-authorization—creates an impression of ambivalence.[8]

This ambivalent response to female authority is pronounced in *All's Well That Ends Well*, where female bonds are strengthened as male bonds are correspondingly weakened: the Countess displays "a more rooted love" (4.5.12) toward

Helena than is possible for Queen Isabel toward her daughter in *Henry V*, while the chivalric ties glorified in *Henry V* (4.7) are denied outright by the satiric exposure of the Parolles-Bertram relationship in *All's Well That Ends Well* (4.3.79–311).[9] The Countess's extraordinary readiness to renounce her son Bertram provides a reminder of Queen Elizabeth's ability to sever relations with her male courtiers.

I

One way of minimizing Helena's effect is to deny the full impact of her power by portraying it as narrowly and exclusively channeled against Bertram as an individual rather than against the social structure as a whole. This version presents Bertram as an isolated target by stressing Helena's alliance with the older generation. But Helena's interactions with the King of France cannot be characterized as cooperation or service. Rather, her rescue of the king calls attention to his ongoing weakness as nominal head of government while dramatizing, by contrast, her own achievement of power to be used for her own ends. The image of male order is vulnerable not simply because Bertram is a weak link in an otherwise solid chain but also because there is no convincing, living embodiment of the ancestral "first father" (3.7.25) elsewhere in the play as the king himself conspicuously demonstrates.

The opening lines of the play focus attention on the King of France as the center of a patriarchal social system, raising high expectations about his capacity to repair breaks in the family network. According to the extended family metaphor developed by Lafew, the king will restore the loss of Bertram's father by offering himself as a paternal equivalent. Thus Bertram is encouraged to see the king as "a father" (1.1.6–7). The first encounter between the king and Bertram in act 1, scene 2, reinforces this logic. The king begins the meeting by recognizing the link between Bertram and his dead father: "Youth, thou bear'st thy father's face" (1.2.19).[10] He ends the session by confirming his ability to serve as a paternal substitute and by this mediation to preserve the po-

tential for the continuity of male heritage: "Welcome, count; /
My son's no dearer" (75–76). Yet the smooth functioning of
this father-son framework is jeopardized by the irritation
aroused in the king by the prospect of his replacement by the
younger generation. The king's nostalgic identification with
Bertram's father leads to a heightened contrast between older
and younger generations at the latter's expense that threatens
to forestall the larger momentum of generational continuity:
"Such a man / Might be a copy to these younger times; /
Which, followed well, would demonstrate them now / But
goers backward" (1.2.45–48).[11] Pursuing this invidious comparison between the noble past "when thy father and myself
in friendship / First tried our soldiership" (25–26) and the
unsatisfactory present of the new generation, the king re-
hearses a set of highly charged emotions: rage over his aging
and demise ("But on us both did haggish age steal on, / And
wore us out of act"—29–30), resistance to yielding control,
defensive antagonism toward his eventual successors, desire
for reassurance and appreciation.

The feelings released in the king by Bertram's presence are
by no means unprecedented. From the perspective of the
Henriad, the unstable mood created by the king's critique of
male youth can be seen as a standard feature of the generational tension fathers and sons must negotiate. Like the King
of France in *All's Well That Ends Well*, Henry IV is a sick king
who initiates contact with his youthful counterpart by lashing
out against him:

> See, sons, what things you are,
> How quickly nature falls into revolt
> When gold becomes her object!
> For this the foolish over-careful fathers
> Have broke their sleep with thoughts,
> Their brains with care, their bones with industry;
> For this they have engrossed and pil'd up
> The canker'd heaps of strange-achieved gold;
> For this they have been thoughtful to invest
> Their sons with arts and martial exercises;
> When, like the bee, tolling from every flower
> The virtuous sweets,

Our thighs pack'd with wax, our mouths with honey,
We bring it to the hive; and like the bees
Are murder'd for our pains. This bitter taste
Yields his engrossments to the ending father.

(2H4, 4.5.64–79)

Henry IV's accusation registers the combined explosive pressure of self-pity and anger to which the King of France gives vent. In particular, citing the "good melancholy" (1.2.56) of Bertram's father, he employs the same despairing image of the beehive:

"Let me not live," quoth he,
"After my flame lacks oil, to be the snuff
Of younger spirits, whose apprehensive senses
All but new things disdain; whose judgments are
Mere fathers of their garments; whose constancies
Expire before their fashions." This he wish'd.
I, after him, do after him wish too,
Since I nor wax nor honey can bring home,
I quickly were dissolved from my hive
To give some labourers room.

(58–67)

The sarcastic play on the term *father*—"mere fathers of their garments"—is reminiscent of Henry IV's challenge to Hal's apparent contempt: "Thy wish was father, Harry, to that thought" (2H4, 4.5.92).

But there is a striking difference in the operation of the bee metaphor that the two kings share. In Henry IV's case, the image conveys richness and abundance: "Our thighs pack'd with wax, our mouths with honey" (2H4, 4.5.76). The language suggests, even during his momentary despair, a conviction about Henry IV's power and desire to give the crown. The King of France, however, confesses utter depletion and inadequacy, as though he were completely lacking in resources: "Since I nor wax nor honey can bring home" (1.2.65). The contrast between fullness and emptiness is emblematic of larger differences in the two situations.

Henry IV's angry outburst is quickly followed by reconciliation, the transmission of royal authority, and the commitment to military action. Henry IV and Hal manage their conflict by themselves without outside interference. The erotic force suggested by the image of Henry IV's "full thighs" is fulfilled in the intimate emotional exchange between two powerful men. The political resonance of the honey image is later realized in *Henry V* in the "sweet and honey'd sentences" (1.1.50) which the Archbishop of Canterbury attributes to the new king and in Canterbury's own elaboration of the male state as a beehive (1.2.187–204).

In *All's Well That Ends Well* decisive action comes from outside male relations. Helena's intervention is what interrupts the sense of drift. She provides the energy and direction needed to overcome the impasse created by the king's listlessness. In the transaction between the king and Bertram, Helena is "this good gift" (2.3.151), the object of exchange parallel to the crown which Henry IV gives to Hal. But Helena herself determines the terms of this gift giving. Not only does Bertram receive for his inheritance something he does not want but also the king gives him something which he did not plan and to which he has been forced to agree by the bargain that revived him. The king tries to transform his test of wills with Bertram into an exclusively man-to-man confrontation, but Helena's prior organizational role is too strong. The occasion will not compose into the standard pattern of male traffic in women who serve as incidental tokens by which men determine their relations of power to one another.

Helena's role as a woman who disrupts the normal procedures of patriarchal power can be registered only by a thorough examination of the extent of the king's—and hence the system's—weakness, for this weakness creates a political vacuum that helps to make Helena's control possible. From the outset, the King of France exudes an overall spirit of lassitude and exhaustion consistent with the specific emptiness communicated by his use of the honey motif in his first appearance. Lafew's idealized encomium invoking the king's "abundance" (1.1.10) is no sooner pronounced than it is undercut by the Countess's abrupt leading question about the king's health (1.1.11), which shifts the emphasis to his incapacity. The king toward whom Lafew directs reparative hopes is himself an empty center in need of restoration. Moreover, his debilitated condition is not merely a physical problem, but is symbolic of a more general malaise.

Even before Bertram's arrival at court, the king's handling of the business of the Florentine-Sienese war raises doubts about his leadership. His decision to avoid committing the state seems less a matter of sound judgment than of abdication because the policy of noninvolvement is compromised by his further decision to endorse private actions whose effect is random and in principle self-canceling since individuals are free to fight on either side. The contradictory nature of the king's policy is underlined by the strained language of his subsequent farewell to the two separate—and opposed—groups of young French nobles: "Share the advice betwixt you; if both gain all, / The gift doth stretch itself as 'tis receiv'd, / And is enough for both" (2.1.3–5). What is being stretched here is the king's logic: the phrase "both gain all" tries unsuccessfully to deny the division that he himself has introduced.

The cynical aspect of this approach is brought out by the attendant lord's observation: "It well may serve / A nursery to our gentry, who are sick / For breathing and exploit" (1.2.15–17). The allusion to sickness generalizes the king's personal ill health, suggesting wider cultural malfunction. The patent inability in a subsequent commentary to explain the king's rationale retroactively exposes the hollowness of the king's decision making:

> The reasons of our state I cannot yield,
> But like a common and an outward man
> That the great figure of council frames
> By self-unable motion; therefore dare not
> Say what I think of it, since I have found
> Myself in my incertain grounds to fail
> As often as I guess'd.
>
> (3.1.10–16)

The king appears to sponsor an ideal of heroic honor, but this honor is vitiated in advance. Through the lack of coherent and principled policy, the king contributes to the conditions for the youthful drift which he goes on to complain about in his initial meeting with Bertram: the king is thus responsible for what he criticizes.

Moreover, the king's attitude toward women exhibits the callousness for which he will later so vigorously prosecute Bertram. Like Polonius's tolerance of his son's "wanton, wild and usual slips" (*Hamlet*, 2.1.22), the king's gratuitous final bit of advice to the departing French nobles gives permission for sexual adventure after military service, if not before:

> Those girls of Italy, take heed of them;
> They say our French lack language to deny
> If they demand; beware of being captives
> Before you serve.
>
> (2.1.19–22)

Bertram's engagement with Diana conforms to this set of priorities, and his later excuse that he "boarded her i' th' wanton way of youth" (5.3.210) fits with the winking spirit of the king's initial formulation. Furthermore, the king's sly generalization about "Those girls of Italy" licenses the contemptuous attitude which Bertram exhibits—she "was a common gamester of the camp" (5.3.187)—and to which the king himself momentarily succumbs—"I think thee now some common customer" (280).

What convinces the king to undergo Helena's treatment is her willingness so emphatically to differentiate herself from the dangerously seductive foreign women the king has warned against (2.1.169–73). But this distinction becomes insecure, blurred by the sexual overtones of the power by which Helena performs the king's rejuvenation. Helena's success confirms her control: she gains the initiative and the king loses it. In designating Bertram as her choice, Helena tries to mitigate her power by moderating her language: "I dare not say I take you, but I give / Me and my service, ever whilst I live, / Into your guiding power. This is the man" (2.3.102–4). But the "guiding power" is all too clearly neither Bertram's nor the king's. Helena's negotiation with the king has already unmistakably established her primacy through the decisive phrase "I will command": "Then shalt thou give me with thy kingly hand / What husband in thy power I will command" (2.1.192–93). By his consent to this proposition, the king shows that he too "lacks language to deny / If they [women] demand" (20–21).

Despite the king's cure, he remains exceedingly vulnerable, truculent and ineffectual for the rest of the play. In between his two meetings with Bertram the king's confidence has been recovered through Helena's agency. His earlier despair gives way to renewed conviction in his "sovereign power and father's voice" (2.3.54). But the second encounter with Bertram in act 2, scene 3, demonstrates the king's continuing weakness because circumstances draw the king into an overreaction that reveals his insecurity, making the restored self seem defensive and unstable. Forced to "produce my power" (150), the king resorts to a harsher version of his earlier tendency to blame the younger generation for all problems when he threatens Bertram: "Or I will throw thee from my care forever / Into the staggers and careless lapse / Of youth and ignorance" (162–64). This outburst dramatizes the king's own flaws as much as Bertram's, for the king's need to apply pressure so heavy-handedly to Bertram stems from the pressure of the king's prior submission to Helena's intervention. Bertram's resistance calls attention to the king's own ongoing dependence on Helena: "But follows it, my lord, to bring me down / Must answer for your raising?" (112–13). By his refusal to cooperate, Bertram upsets the smooth operation of a scenario that would allow the king to deflect his dependence by passing it on to the younger man and making him share it.

Helena's relations with the king and with Bertram form parallel actions: in both cases, she meets with resistance which she successfully overcomes by manifesting her superior power. Uneasiness about the triumph of a woman's demand is by no means confined to Bertram. The king's psychological and institutional discomfort is suggested by the lengths to which he goes in his coercion of Bertram. It is as though the king is constrained to deny his own doubts by aggressively suppressing them in Bertram. Yet the completion of the process in which Bertram is "crush'd with a plot" fails to satisfy the king because it does not bring relief from the fundamental problem of his own dependence on a woman. The king's offer to Diana at the end of the play—"If thou beest yet a fresh uncropped flower / Choose thou thy husband and I'll pay thy dower" (5.3.321–22)—is not a simple repetition. Rather, it represents a compulsive effort to redo the plot to make it come out right: this time he, not the woman, seizes the initiative. If the proposal is his, then the male control that he has lost can be reasserted. The irony of this logic is that his proposal is so closely modeled on Helena's original proposition that it testifies to her power rather than to his. But the irony is not a lighthearted one. Though brief, this moment signals a deep and continuing uneasiness with female control.

II

The course of Helena's love in *All's Well That Ends Well* has the effect of reconstituting a combined image of Venus and Diana;[12] she therefore reconnects the female attributes that the poetic sequence from *Venus and Adonis* to *The Rape of Lucrece* had split apart. Helena succeeds, where Venus spectacularly failed, in the conquest of a resistant male. Moreover, Helena also recuperates Lucrece's humility and passivity; for Helena's occasional hesitation and submissiveness, which seem to compromise her assertiveness, act rather as a sign of the virtue that sanctions and strengthens her position. The difference between Venus's and Helena's ambition is that the latter is more difficult, virtually impossible, to fault. Venus's violation carries with it a suggestion of illegitimacy that permits us to label her action as in some sense wrong. Helena's triumph is licensed by a moral justification akin to the merry wives' riddling self-defense that they "may be merry and yet honest too" (*The Merry Wives of Windsor*, 4.2.96):

> Why then tonight
> Let us assay our plot; which, if it speed,

Is wicked meaning in a lawful dead,
And lawful meaning in a lawful act,
Where both not sin, and yet a sinful fact.
(3.7.43–47)

Two critical formulations lead to an underestimation of Helena's disruptive social significance. The first, exemplified by G. K. Hunter's introduction to the New Arden edition, diminishes the threat of Helena's initiative by stressing her personal submissiveness and her religious reliance on divine agency. Too neatly dividing the play into two parts, Hunter sees Helena's pilgrimage—"a journey of contrition and abnegation" (p. xxxi)—as the turning point and confines her active role to the first half: "In the second half of *All's Well*, Helena is a 'clever wench' only in the sense in which Griselda is— clever enough to be virtuous, pious, and patient till Destiny and Justice work things out for her" (p. xxxii). Recent feminist critics have challenged and refuted this characterization of Helena by noting that the consistent forcefulness of her actions impressively outweighs her occasional recourse to passive language or diminutive tone. While acknowledging Helena's mixture of "aggressive initiative and passivity," Susan Snyder convincingly argues that upon arrival in Florence Helena "takes forceful control of the action, persuading the Widow to agree to the bed-substitution, instructing Diana, pursuing Bertram back to France, seeking audience with the king, and through her agent Diana manipulating the final revelation-scene to expose Bertram, prove her fulfillment of the impossible tasks, and claim her reluctant husband all over again."[13] Helena's oxymorons—"humble ambition, proud humility" (1.1.167)—apply to her actions at the end as well as the beginning; she is never humble without also being ambitious and proud. There is no mistaking the crisp energy with which Helena manages Bertram's taming: "But let's about it" (3.7.48).

A second formulation by which Helena's dominance is tempered is to treat it as a temporary and transitional anomaly whose resolution can be found in the late romances. This motif of the postponed resolution is represented by G. K. Hunter's use of a larger developmental perspective retroactively to solve the problems of *All's Well That Ends Well*: "Viewed in this context [of the romances], much that seems perverse in *All's Well* begins to fall into focus"; "much of the perversity of the denouement disappears if we see it as an attempt at the effects gradually mastered in the intervening comedies, and triumphantly achieved in *The Winter's Tale*" (introduction, New Arden edition, p. lv). This approach creates difficulties, however, because it leads in my view to an inaccurate account of *The Winter's Tale*[14] and because it mutes the effect of *All's Well That Ends Well* by recuperating it in terms of another play and thereby reducing our ability to see its own terms. What is lost when *All's Well That Ends Well* is redirected toward and transposed onto the late romances? One answer is that Helena's power is discounted, since the gender dynamic of the romances requires her transformation into an enabling, cooperative heroine. But the Helena of *All's Well That Ends Well* cannot be easily translated and assimilated into the sublime female comfort exemplified by *The Winter's Tale*. In the distinctive play she dominates, Helena makes her own demands and, however cautiously, advances her own power.

The force of Helena's challenge is illustrated by the change in the king's rhetoric about class. Prior to Helena's arrival at court, the king evokes an ideal of hierarchy based on the behavior of Bertram's dead father:

> So like a courtier, contempt nor bitterness
> Were in his pride or sharpness; if they were,
> His equal had awak'd them, and his honour,
> Clock to itself, knew the true minute when
> Exception bid him speak, and at this time
> His tongue obey'd his hand. Who were below him
> He us'd as creatures of another place,
> And bow'd his eminent top to their low ranks,
> Making them proud of his humility
> In their poor praise he humbled.
>
> (1.2.36–45)

The witty reversal of "proud" and "humbled" in the final two lines depends on the firm, fixed distinction between ranks that admits no ambiguity between "His equal" and "Who were below him." What is striking about this image of clear-cut class structure is that it has no room for Helena. Neither Bertram nor the king can follow this decorum because Helena refuses to accept her position as one of the "creatures of another place."

After Helena's decisive intervention in the court world, the king projects a very different image of class relations, now adjusted to reflect the situation into which he has been maneuvered by the pressure of Helena's upward initiative:

> 'Tis only title thou disdain'st in her, the which
> I can build up. Strange is it that our bloods
> Of colour, weight, and heat, pour'd all together,
> Would quite confound distinction, yet stands off
> In differences so mighty. If she be
> All that is virtuous, save what thou dislik'st—
> A poor physician's daughter—thou dislik'st
> Of virtue for the name. But do not so.
> From lowest place when virtuous things proceed,
> The place is dignified by th' doer's deed.
>
> (2.3.117–26)

In shifting from his earlier image of "creatures of another place" who remain in "their low ranks" (1.2.42–43) to this more positive version of "lowest place" (2.3.125), the king legitimizes social mobility instead of ordered stability. In so acting on Helena's behalf, however, he inadvertently names the danger that her advancement as a lower-class woman may "quite confound distinction."

The king emphasizes his own agency—"the which / I can build up"—but he is Helena's creation more than she is his. With Helena as prime mover and the king as the figurehead through which she pursues her own ends, the play's action confounds the conventional organizing distinctions both of class and of gender.[15] The intertwined gender aspect remains pertinent because while the king enunciates a philosophical endorsement of class flexibility, Helena's practical realization of her aspiration depends on strong support from female sponsors, one of whom, the Florentine widow, suggests an experience of class that validates Helena's enterprise. The Widow provides a living example of class fluidity, though in the reverse direction ("Though my estate be fall'n, I was well born" [3.7.4]), and thereby serves as a mediating figure who breaks the barrier between high and low.

Following J. Dover Wilson's suggestion that the class disparity expressed by Helena's view of Bertram as "a bright particular star / . . . so above me" (1.1.84–85) is equivalent to "the social relationship between Shakespeare and his patron,"[16] C. L. Barber develops a parallel between the poet and the young man of the sonnets and Helena and Bertram. According to this analysis, *All's Well That Ends Well* represents an aggressive disengagement from the bourgeois poet's paralyzing deference to the aristocratic youth in the sonnets. Feelings about the youth, who is now recast as Bertram, are released in two ways. The first exorcises the poet's adulatory stance by self-critically parodying it in the form of Parolles's empty words of affection for Bertram. The satiric treatment of Parolles is a relatively routine replaying of issues more deeply expressed in the rejection of Falstaff. The second attempts to enact the poet's vindication through Helena's highly charged conquest of the young aristocrat, despite his efforts to ignore and resist her. But this wished-for triumph is secured by a psychological shortcut: since "Helena's project culminates in the moral aggression expended on Bertram before he accepts marriage to her, we can feel . . . that the play is being *used*, rather than that its full human implications are being worked out into the light."[17]

This interpretation presupposes an alignment between Helena and Shakespeare, who share the same "moral aggression" against Bertram. I want to modify this version of the balance of forces by emphasizing the structural ambivalence of Shakespeare's position. Helena's gender makes impossible any one-sided identification with Helena against Bertram. However enthusiastic Shakespeare's participation in the discomfiting of Bertram, there is also an undertow of residual sympathy for Bertram's plight and concomitant anxiousness over Helena's power.[18] However substantial Shakespeare's promotion of Helena's enterprise, there is no total, unimpeded, unqualified cross-gender identification on his part.[19] Helena's aggression against Bertram is different from Shakespeare's; the latter is more limited than the former, creating a boomerang effect that pulls Shakespeare's investment in Helena up short and makes his ambivalence run both ways, toward Helena as well as toward Bertram. In this sense it is possible to reverse Barber's formulation and say that the play uses Shakespeare.

Reacting against Helena's triumph, Shakespeare remains in part sympathetically bound to the besieged male positions of both Bertram and the king; the play thereby gives voice not only to the two male characters' discomfiture but also to Shakespeare's. The authorial division that blocks a convincing resolution is significant because it dramatizes a much larger cultural quandary: the society's inability to accommodate, without deep disturbance, decisive female control. If the underlying restiveness of *All's Well That Ends Well* gives way in *Hamlet* to open misogynist attack, this shift is made possible in part by the drastic decrease in female power and control. Deprived of the delicate balance between sexuality and purity by which Helena wins her position as wife, the wife in *Hamlet* is left isolated, exposed, and vulnerable.

4

Gender, Genre, and Nation
in *Hamlet*

In an extraordinary commentary on *Hamlet*, C. L. Barber observes that the play demands a sympathetic identification with the hero so total as to forestall and all but block any critical perspective. The absence of a counterbalancing "ironic control" makes *Hamlet* a "failure" compared to subsequent tragedies: "What the play does not provide is ruthless awareness of Hamlet, such awareness as we are to get of Othello, Lear, Macbeth, Antony, Coriolanus."[1] Barber explains this shift primarily as an internal development, part of the ongoing process of Shakespeare's "whole journey" as an individual artist. However, since the later tragedies belong to the Jacobean period, I want to redirect the question along different lines: if *Hamlet* "is a play in which something gets out of hand," is there a specifically Elizabethan context that could help to account for the "something" not under control? In particular, I want to pursue a correlation between *Hamlet* and the conflicting social forces exemplified by the tension in the relationship between Elizabeth and Essex.[2]

The basis for making a connection between the cultural phenomenon of Essex and the theatrical phenomenon of *Hamlet* is their historical overlap: the final crucial years of Essex's career (1599–1601) coincide with the dates for *Hamlet*.[3] The problem is how, and at what level, to formulate the connection. The association of Essex with Hamlet made by J. Dover Wilson has been persuasively challenged by David Bevington's demonstration of the danger of arbitrary, misplaced specificity in topical interpretation.[4] For example, Hamlet's situation with respect to his father and mother bears some resemblance to Essex's family circumstances. Like Hamlet, Essex is called upon to repair the abrogated paternal heritage of a prematurely deceased military father. The pull of this burden is indicated by Essex's gravitation to Ireland, the site of his father's failure, as the scene of his own demise. In a further echo of Hamlet's predicament, Essex's mother promptly remarries a man at the center of political power. Yet these similarities serve only to highlight a more fundamental difference: while Essex finds a fully acceptable sponsor in his new stepfather Leicester, Hamlet's identity is founded on absolute rejection of Claudius. The overall result of the comparison is thus to undercut a direct topical equation of Essex with Hamlet.

Nevertheless, Annabel Patterson has recently renewed the argument for linking *Hamlet* with Essex. She does so by setting aside J. Dover Wilson's "characterological" approach in favor of a "cultural" interpretation.[5] I propose to follow and to expand Patterson's cultural emphasis. I shall suggest a connection between Essex and *Hamlet* on the grounds of genre and focus in particular on the generic effects of pastoral, where pastoral is understood as a social institution rather than purely aesthetic form.

I

The three terms in the title of this chapter—gender, genre, and nation—are brought into conjunction by the pastoral mode:

> The Tudor state was reformulated within nationalist ideology as a *hortus conclusus,* an enclosed garden walled off from its enemies. In the Ditchley portrait, Elizabeth I is portrayed standing upon a map of England. As the virgin who ushers in the golden age, she symbolizes at the same time as she is symbolized by an island which resists all 'foreign bodies.' . . . The conjuncture of imperial virgin and cartographic image . . . constitute[s] the terrain of Elizabethan nationalism.[6]

Pastoral is thus the site where the concepts of nation and gender intersect: the image of the garden enacts England's national self-definition, while this national identity is in turn symbolically secured by the superimposed image of Elizabeth's female body. However, the same set of mutually reinforcing images that implies national harmony also marks an area of cultural tension concerning gender. For this imagery simultaneously makes Elizabeth the guarantor of England's integrity and a potential threat. If she represents the firm boundaries that keep external enemies out, she also figures the limits that hold in, even overwhelm, indigenous male initiative. Is England's invincibility due to Elizabeth's magical potency or to the male soldiery that her Ditchley portrait has erased?[7]

Hamlet, I shall argue, engages in an exploration of national identity in which the pastoral genre and female gender are crucial terms. The sense of an unsettled, disturbed image of the collective identity vested in the state—a note sounded from the outset in "This bodes some strange eruption to our state" (1.1.72)—takes on this larger meaning of cultural disturbance. England explicitly has a minor, marginal role in the play; but *Hamlet* is more centrally about England if, on the principle of "indirections," Denmark itself is experienced as a metaphor for the British state. Yet, *Hamlet* might seem an unpromising candidate for a specifically pastoral fashioning of national identity. I therefore turn to a striking, but apparently incidental, pastoral appeal early in the play—Marcellus's wistful invocation of the harmony that perhaps accompanies the celebration of "our Saviour's birth" (1.1.163–69).

At first sight, the function of this brief pastoral interlude is to provide a stark generic counterpoint: this wished-for pastoral is what will be conspicuously excluded by the tragedy that is in fact to ensue. However, as it unfolds, the action of *Hamlet* intertwines rather than separates the two modes. Marcellus's throwaway pastoral gesture toward a protected space of psychological reprieve is actually a "harbinger" and "prologue" (125–26) for the play's eventual destination. A key detail in Marcellus's speech is the disarming of female force: "nor witch hath power to charm" (168). *Hamlet* as a whole enacts a far more complex escape from female power to charm, but Marcellus's set piece represents a tentative, preliminary move in an overall pattern: the sustained production of an insulated area for the free play of male bonds. *Hamlet* is a pastoralized tragedy that employs pastoral to reform the relation between national and gender identity. On a much larger, more subtly affecting scale than *The Rape of Lucrece* as described in chapter 2, *Hamlet* creates a gendered version of tragedy that skews pity in the twin directions of male emotional preserve and of political bulwark for a male state.

C. L. Barber raises the question of genre when he qualifies the play's status as tragedy: "*Hamlet* is not, I think, a fully achieved tragedy, but rather a heroic-prophetic play with a 'tragical' ending."[8] In this regard, Polonius's generic equivocation appears less exclusively parodic, for his rambling inventory gives inadvertent testimony to the power of pastoral: "tragedy, comedy, history, pastoral, pastoral-comical, historical-pastoral, tragical-historical, tragical-comical-historical-pastoral." (2.2.392–95). Pastoral here operates as an omnibus term that not only modifies but also subsumes the categories with which it is hyphenated. Initially, *Hamlet*'s pastoral dimension is entirely negative. The play ruthlessly denies and systematically cancels any possibility of a supportive pastoral landscape: to Hamlet the world is "an unweeded garden" (1.2.135); his father's murder occurs in the vulnerable pastoral setting of his "orchard" (1.5.35, 59); Hamlet is reduced to the dispirited perception of "this goodly frame the earth" as "a sterile promontory" (2.2.298–99); his re-creation of the scene of his father's death pointedly includes the violated pastoral motif: "A poisons him i' th' garden for his estate" (3.2.255). But *Hamlet* empties out the pastoral mode only to revive and rebuild it.

A crucial turning point in the play—Hamlet's departure for England and his "sudden and more strange return" (4.7.45)—hinges on the pastoral movement of withdrawal and return. Though the journey is abbreviated and not directly dramatized, its effect is not compressed but is strategically drawn out. Hamlet's release from the claustrophobic "prison" he feels Denmark to be (2.2.243) is all the more spectacularly expansive for being so long delayed. Claudius first broaches

Hamlet's trip as conventional pastoral recreation—a change-of-scene therapy: "Haply the seas and countries different, / With variable objects, shall expel / This something settled matter in his heart" (3.1.173–75). But even this initial proposal is given dramatic point because it reverses Claudius's earlier denial of Hamlet's leave (1.2.112–16). The king's desire to keep his nephew under close watch is ironically replaced by an increasingly urgent need to send him away. Claudius's new plan gathers emotional force with each subsequent mention (3.3.1–7, 24–26; 3.4.202–12; 4.1.29–30; 4.3.40–71; 4.7.30–33), becoming a vivid measure of his growing insecurity.

Hamlet's surprise return is equally exploited for maximum impact; the events of the voyage are elaborately rehearsed, twice announced prior to Hamlet's actual appearance (4.6.1–31; 4.7.36–51) and then taken up by Hamlet in person at the beginning of the play's last scene (5.2.1–62). So magnified, this episode provides a catalyst for Hamlet's dramatic change of mood in act 5. The play's structure is organized around three galvanic moments, each of which energizes Hamlet with a sense of purpose. However, the first two—the aftermaths of his encounter with the ghost (1.5.113–98) and of his entrapment of Claudius through the play-within-a-play (3.2.255–88)—become bogged down and diverted. The third moment—Hamlet's new mobility and his return to Denmark—is different because this time Hamlet's resolve carries through to the end. It is not simply the note of confidence registered in the amused defiance with which Hamlet now challenges Claudius: "High and mighty, you shall know I am set naked on your kingdom" (4.7.41–42). Hamlet's shift in tone embraces a much larger spirit of equanimity manifested in his two great speeches on "rashness" and "readiness" in the last scene (5.2.6–11, 215–20).

The play's final pastoral modulation is convincing even though Hamlet's journey takes place on sea rather than in the more familiar green world. The central feature of pastoral is neither the figure of the shepherd nor the image of the green world, but its focus on courtly matters: *Hamlet* employs pastoral in its capacity as a medium for negotiating one's position in relation to the court. Right up to the very end, the play supplies a constant parade of hollow court-grown characters—not to mention Claudius, there are Polonius, Rosencrantz and Guildenstern, and finally the "water-fly" Osric (5.2.82–83)—who afford occasion for Hamlet's virtuoso displays of contempt. As self-appointed "satirical rogue" (2.2.196), Hamlet keeps up a running commentary on the vagaries that attend the pursuit of courtly advancement: "No, let the candied tongue lick absurd pomp, / And crook the pregnant hinges of the knee / Where thrift may follow fawning" (3.2.60–62). Yet this expression of disdain is itself a standard pastoral line: "Renaissance pastoral takes the court as its cynosure. Although many of these works direct criticism or hostility against courtly decadence or the iniquities of courtly reward, such anti-courtliness tends to measure either the court's distance from its own high ideals or the courtier's distance from the satisfaction of his ambitions."[9]

Hamlet's ambitions are more profound than those of the easy targets he mocks, but Hamlet's ambitions also have the court as their frame of reference. Within this orbit, Hamlet masterfully manipulates the repertoire of courtly forms and rituals to his own ends: he does "make love to this employment" (5.2.57). Pastoral enables both Hamlet's bitter critique and his more positive accommodation, the dramatic weight gradually shifting from the former to the latter. Hamlet's change of heart resists explanation at the level of character. His lengthy apology to Laertes (222–39) is opaque, inadequate, unearned; as an expression of character, it is too limited by his narrow formulation: "I'll court his favours" (78). Hamlet's appeal to Laertes's "most generous thoughts" is motivated less by character than by genre. The generosity that permeates the conclusion evidences the power of pastoral in governing the play's final disposition. To rephrase Hamlet, there's a genre "that shapes our ends" (10).

II

At this point I return to the issue of a connection between Hamlet and Essex by positing a generic correspondence between *Hamlet*'s end and Essex's end. The latter presents a similar experience of sudden composure: under the pressure of his death sentence, Essex's jumble of emotions, ranging from haughty self-justification to groveling despair, is reorganized into a final stance of steady penitence and serenity.[10] This moment is for Essex not only the closing out, but also the rounding off, of his career; as the endgame in his relation with Elizabeth, it constitutes both his final appeal to the queen and his ultimate declaration of independence. To say that Essex's self-presentation is a literary posture is not merely metaphorical. Not only can Essex's letters to the queen be considered literary productions but also his final approach is consistent with his previous use of his own poetry as a means of access to the queen. Though not actually sent to the queen, Essex's longest poem was written in the Tower in the last four days of his life.[11]

The argument here is neither that Essex holds up the mirror to Hamlet's nature nor, conversely, that Essex's final moment is modeled on Hamlet. Rather, to adapt Hamlet's terms "form" and "pressure" (3.2.24), both actions bear the imprint of the cultural pressure of generic form—in particular, the convention of *ars moriendi*,[12] a version of pastoral in which the other world is the "undiscover'd country" after death "from whose bourn / No traveller returns" (3.1.79–80). Because there is no return, emphasis may fall less on the destination than on the process of preparation, and *ars moriendi* may become not just a tradition but also a strategy and a practice. In Harry Berger's account, two key features of Shakespearean *ars moriendi* are victimhood and theatricality.[13] It would not, in this view, be sufficient to say that Essex and Hamlet both exhibit equanimity in the face of death. A fuller analysis would add that both Essex and Hamlet are self-styled victims and that both possess finely tuned theatrical sensibilities with which to act out the victim's role.

The motif of *ars moriendi* is announced in *Hamlet* by one victim (Ophelia) speaking of another (Polonius): "They say a made a good end" (4.5.183). This piety has been undercut in advance by Hamlet's blunt eulogy: "Thou wretched, rash, intruding fool, farewell" (3.4.31). Yet, though Ophelia's appeal to convention is ironic in its immediate application, the motif retains a deeper resonance. As with pastoral in general, so with *ars moriendi*: what is initially unsparingly mocked is later recovered for positive use. However brutal his summing up of Polonius's life (3.4.215–17), Hamlet himself will be handsomely eulogized—a procedure that he not only insists is his right, but also actively shapes in the final scene after his contemplation of the graveyard. From this standpoint, the action of the play is to move Hamlet from the hestitation of "Must give us pause" (3.1.68) to the conviction of "The readiness is all" (5.2.218).

Part of the cultural work the play performs is to satisfy Hamlet's original image of death as "a consummation / Devoutly to be wish'd" (3.1.63–64) by finding and fashioning a more legitimate, less obviously escapist, version. Pastoral offers the means for realizing this ambition, though the moment when the shift from negative to positive pastoral begins to take hold is slight. In his exhilaration after catching the king in *The Mousetrap* (3.2.232), Hamlet indulges in generic high jinks that not only transform tragedy into comedy (286) but also include a glance at pastoral. Harold Jenkins is right in seeing Hamlet's gleeful address to Horatio as "O Damon dear" (275) as a pastoral touch that evokes Damon and Pythias as a model of male friendship. This detail is consonant with the role of male bonds in fulfilling the pastoral design that emerges at the play's end. However, the burden of the design falls on Ophelia: she serves as the principal vehicle for establishing the pastoral mood. For this reason, genre becomes an expression of gender relations.

Ophelia's elegy (3.1.153–63) effects a shift in the central object of mourning from old to young Hamlet. The price she pays for this choric function is to become an embodiment of elegy herself. The floral imagery and lyricism that symbolize her reduced state bring pastoral convention into the mainstream of the play in act 4. Her funereal singing of "grassgreen turf" and "sweet flowers" (4.5.31, 38), the tableau of her distribution of flowers (4.5.173–83), the set piece pastoralism of her death (4.7.165–82), and the flowery tribute at her grave (5.1.236–39) all set the stage for the play's strong generic turn, but at Ophelia's expense. The play allows Hamlet to ride the current of pastoral feeling that destroys Ophelia. Their divergent courses are indicated by the contrasting vertical imagery of Ophelia's sinking and Hamlet's elevation as figured in Horatio's image of ascension (5.2.365). The accidental quality in the "rashness" (7) that ennobles Hamlet demeans Ophelia, whose accidental death leaves uncertain whether she consciously committed suicide and hence denies her the dignity of having chosen her destiny. It is as though there are two versions of pastoral: Ophelia represents the external pastoral of "the trappings and suits of woe" while Hamlet expresses the inner pastoral of "that within which passes show" (1.2.85–86). Yet even this distinction understates the case, for, in contrast to the "maimed rites" (5.1.212) accorded to Ophelia, Hamlet is respectfully granted proper ceremony: "and for his passage, / The soldier's music and the rite of war / Speak loudly for him" (5.2.403–5).

Ophelia's fate points back to the queen as the primary female figure, for it is Gertrude's voice that speaks for Ophelia by reporting her death and by observing the formality of "her maiden strewments" (5.1.226). This link between the two women reinforces the division of pastoral labor according to gender. Because the loaded generic deck stacks the cards against women, the feminist defense of Gertrude as an individual character is insufficient.[14] It is necessary to shift the ground of analysis to a critique of the overall dramatic structure. The gendered shape of the play's action is indicated by its marginalization of both women. At Ophelia's grave, the main business is Hamlet's competition with Laertes: Hamlet's "I lov'd you [Laertes] ever" (5.1.285) speaks louder and to more lasting effect than the brief "I lov'd Ophelia" (264) with which he started. Hamlet's equally brief recognition of his mother—"Wretched Queen, adieu" (5.2.338)—is terse compared to his dealings with Laertes, Horatio, and Fortinbras, the three male counterparts who provide the main line of communication in the final scene.

Hamlet offers two measures of the degree to which Gertrude as "queen-mother" (3.1.184) has earlier served as a lightning rod for Hamlet's highly charged outrage. First, the play twice (1.1.116–23; 3.2.102–3) refers us back to *Julius Caesar* (1599), an exclusively male-male conflict that lacks the greater dramatic intensity created in *Hamlet* by the addition of Gertrude's role. Second, the need that drives Hamlet's relation to Gertrude is so powerful that it causes him to disobey the ghost's express instruction to "leave her to heaven" (1.5.86). Even when the ghost intervenes in the closet scene to reassert the taboo protecting Gertrude (3.4.112–15), Hamlet is hardly able to contain the anger he directs toward her. This rage can be partly illuminated by reference to Queen Elizabeth, for Gertrude represents the convergence of three issues—sexuality, aging (3.4.68–70), and succession—that produced a sense of contradiction, even breakdown, in the cult of Elizabeth in the final years of her reign and that were brought into particular focus by her association with the much younger Essex. The connection between Gertrude and Elizabeth provides a way to expand consideration of Gertrude's position that is neither characterological nor authorial; I am not claiming that the two women are similar in every respect or that Shakespeare necessarily intended this connection. What is cognate is rather the interrelations of genre and gender by which the women's identities are shaped. As a specific case, I turn to a device Essex presented to Elizabeth in 1595 on the occasion of the tournament celebrating the thirty-seventh anniversary of her accession to royal power.[15]

III

Essex's device has thematic and structural links with *Hamlet*, which it precedes by approximately five years. Both dramatize the difficulty of trying to encompass multiple roles. The three options of hermit, soldier, and statesman with which Essex is confronted are roughly equivalent to the triple expectation—"The courtier's, soldier's, scholar's, eye, tongue, sword" (3.1.153)—apparently nullified by Hamlet's collapse.

Ironically, Hamlet belatedly achieves this synthesis when he encompasses Laertes, Fortinbras, and Horatio—the figures of courtier, soldier, and scholar—at the play's end, though he does so only in death. In a sense that remains to be explored, Hamlet is thus more successful than Essex.

Both works depend on a play-within-a-play effect. Like Hamlet's play, Essex's device begins with a dumb show. Like Hamlet (2.2.535–36), Essex contributes his own writing.[16] Like Hamlet, Essex has a political purpose—to catch the conscience of the queen. Court entertainment designates a special space within a larger field of symbolic play that includes the play of ambition and jockeying for power. Essex's masque is part of the larger program of the tilt and the Accession Day celebration, which are in turn facets of the cult of Elizabeth by which power is maintained and distributed.[17] The sense of courtly entertainment as courtly plotting carries over to *Hamlet* not only in the performance of Hamlet's play but also in the match between Laertes and Hamlet in the final scene. The two entertainments staged in the king's presence form a pair: the latter is Claudius's countermove to Hamlet's mousetrap. Like the tilts for Elizabeth, the match presents the stimulation and purgation of leading subjects' aggressive impulses so as to reaffirm the authority of the monarch who oversees this scenario of staged conflict. However, Claudius's "device" (4.7.63) involves the devious "practice" (66) of the unbated sword and poison, which use of the term (4.7.137, 5.2.323) plays off Hamlet's more innocent sense: "I have been in continual practice" (5.2.206–7). Nevertheless, despite his death, Hamlet dominates the final scene; his triumph over Claudius draws on Hamlet's own deeper deployment of practice as rhetorical and theatrical strategy.

Seen as a medium of negotiation, Essex's device raises two questions: what is being negotiated? and why does Essex fail? The criterion for success or failure is the queen's response. Her studied indifference—"the Queen said, that if she had thought their had bene so moch said of her, she wold not have bene their that Night, and soe went to Bed"[18]—pronounces a verdict of failure. But if the fact of failure is clear, the cause needs explanation. On the face of it, the device's apparatus seems predictably conventional and hence unexceptionable. The pastoral atmosphere is not restricted to the option offered by the hermit but extends to the whole mode of organization and resolution, which reproduces the mechanism of *discordia concors* described by Edgar Wind.[19]

A clue is provided in a firsthand witness's cryptic qualifying reference to the device's style as "an excellent, but to plain *English*."[20] The basis for Essex's attempt to solicit the queen's sympathetic and favorable hearing is his complete submission to her service: "Then your Majesty shall first see your own invaluable value, and thereby discern that the favours you vouchsafe are pure gifts and no exchanges. And if any be so happy as to have his affection accepted, yet your prerogative is such as they stand bound and your Majesty is free." Despite its submissive posture, this passage is superfluous, even indiscreet, in spelling out what might better remain tacit.[21] Moreover, though apparently renouncing any idea of bargaining or reciprocity, Essex nonetheless insists that he has something worth giving. Overall, Essex's stance of ostentatious subservience is in tension with an equally strong note of self-assertion. While designed to assuage the queen's concerns about Essex's ambitions, the device only exacerbates the problem. To translate Whyte's "to plain *English*" into *Hamlet*'s terms: Essex appears to "protest too much" (3.2.225).

Two aspects of Essex's device erode the queen's hierarchal authority to which it professes allegiance. First, the balanced use of Philautia intimates that the situations of Essex and Elizabeth are comparable: she figures the danger of self-love to "the alone Queen" as much as to Essex.[22] The implied solution is that both should give up self-love and turn to each other. This conclusion would place Essex and Elizabeth on the same level. Second, Essex's device is remarkably self-involved and self-centered, not only in dwelling at such length on his own personal dilemma but also in availing itself of a resolution that had previously been the queen's prerogative. In presenting himself as the man who can harmoniously integrate the qualities of soldier, scholar, and statesman, Essex replicates the structure of Peele's *Araygnement of Paris*, in which Elizabeth assimilates the three goddesses. Essex thereby suggests that his synthetic power is equivalent to the queen's. Were Elizabeth to accept the symbolic representation of their relations as offered in Essex's device, she would accede to an equalizing of their positions. Hence her acid rejection.

A major difference between court entertainment and public drama is that the former is built around the queen's presence while the latter is not. The queen may of course witness a public theatrical performance, but her attendance is not an integral part of the design: there is no direct appeal to the queen and no direct response from her. Though all public theater is affected by the implied cultural presence of Elizabeth, her presence in this sense is sufficiently distant and mediated to permit dramatic gaps and swerves into which cultural fantasies antagonistic to the official cult of Elizabeth can insinuate themselves. The latent cultural fantasy in *Hamlet* is that Queen Gertrude functions as a degraded figure of Queen Elizabeth.

The key to the operation of this fantasy is Gertrude's powerlessness, which contrasts so sharply with the actual situation of Elizabeth's preeminence. The drastic curtailment of female authority gratifies the male imagination by underwriting a gender-role reversal: Gertrude is reduced to a captive audience subject to male manipulation; while Gertrude defers and capitulates, Hamlet viciously attacks not only with impunity but with righteousness. Essex could not play the role of Elizabeth's "scourge" (3.4.177), but Hamlet's fiction indirectly fulfills this fantasy. Hamlet's license thus makes amends for Essex's tribulation.

Hamlet's performance in the closet scene teasingly walks the precarious line between verbal aggression and physical violence. Hamlet primes himself by drawing a firm distinction: "I will speak daggers to her, but use none" (3.2.387). Gertrude's submission ratifies Hamlet's image: "O speak to me no more. / These words like daggers enter in my ears. / No

more, sweet Hamlet" (3.4.94–96). This pat compliance with
Hamlet's perspective, however, is not the whole story. In a
more volatile moment, Gertrude has earlier feared for her life:
"What wilt thou do? Thou wilt not murder me?" (20). The
moment quickly passes: Hamlet's violence is harmlessly de-
flected to Polonius, whom we are encouraged to regard as an
expendable windbag, and Hamlet soon settles down in ear-
nest to the business of strictly verbal harassment of Gertrude.
Nevertheless, Hamlet's enactment of literal violence in her
presence sets off wider cultural reverberations. The scene
briefly calls up the potential for male violence against Elizabeth as expressed in Essex's quarrel with the queen in 1598
when he angrily reached for his sword or in the sexually
toned violation of her private chambers when, against orders,
he secretly returned from Ireland in 1599:

> He brushed through the Presence Chamber to the Privy
> Chamber and right on through that, without knocking, into
> the royal bedroom. The Queen had no idea, as she turned at
> the sound of scuffles and commotion, that the Earl of Essex
> was in England, let alone in her palace, let alone in her own
> private bedchamber to which no male subject had ever been
> invited. . . .
> She was only just up—grey, wrinkled, her wig off, her hair
> straggling down over her unmade-up face. She had not fin-
> ished dressing. She was alone and defenseless, deprived of
> the physical artifices that turned a wizened old woman into a
> robed, crowned, painted Queen. Essex had stripped away the
> facade that was Gloriana and had dared to thrust himself
> unprepared and uninvited upon the vulnerable, decaying
> woman that wore the mask.[23]

I cite these instances not to suggest that they are present in
Hamlet as direct topical echoes but rather to indicate the general context of cultural tension in the 1590s with which the
play resonates.

Even more important than the figurative dagger that Hamlet wields in the closet is the image of the mirror. The tech-
nical operation of mirrors was not conceived as a straightfor-
ward procedure of reflecting exact likeness:

> But the Renaissance glass was invested with dioptric and pris-
> matic powers deriving from the interpretive activity of the
> human mind. Its exclusiveness was therefore prized as a guar-
> antee of the mind's freedom from the tyranny of the actual
> world.

> For the Renaissance more is at stake in mirrors than an abstract
> and bodiless reflection. Both optics and mirror lore in the pe-
> riod suggested that something was actively passing back and
> forth in the production of mirror images, that accurate repre-
> sentation depended upon material emanation and changes.[24]

The idea that mirroring involves an active process of exchange and that mirrors themselves have a shaping force
provides a model for the swerves, the distortive cultural fantasies, that art may generate. Hamlet's use of the mirror is a
case in point, for his view of it is gendered: "the purpose of
playing . . . is to hold as 'twere the mirror up to nature; to
show virtue her feature, scorn her own image" (3.2.20–23).
This statement names Hamlet's agenda in the closet scene.
The purpose of his playing there is to present Gertrude with
her own image as scorn: "You go not till I set you up a glass /
Where you may see the inmost part of you" (3.4.18–19). Gertrude signals her reception of Hamlet's message: "Thou
turn'st my eyes into my very soul, / And there I see such
black and grained spots / As will not leave their tinct" (89–91).
Essex's device attempts to hold up a mirror to Elizabeth's
nature through the image of Philautia, but conspicuously fails
to induce a similar confession. Unlike Elizabeth, Gertrude
conveniently offers a weak character whose vacuousness in-
vites filling in by the male imagination. Hamlet's male mirror
plays a busy role in creating the female nature it ostensibly
reflects.

The further question of how the mirror applies to Hamlet
himself can be raised by way of comparison with Lucrece.
Both Lucrece and Hamlet find in Hecuba a mirror image that
affords identification and support. Like Lucrece, Hamlet
finds in Hecuba an image adequate to express the grief that
overwhelms him. The eagerness behind his "Say on, come to
Hecuba" (2.2.497) marks the urgency of his need for her

"passion" (514): hers is the "passionate speech" (428) he has been waiting for. There is, however, a significant difference in the respective uses Lucrece and Hamlet make of Hecuba. For Lucrece, Hecuba provides closure; for Hamlet, Hecuba occasions acute anguish as much as relief:

> What's Hecuba to him, or he to her,
> That he should weep for her? What would he do
> Had he the motive and cue for passion
> That I have?
>
> (553–56)

Unlike Lucrece's, Hamlet's identification with Hecuba is problematic for reasons of gender.

The association with Hecuba overruns his masculine identity, rendering him negatively female: "Must like a whore unpack my heart with words" (581). Hamlet is able to obtain relief from his self-torturing relation to language when he employs the mirror to transfer the whore image to a cooperative Gertrude and thus to reinstitute an orderly division of gender categories. Having expunged the internal whore by projecting it outward onto a certifiable whore, Hamlet purifies his language, regains faith in his rhetorical powers. Sexual and linguistic purity go hand in hand. Despite his antipathy to Claudius, Hamlet shares with him a reliance on the stereotype of the prostitute as an emblem for female deception and hence actively participates in the general denigration of women. Claudius's clever accusation of "unmanly grief" (1.2.94) hits home. The closet scene opens up a protected play space in which Hamlet can recover his manliness. Whereas Lucrece fixes on and stops with Hecuba, Hamlet moves on. Having rehearsed Aeneas's past (2.2.442–43), Hamlet, like Aeneas, goes on alone to found a new realm, leaving Dido behind to her fate. As at the end of *The Rape of Lucrece*, but with far greater emotional power, *Hamlet* creates a self-enclosed male state.

Not only does Hamlet enforce the negative connection between Elizabeth and Philautia that Essex's device attempted to make, but also the sexual politics of the mirror recover a positive significance in Essex's link with Philautia. Hamlet's final identity is carried primarily by the mirror-like exchanges with Laertes, Horatio, and Fortinbras. This interactive self-affirmation—"For by the image of my cause I see / The portraiture of his" (5.2.77–78)—dramatizes the mirroring effect as a positive male power. Most surprising is the force of Hamlet's exchange with Fortinbras, a reconciliation strong enough to sustain the renewal of the state. Despite Hamlet's quibbles about Fortinbras's "divine ambition puff'd" (4.4.49) in his final soliloquy prior to departure for England, Hamlet throws his political support to Fortinbras: "He has my dying voice. / So tell him, with th' occurrents more and less / Which have solicited—the rest is silence" (5.2.361–63). This sublime silence is soon filled when Fortinbras returns the compliment with his tribute:

> Let four captains
> Bear Hamlet like a soldier to the stage,
> For he was likely, had he been put on,
> To have prov'd most royal; and for his passage,
> The soldier's music and the rite of war
> Speak loudly for him.
>
> (400–405)

This ritual does speak loudly for Hamlet. Fortinbras's mirror endows Hamlet with a military image that he did not have in life, but the effect is not ironic.[25] The fraternal context confirms Fortinbras's gesture as fitting.

The restoration of a grand military image has Essexian cultural overtones. The play satisfies in fantasy the regal image that Essex "put on" and dismally failed to realize. *Hamlet's* generic twist as pastoralized tragedy contributes to the effect of fantasy since the pastoral element mitigates the tragic impact. Hamlet has to pay the tragic price of death, yet it is not only worth it but is actually pleasing and gratifying. Dying well means the ability to stage a traditional masculine self-image uncompromised by female intervention. The integrated network of gender, genre, and nation in *Hamlet* eludes Elizabeth's "power to charm" (1.1.168).

IV

Literary critical studies of Essex have often engaged in romanticized, uncritical defenses of Essex's position. In the mid-1930s, Ray Heffner saw Essex as "the ideal courtier."[26] In 1945, putting a liberal spin on the Essex mythology, E. P. Kuhl enlisted Essex as a progressive force: "Like Bruno, he was also a martyr to science, reason, liberty."[27] In far more sophisticated criticism at the close of the 1980s, a version of Essex has emerged that answers to the terms subversive and radical. There is a tendency in such work to construe as heroically protodemocratic Essex's protest in the dispute with Elizabeth in 1598: "What, cannot princes err? Cannot subjects receive wrong? Is an earthly power of authority infinite?"[28] This approach too easily constructs a continuity that makes Essex a democratic forerunner of later parliamentary developments and an anticipation of Milton's political voice.[29] In addition to collapsing the boundaries between distinct historical periods, this formulation ignores gender as an analytic category. Essex's resistance to Elizabeth has a strong masculinist and misogynist aura that should not recommend it as a model and inspiration for our own ideal of subversion. The development of political criticism in literary studies cannot be confined to the Renaissance; instead of making more than can be made of Essex's, or Shakespeare's, radical potential, we must be able to look elsewhere to more contemporary literature for possible images of subversion.

PART TWO

WOMEN WRITERS' REPRESENTATIONS OF SHAKESPEARE

Above all, once he removed the make-up, his
face was without expression, bland, as though
only on stage made up as Caliban in the
scarlet shirt and baggy trunks was he at all
certain of who he was. Caliban might have
become his reality.

Paule Marshall,
Soul Clap Hands and Sing (1961)

And tonight

every song he sings
is written by Shakespeare
and his mother-in-law.

Rita Dove, *Museum* (1983)

5

Some Versions of Tradition

This chapter marks the shift from Part 1, which focuses on Shakespeare's representations of women, including Queen Elizabeth, to Part 2, which concerns twentieth-century women writers' representations of Shakespeare. Just as Shakespeare's versions of women are multiple, so the use of Shakespeare in contemporary literature produces varied effects, as the juxtaposition of quotations from Paule Marshall and Rita Dove in the epigraph to Part 2 can begin to suggest.[1]

In both Marshall's short story "Brazil" and Dove's poem "Shakespeare Say," the main character is a performing artist who serves as a partial metaphor for the author. The former assesses the career of the nightclub entertainer known as Caliban; the latter's speaking voice belongs to "Champion Jack Dupree, black American blues singer," who "is now living and touring in Europe" (Dove's note). In both cases, Shakespeare plays a crucial part in the performance. But these similarities only heighten the differences between the two situations. For although both hinge on naming, they do so with sharply contrasting results.

In Marshall's story, the prospect of retirement precipitates a crisis of identity dramatized as a conflict between Caliban's stage name and his original name, Heitor Baptista Guimares. With increasing panic, Caliban tries to recover his origins by obtaining recognition of his real name. His failure to achieve this validation brings the realization that his act has taken over his self, canceling his individual identity: "Caliban had become his only reality and anything else he might have been was lost" (p. 175). His final act of desperation—the destruction of his partner Miranda's apartment—can only confirm his "emptiness" (p. 176). His attempted self-assertion—"I am

Heitor Guimares" (p. 174)—is countered not only by Miranda's, but also by the narrator's insistence that he is Caliban. It is no accident that the name whose power he is unable to escape and which consumes him is specifically Shakespearean. Though resolutely impersonal, Marshall's meditation on Caliban's entrapment may reflect a doubt, a worry, about the investment in literary tradition expressed in her own Yeatsian self-definition in the collection's title, *Soul Clap Hands and Sing.* In this story at least, the Shakespearean heritage has obliterated rather than facilitated the singing.

The response to Shakespeare in Rita Dove's poem is both more direct and more tricky. Marshall's story focuses on a single Shakespearean character; Shakespeare is named only once and only in passing (p. 151). Dove more boldly addresses the author's name and authority, placing them up front in the title "Shakespeare Say." However, Dove cites the ritual of quoting Shakespeare to ironic effect, for Shakespeare is present in name only. He presides over the poem as an empty signifier who is conspicuously not there in the body of the poem. The vacuum left by Shakespeare's absence is filled by Dove's deft, irreverent presence. The only direct quotation occurs in the poem's final line, which alludes not to what Shakespeare say but to what "Mama Said," a rock-and-roll lyric by the Shirelles, a black female group from the early 1960s: *"my mother told me / there'd be days like this."* The last line literally sings; its music is non-Shakespearean because it derives not only from pop culture but also from the mother in counterpoint to the mother-in-law with whose constraints the poem associates Shakespeare. If Marshall's story exemplifies the aesthetic confinement to which Shakespearean influence can lead, Dove's poem suggests the performance of an escape artist who says there'll be days when Shakespeare doesn't signify, is beside the point.

My reason for beginning with this comparison is to stress the contribution that detailed analysis of particular cases can make to the overall project of canon studies. The central question remains: what impact does the contemporary revision of the literary canon have on our understanding of Shakespeare's status? Public discourse on this issue has frequently been superficial because nebulous and out of touch with actual instances. Close reading (as defined in the Introduction) helps to anchor general discussion by putting it to the test of specific case studies. But close reading can be a way to avoid explicit consideration of theoretical implications. I therefore emphasize the importance of a balance between analytic and theoretical dimensions and the need to go back and forth between these two levels. The organization of chapters in Part 2 reflects this methodological combination: chapter 5 presents a conceptual discussion of the canon problem, chapters 6–8 offer in-depth case studies, and the Afterword returns to general theoretical issues.

I

My consideration of the concept of canon begins with a review of Frank Kermode's discussion of the topic. I acknowledge some common ground with Kermode. I share his commitment to the continual reconstruction for the present of the cultural past.[2] I also believe in Kermode's ideal of an ongoing critical conversation that forms a tradition of commentary about individual works, though I see this process as thoroughly historical rather than transhistorical. However, since I apply these ideas in a direction different from Kermode's, I find the areas of disagreement larger and more important than the similarities.

By his own account, Kermode has been writing about the issue of the canon for fifteen years, his first paper on the subject having been presented in 1974.[3] The content of this writing has remained largely constant over this period. What has changed dramatically is the tone. This change is especially significant in Kermode's case because tone plays a major role in carrying the weight of his argument, poise and understatement being the principal means by which he establishes an authoritative voice. Kermode's initial statement conveys confident control:

> A few years ago the MLA suffered something that looked for a moment like a revolution; but it was only a saturnalian interlude (appropriate to the season of their meeting), an episode of Misrule, tolerated because in the end reinforcing the stability of the institution. The boy bishops had their day, and the more usual, more authentically prelatical figures have resumed their places. We can tolerate even those who believe the institution should be destroyed.[4]

Kermode's dismissal proves premature, however.

As it becomes apparent that the impact of the sixties on the MLA was not a passing phase, the anxiety latent in his early confidence comes to the fore with surprising force in Kermode's subsequent writing. His equanimity is increasingly disrupted by a tonal mixture ranging from irritation and sarcasm to resignation and pessimism. The price Kermode now feels obliged to pay to secure even the semblance of continuity leaves him disconsolate:

> That the conversation, the game, must go on, I have no doubt at all, for it is the means by which the primary objects of my own attention have to be brought to the attention of another generation. Thrilling new turns in the talk are the prerogative, no doubt, of the young. . . . But I agree with those who say that the idea of tradition has never been so weak as it is now, the sense of a literary past less strong.[5]

Having lost his faith in the capacity of professional institutions to absorb radical challenges, Kermode is no longer satisfied by the expectation that "the new theories and methods" will "be routinized, and defused not by opposition or repression but by assimilation."[6]

Kermode's response to this more urgent situation is to attack proponents of canon revision by ridiculing their lack of "real political power":

> Culler, for one, believes that theory will do good to suffering minorities. The days when the editors of *Tel Quel* supposed they could help with the revolution by turning up at the Renault factory and reading their pieces to the workers over lunch are presumably over. . . . And it is hard to avoid the doubtless over-simple reflection that if one feels strongly

enough about the matter there are probably more effective ways of drawing attention to political injustice than by deconstructing Hegel and Freud. Another crude reflection is that if this adversarial enterprise ever seemed likely to upset the cultural and political arrangements preferred by the patrons on whose benevolence it depends, they would soon find ways of putting a stop to it.[7]

Kermode thus proves that canon revision is not a threat, yet still feels extremely threatened by it. The emphatic denial of political efficacy sits uneasily with Kermode's alarmist warnings elsewhere about the political potential of canon revisions: "What is certain is that revolutionary revisions would require transfers of powers, a reign of literary terror."[8] Not only are these two versions—canon revision has no effect; canon revision has dire consequences—contradictory, but both are caricatures. Kermode's attempt to put a stop to large-scale revision of the canon rests, finally, on the all-or-nothing proposition contained in the words "absolute" and "perfection": "Absolute justice and perfection of conscience are unlikely to be more available under that new dispensation than they are now."[9] Nobody's perfect, even revisionists can agree. But the project of revision need not claim absolute perfection in order to argue for relative and significant improvement.

Tacitly abandoning the argument, Kermode adopts a different tack in a recent essay on T. S. Eliot. Here Kermode effectively gives up and concentrates instead on the elegiac note announced in the title "The Last Classic."[10] The mood shifts from fighting for the tradition to mourning its passing in "a world where the idea of the classic is dying or has died" (p. 165). To be sure, Kermode is using the term "classic" in the specialized sense defined in his previous study *The Classic*.[11] But the emphasis on Eliot as a historical termination produces a definitive sense of an ending that has much larger emotional reverberations because of Kermode's personal identification with Eliot's status: "It would be hard to discover a poet or critic now living who shared these views or held to any that even slightly resembled them. . . . And that is why we may think of Eliot as the last classic, at any rate until some new civilization should construct its own idea of the classic and its own canon" (p. 163).[12] The "at any rate" escape clause does not alter the prevailing melancholy, funereal tone; for the hypothetical future briefly postulated is indefinitely postponed and has no connection with the present cultural upheaval.

The cultural change through which we are living is substantial enough to warrant the term "new civilization," but Kermode, having no productive way to move from Eliot to contemporary literature, is unwilling positively to engage the new civilization that has already arrived. In effect, Kermode's elegy for Eliot doubles as his own elegiac opting out. There are two reasons for this impasse: Kermode's idea of the canon both restricts the set of objects under discussion and restricts the kinds of things that can be said about them. My goal is to reopen the conversation by reconsidering these restrictions. First, it is necessary to extend the same attentiveness to works that Kermode's canon would automatically exclude. The intrusion of black women writers carries a heavy symbolic charge for Kermode, but he shows no evidence of firsthand acquaintance with this literature.[13] Yet the tradition of vital critical commentary on this work is building itself in exactly the way that Kermode under other circumstances would celebrate. Second, in addition to expanding the range of the works that can be fully accorded the most privileged form of attention, it is necessary to provide for more fundamental criticisms of established authors. Kermode's only concession is to admit the possibility of "subcanons," a concept that implies the continuation of a primary canon to which minority literatures have an ancillary, subordinate relation, with perhaps the hope of eventually producing a writer good enough to enter the main canon.[14] This rigid hierarchical structure must be replaced with a more active conception of the interrelations between established and emergent literature in which the former is no longer held apart from the latter.

This alternative to Kermode's approach involves a shift

from T. S. Eliot to Adrienne Rich as a principal critical resource. In my view, Rich offers a different concept of canon
from the one Kermode derives from Eliot. Hence I disagree
with Kermode's claim that "the contents of these categories
may be challenged, but the concepts of themselves remain in
place."[15] In order to delineate the conceptual differences between Eliot and Rich, I shall first survey developments in
British and American criticism, for which Eliot was a key
reference point.

II

Raymond Williams's discussion in 1961 of "the operation of a
selective tradition" prefigures the current focus on what we
now call canon formation.[16] The criticism of F. R. Leavis illustrates the act of selection: in *New Bearings in English Poetry*
(1932) and *Revaluation* (1936), Leavis systematically established a revised great tradition with T. S. Eliot's pivotal work
at the center. This version of the tradition, which in its moment came to seem authoritative, even unassailable, is actually constructed; Leavis is highly explicit about the process of
its construction through conscious decisions about inclusion
and exclusion. The most pressing difficulty in the process as
practiced by Leavis is exemplified by his treatment of Ronald
Bottrall in the epilogue of *New Bearings in English Poetry*. The
account appears weakest at the point where Leavis tries to
extend this new tradition into the immediate future. Bottrall's
poetry could not sustain the weight of Leavis's claim for it, as
Leavis himself ultimately admitted when he gave up on the
future: "by the later thirties, *Scrutiny*'s hopes for the new generation were near collapse."[17]

Though Leavis's use of Eliot's work included a substantial
critical element, Leavis nonetheless remained definitively indebted to Eliot.[18] Raymond Williams's critical framework, as
presented in *Culture and Society, 1780–1950* (1958), encompasses both Eliot and Leavis.[19] Consequently, Williams's departure from Eliot's values is more decisive, the turn to an
alternative tradition announced in the displacement of Eliot

when *Drama from Ibsen to Eliot* (1952) becomes *Drama from Ibsen to Brecht* (1968). However, important as Williams's work has been in demonstrating the potential for the revision of the canon, there remains a gap between his theoretical breakthrough and its concrete application.

While Williams is far more successful than Leavis in responding to new cultural developments in the present, his work nonetheless suggests a difficulty analogous to Leavis's problem with Bottrall. The realization of a full-scale change in the literary canon depends on the emergence of literature by black and women writers as major areas in the seventies and eighties. Williams's writing does not centrally address this new material. Terry Eagleton's attempt to discern a feminist element in Williams's work is unconvincing; more accurate is the acknowledgment of the absence of a feminist perspective as one of the limitations in Williams's otherwise crucial contribution.[20] The limitation here is less a question of personal failure than of historical and cultural location, for the intensive focus on the literary implications of race and gender originates primarily in the United States rather than in England.[21]

From the vantage point of our own critical moment, F. O. Matthiessen and Lionel Trilling can each be seen as having found it necessary to suppress or neutralize, within his critical work, an element of his identity—Matthiessen his homosexuality, Trilling his Jewishness. Both conducted critical projects influenced by the cultural presence of T. S. Eliot.[22] *American Renaissance* (1941), Matthiessen's effort to compose a great tradition for American literature, was preceded by, and dependent upon, his study of *The Achievement of T. S. Eliot* (1935).[23] Trilling participated in *Partisan Review*'s appreciation of Eliot as an exemplar of modernism.[24] Trilling's criticism in his review of Eliot's *The Idea of a Christian Society* is restrained both by self-conscious "respect" (p. 379) and by the recourse to Eliot as a philosophical counterweight to the Marxist perspective that Trilling had found wanting.[25] As late as 1967, Trilling includes *The Waste Land* as "the most famous and influential poem of our time" in the canon formed by his textbook *The Experience of Literature*. In Trilling's view the poem transcends its Christian sensibility because it predates Eliot's "religious decision" and because it draws on other religious traditions.[26] Trilling's need to accommodate Eliot is linked to the general process of assimilation by which Trilling established himself in a field dominated by an Anglo-Christian mentality inhospitable to Jews.[27] Particularly telling accounts of the intellectual costs of this assimilation are the analyses by Mark Krupnick and Alan Wald of Trilling's two short stories, "Of This Time, Of That Place" (1943) and "The Other Margaret" (1945).[28] The latter's fixed racial divide implies a cultural exclusion of blacks that must be confronted in order to move beyond Trilling's predicament.

Don E. Wayne has recently given a sympathetic view of Trilling's assimilation, seeing it as a necessary step in the entry into the profession of English literary studies of "first-generation Americans of non-English ancestry."[29] The example of Harold Bloom in the next generation bears out Wayne's analysis but also, in part, gives occasion to question it. An important aspect of Bloom's career is the development of his Jewish identity as an explicit element of his criticism, a development culminating, for example, in his study *The Strong Light of the Canonical: Kafka, Freud and Scholem as Revisionists of Jewish Culture and Thought* (1987). The significance of this achievement must be measured against the opposition to Jewish intellectuals described by Geoffrey Hartman.[30] Louis Montrose comments specifically on "the genteel Protestant and Anglo-Saxon ethos that pervaded and still pervades Spenser studies" in the form of "Christian Humanist apologetics."[31] Moreover, the emergence of ethnic consciousness in Bloom's work is explicitly associated with resistance to T. S. Eliot, as Bloom makes clear in his opening remarks in "Reflections on T. S. Eliot."[32]

The limitations of Bloom's development in this direction can be brought out by considering the parallel insistence on her Jewish identity in the work of Adrienne Rich. Like Bloom, Rich has given increasing attention to the articulation of her Jewishness. In this connection, Rich's response to *The Mer-*

chant of Venice overlaps with that of Bloom, who regards the play as "an anti-Semitic text," adding that "there is no real reason to doubt that the historical Shakespeare would have agreed with his Portia."[33] Rich, for similar reasons, critically dissents from Portia's role.[34] This shared response, however, serves only to highlight a crucial difference: where Bloom elaborates his Jewish heritage but stops there, Rich's exploration of her Jewish identity is part of a much larger framework that is attuned not only to other elements of her identity but also to features not her own. Moreover, this contrast has direct implications for their respective versions of canon formation.

Despite Bloom's antipathy for Eliot, he nonetheless shares Eliot's model of tradition; while revising the contents of the tradition, Bloom adheres to similar principles of canon organization.[35] Bloom's version places greater emphasis on conflict between individual artists, but Eliot's main thrust is maintained because Bloom portrays conflict as a psychological confrontation occurring in an aesthetic vacuum, virtually without reference to social issues and political values. Whereas Bloom remains tied to Eliot, the approach of Adrienne Rich represents a fundamental departure from Eliot's model.

Like Eliot, Rich has made significant contributions in two areas: critical essays as well as poems. The relation between the two modes is similar: in both cases, the function of the prose is to create an audience for a new kind of poetry. In particular, I want to compare Eliot's "Tradition and the Individual Talent" (1919) with Rich's equivalent essay a half-century later, "When We Dead Awaken: Writing as Re-Vision" (1971).[36] The difference is not that Eliot opposes change while Rich advocates it. Change is built into Eliot's model of tradition: "The existing monuments form an ideal order among themselves, which is modified by the introduction of the new (the really new) work of art among them. The existing order is complete before the new work arrives; for order to persist after the supervention of novelty, the *whole* existing order must be, if ever so slightly, altered" (p. 44). The touch of humility that Eliot adds in the phrase "if ever so slightly" should not distract us from his ambitious design to alter the tradition substantially.

The point is rather that the terms and scope of change envisioned by Rich differ from Eliot's not only in degree but in kind. What is involved for Rich is not simply changing individual figures in the canon or substituting one set of authors for another, while preserving the standard procedures for canon formation. Instead, the issue is a fundamental revision of the concept of canon itself. The process of selection is different because the basic units are different: in Eliot's case, the emphasis is on the author as "individual talent"; in Rich's case, the emphasis is on distinct cultural traditions of historically oppressed and newly emergent groups in American society. In the latter instance, it is the artistic production of the group as a whole that merits inclusion. Each cultural grouping has its own integrity and its own terms, though these terms are emphatically not essentialist; that is, a particular tradition is neither internally uniform nor cut off from interaction with outside forces. Rather, the literary expressions of new cultural groups are not ranked such that they are relegated to subsidiary secondary status. There is no overarching master tradition that organizes the others. The result is that Eliot's image of a self-adjusting "ideal order" or Leavis's assertion of *the* "great tradition" is not attainable within this critical perspective. If plural traditions cannot be synthesized into a single tradition, Eliot's framework for the canon breaks down because it is unable to deal with the question of how to conceive of the relations, within a culture, among irreducibly multiple traditions.

Rich's own poetry provides a test that shows the inadequacy of Eliot's version of tradition. Though Rich's account of her poetic development stresses the struggle to achieve a first-person speaking voice, it would be misleading to treat Rich as an individual talent who could be added to an ongoing orthodox tradition. Despite the power of her personal voice, Rich has in other ways counteracted the institutions of individual authorship. Rich's response to the National Book

Award for *Diving into the Wreck* in 1974 may be seen as a symbolic gesture: she "rejected the award as an individual, but accepted it, in a statement written with Audre Lorde and Alice Walker, two other nominees, in the name of all women."[37] But this formal stance is incorporated into her poetry, making it at very deep levels the expression of our cultural moment. As a more recent statement puts it, "Rape-crisis hot lines, battered-women's shelters, houses for women emerging from psychiatric abuse, feminist health and abortion clinics, grass-roots feminist publications, the work of dedicated activists fueled my understanding, my images, and my words. I wrote and signed my words as an individual, but they were part of a collective ferment."[38] Rich examines another aspect of this "collective ferment" in "'Wholeness Is No Trifling Matter': Some Fiction by Black Women," where she finds a "powerful and corrective vision of reality."[39] In the new edition of *Of Woman Born,* she extends her awareness of other cultural perspectives to include Caribbean American, American Indian, Asian American, and Latina women writers.[40]

Since Rich's work is so intimately affiliated with her chosen multicultural contexts that she cannot be understood apart from them, Rich cannot be singled out and, as an isolated great poet, be added to an evolving tradition. Instead, the collective force of her work makes it necessary to recognize a major new development and to undertake a systematic reassessment of the overall process of canon formation. In the short term, it may be possible to fend off this reappraisal by assuming the existence of dual traditions—one mainstream, the other a subculture—that do not come into contact with each other. This tactic will, however, only postpone the need to deal comprehensively with both established and emergent traditions. The need is pressing because our culture is created from both. In T. S. Eliot's account, artistic "change is a development which abandons nothing *en route,* which does not superannuate either Shakespeare, or Homer" (p. 46), but Adrienne Rich's different concept of canon produces a different view of Shakespeare: "We know . . . more than Shakespeare because we know more about the lives of women" (p. 49). Rich's challenge forces a clarification of the precise meaning of the term "superannuate."

III

As a transition to the consideration in the following three chapters of the reception of Shakespeare in the work of Maya Angelou, Gloria Naylor, and Adrienne Rich, I provide here a brief example of a response to another canonical figure. The comparison of Yeats's "Leda and the Swan" with June Jordan's "The Female and the Silence of the Man" suggests what is involved in a process of canon revision that stems from the interaction between established and emergent traditions. Jordan's poem closely approximates Yeats's lineation and rhyme scheme, but the effect of her imitation is to expose the mood and tone of "Leda and the Swan" as overly precious.[41]

Yeats's language is explicit and precise about the violence and callousness of Zeus's rape of Leda. The words "mastered," "brute," "power," and "indifferent" in the tremulous final question—"Being so caught up, / So mastered by the brute blood of the air, / Did she put on his knowledge with his power / Before the indifferent beak could let her drop?"— display a matter-of-fact awareness of the stark imbalance of power which the encounter between girl and god enacts. Yet Jordan outdoes Yeats in blunt, plain terms. Her declarative sentences—"The big fist shattering her face"; "She vomits out her teeth"—emphasize the crudity of aggression. The verbal action is reduced to the sparest possible structure: "He tears," "his rage destroys," "He lacerates," "he claws and squeezes out."

By thus stripping the artifice from Yeats's poem and disrupting its aesthetic distance, Jordan shows up the limitations of awareness in "Leda and the Swan." Jordan's contrasting style demonstrates that there are two kinds of matter-of-factness. The clarity of Yeats's depiction comes from his taking the rape for granted as a given; Jordan's terseness expresses instead both her anger at finding the same situation unacceptable, and her drive to oppose and change it. Yeats coolly assumes that the male god's knowledge, as well as his power, is absolute: if Leda gains any knowledge, it would be the same as his. "Did she put on his knowledge with his power . . . ?" is as far as Yeats's question goes. Jordan picks up the motif of knowledge, but shifts the point of view. "And now she knows" her poem abruptly and flatly begins. The difference is that in Jordan's version Leda's knowledge is not derived from Zeus, but is her own.

For Yeats the overriding concern is specifically literary knowledge. His term "engenders" carries a double resonance. It refers to Leda's biological role as the common maternal origin of Helen and Clytemnestra. But more important, Yeats's allusions evoke their literary reproduction by the tradition of Homer's *Iliad* (Troy's "burning roof and tower") and its aftermath in Aeschylus's *Orestia* ("And Agamemnon dead") and establish his own derivation from the classical source. Jordan's intervention challenges this male literary line. In Jordan's account, Leda is neither the simple victim nor the potential repository of canonical wisdom that Yeats's poem makes her. Though Yeats's tacit reference to the unnamed Clytemnestra hints at the prospect of female revenge, he portrays the revenge as the impersonal working out of a tragic cycle that must run its fated course. In Jordan's poem, this revenge is not the guaranteed outcome of a prior tradition, but is actively constructed in the present from the far more immediate and galvanizing resource of a feminist perception of her personal experience.

The last three lines of Jordan's poem are set off by the succinct turn from "She vanishes" to "She reappears." This shift has the effect of a coda that transforms Leda, making her capable of a level of resistance and retaliation not imagined by Yeats: "A lovely girl protected by her cruel / incandescent energies." The images of protection and energy are important for Jordan's work as a whole; this line speaks deeply to her concern with self-defense against violation and to the energies on which her poetry draws to insist on the full empowerment of her identity as a black woman.[42] Most specifically, this poem connects with Jordan's incandescent poem about her own rape, "Poem about My Rights," from *Passion*. The comparison of Yeats's and Jordan's poems has two implications that are relevant to canon revision as a general issue. First, the reformulation of the canon cannot be regarded exclusively as the product of a set of maneuvers in literary criticism and theory. As Jordan's poem shows, this phenomenon is an explicit occurrence within literature itself. Second, altering the relations among elements in the literary field involves direct and unavoidable conflict. It is not enough to say that, despite their differing poetic visions, Yeats and Jordan both start in "the foul rag-and-bone shop of the heart." The differences do not simply coexist in harmonious diversity, but actively conflict. Yeats must move over in order to make space for the full play of these differences, and Yeats will not move without the critical pressure applied by Jordan's poem. This aspect of confrontation is what makes the activity of canon reconstruction so emotionally charged and so susceptible to oversimplification. In Ursula K. LeGuin's exuberant hyperbole, canon revision becomes "send[ing] Bronx cheers to the Great Tradition," while Richard Poirier acerbically belittles all such efforts as "treating the canon as if it were a water pistol."[43] Jordan's poem does not achieve its triumph as easily as sounding a Bronx cheer, nor does she dismiss Yeats's poem as a mere water pistol; the engagement between the two occurs at a deeper level of seriousness. This more serious encounter between established and minority literatures is the subject explored in the remainder of this study.

The nature of my argument favors art in which the engagement with the established tradition and especially with Shakespeare is highly visible. This principle of selection is a matter of logistical convenience, however, not a statement of philosophical position. I do not see the inclusion of Shakespearean allusions as an artistic requirement, nor do I believe that literature with such allusions is better, higher, or more complex than literature without. The work of Toni Morrison and Alice Walker, in which Shakespearean references are relatively absent, constitutes an equally possible and successful approach. It is by no means imperative that a black writer's work incorporate the orthodox great tradition. Both patterns are valid, and both contribute to the overall effect of a new tradition that compels a revision of the existing canon.

6

Shakespeare, Angelou, Cheney: The Administration of the Humanities in the Reagan-Bush Era

The emotional high point of Lynne V. Cheney's *Humanities in America* is her quotation of an extended passage from an address by Maya Angelou in which Angelou quotes Shakespeare's Sonnet 29 and asserts: "'I *know* that William Shakespeare was a black woman.'"[1] In this heightened moment, Cheney links and fuses three voices—Shakespeare's, Angelou's, and her own—thus creating the conjunction to which my title refers. However, my purpose is to challenge the impression Cheney conveys of a unified canon of Western literature, and I shall do so by suggesting that there are significant differences between Angelou's use of Shakespeare and Cheney's representation of Angelou's Shakespeare. My procedure will be, first, to examine the overall structure of the report of which the Angelou quotation is a part and, second, to consider this quotation in the larger context of Angelou's work as a whole.

I

Humanities in America touches on a number of educational issues, including the priority given to research over teaching and the arcane nature of post-structuralist theory. But these have little bearing on Cheney's core concern—the emergence of political interpretation in the humanities. Political analysis is very clear, not arcane; and it is conducive rather than resistant to the increased emphasis on teaching that Cheney advocates. As she herself warns, "teaching becomes a form of political activism" (p. 12).

Cheney's specific focus is on political interpretation as it relates to the status of the traditional canon. The title of the section for which the Maya Angelou passage serves as climax makes this connection between "Politics and the Curriculum" (p. 11). In Cheney's view, the whole educational structure is threatened because political analysis erodes support for the established classics: "It makes more difficult a task that is already hard: determining a substantive and coherent plan of study for undergraduates" (p. 12); "the newly politicized nature of debate in the humanities has made it more difficult" (p. 14). Cheney's objective is to remove this difficulty.

Despite her opposition to the intrusion of politics into the humanities, Cheney's own argument is explicitly political in two ways. First, given her administrative power as a presidentially appointed head of a federal agency that disburses funds, Cheney has an agenda that can fairly be called political in the familiar sense of politics as governmental activity. Her report is an intervention and intended as such. As the final heading, "Recommendations" (p. 31), makes plain, she is not merely presenting a neutral description but rather actively signaling the views to which she wishes to lend her institutional support.

Second, the report directly acknowledges the political dimension of literature: "The humanities provide context for the decisions we must make as a people by raising questions of social purpose: What is a just society, and how is it achieved?" (pp. 2–3). In this opening moment, the terms of Cheney's approach overlap with those of the political critics she opposes. The concepts of "social purpose" and of "a just society" are relevant, Cheney agrees, to the study of literature. The contrast, then, is not between political and nonpolitical approaches but between different political views. It is therefore appropriate to pursue the question "What are Cheney's politics?" where politics are understood as the intellectual vision that gradually unfolds over the course of the report.

The body of Cheney's discussion is organized as an evaluation of three areas—higher education, television, and cultural institutions such as museums, libraries, historical societies, humanities councils, and theater festivals. The order of this three-part structure dramatizes a distinct progression from the negative review of higher education through the ambivalent survey of television to the decidedly upbeat assessment of the other cultural institutions. Shakespeare figures as an index to the tone of each of the three sections, which may be summarized, respectively, as Shakespeare endangered, Shakespeare abundant, and Shakespeare redeemed.

In the middle section, television occasions mixed feelings: reservations are strongly expressed; benefits, however tentative, are duly noted. In general, the effort here is to put the best face on things. Shakespeare, for example, is given the limited test of commercial availability:

> Classics are amazingly easy to obtain. In neighborhood bookstores, one can find volumes of Aeschylus and Sophocles, Dickens and Shakespeare selling for under five dollars. Observed Michael Novak, "The very best books ever produced in the history of the human race are available for many times less than a pair of basketball shoes. . . ."
> . . . Facets, a nonprofit Chicago organization, . . . is able to rent videotapes by mail for $10. Four versions of "Macbeth" are available, three of "King Lear."
>
> (pp. 19–22)

This reassurance about the successful operation of our cultural economy may seem an inconsequential digression. However, the conspicuous avoidance of larger economic problems in the analysis of television is relevant to the political stance of the report as a whole, for it suggests how constrained Cheney's intellectual vision is by the need to affirm an economic philosophy congenial to the Reagan administration. The role of commercials in television and the contrast in this regard between commercial and public television require a deeper economic discussion than Cheney is prepared to give. Moreover, her treatment of economic issues here is consistent with her economic thinking elsewhere in the report: for example, in the praise for the role of private philanthropy in the creation of the Alabama Shakespeare Festival theater complex (pp. 24–25); in the application of market principles to college education so that parents can be encouraged to use their purchase power to influence the curricular products that are offered to their children (pp. 14, 32).

At the beginning of the third part of the report, Cheney invokes the motif of an expanding economy to underwrite a more general image of social unity:

> Carl Raschke, a philosophy professor from the University of Denver, pointed to similarities between our own time and the late 1870s. . . . "We were then, as we are now, about fifteen years after a devastating war that had divided the country," Raschke noted. "The American people seemed to have been emerging out of a kind of cynicism and slumber and dispiritedness with a hunger for a new vitality and vision. There was a hunger to reappropriate and to understand anew values, traditions, and history that had been set aside during the period of conflict."
>
> (pp. 23–24)

Details of this analogy between the Civil and Vietnam wars and their aftermaths are never specified and clarified, but the gist of the attitude adopted toward the period of the 1960s through 1980s is evident. The divisiveness associated with the Vietnam War has been put behind us, superseded and canceled by a reawakening of social harmony. Reinstatement of the canon fits into and reinforces the purported historical shift by fulfilling the desire to recover traditions. This projected overview of the past three decades receives its gesture of confirmation in the quotation from Matthew Arnold that concludes the report's third section: " 'Again and again I have insisted,' he wrote, 'how those are the happy moments of humanity, how those are the marking epochs of a people's life, how those are the flowering times for literature and art and all the creative power of genius, when there is a *national* glow of life and thought' " (p. 29).

Cheney's interpretation of the present as one of "the happy moments" hinges on the contrast—around which the entire report is constructed—between the negative view of higher education in part 1 and the positive view of "public programming in the humanities" (p. 27) in part 3. According to Cheney, we face a situation in which the new " 'two cultures' are the academy and society" (p. 10). The public cultural institutions have filled the gap, becoming "a kind of parallel school, one that has grown up outside established institutions of education" (p. 27). Since public humanities organizations are more closely involved with and responsive to diverse general audiences, they represent a populist trend that can be trusted to counteract the political interpretation prevailing in the academy.

How the constituencies cultivated by public humanities institutions operate as a corrective, Cheney indicates by example:

> Overly narrow interpretations are also likely to be challenged by an audience that has the authority of maturity. "I once watched a young scholar try to draw an ideological conclusion from a passage in a Doris Lessing novel," says Victor Swenson, executive director of the humanities council in Vermont. "The discussion group wasn't confrontational about objecting, but they weren't having any of it either."
>
> (p. 29)

Cheney implies that this disagreement proves that the scholar's position was invalid and should be retracted, but this does not necessarily follow. Cheney goes on, however, openly to encourage the development of a pressure group capable of supplying political leverage: "Millions of adult Americans, through their participation in public programs, have come to affirm the importance of the humanities. They can be a force for change" (p. 33).

This movement also secures the recuperation of the 1960s because managers of public humanities organizations are drawn from graduate students for whom the academy could not provide employment: "Many of those who received humanities Ph.D.'s in the 1960s and 1970s when the academic job market was tight, now work in public humanities institutions" (p. 26). These "new scholars"—in Cheney's phrase (p. 26)—are supposed to have adjusted their views to the requirements of their new environments and, in particular, to have rejected subservience to academic scholars.

Two difficulties remain, however. Quoting Sidney Hook's assertion in her initial defense of the canon, Cheney appears to value the criticism it incorporates: "The Western tradition *is* a debate. . . . 'It would hardly be an exaggeration to say that of all cultures of which we have knowledge, Western culture has been the most critical of itself'" (pp. 12–13). Yet Cheney celebrates and denies this critical inquiry in the same breath. In a characteristic move, she first concedes, then negates, the importance of a critical perspective: "There will probably always be in our colleges and universities some sense of estrangement from society, a sense that flows from a critical attitude toward human affairs which is crucial to preserve. But the extreme alienation of some faculty members may well be tempered by closer involvement with our culture" (p. 29). Cheney's previous appreciation of criticism is converted by the vaguely negative terminology of "estrangement" and "alienation" into a dangerous tendency that should be curbed. In the end, Cheney's scheme can provide no adequate account of, or place for, the critical spirit she had earlier seen as an essential feature of Western tradition.

Moreover, the antidote suggested by Matthew Arnold's "happy moments of humanity" is itself immediately undercut by a less sanguine version of the role of the classics in a democratic society:

> With no small and permanent ruling class to uphold standards, democratic literature, he [Tocqueville] thought, would exhibit "a rude and untutored vigor of thought," a fascination with the facile and vivid, rather than the rigorous and subtle. Loving liberty as he did, Tocqueville sought ways to counterbalance such tendencies. He recommended looking back to classical literature, for example, for models of excellence from which we could learn.
>
> (p. 31)

Gone is Cheney's original view of the social purpose of the humanities as facilitating explorations of "a just society" (p. 3). Emphasis now falls on literature as a vehicle for maintaining social order. The phrases "uphold standards" and "such tendencies," eloquent in their vagueness, communicate a built-in bias against the lower-class instability potential in a democratic system. The tension in Matthew Arnold's polarized title *Culture and Anarchy* comes to the fore, with democracy as the anarchy and culture as the equivalent of ruling-class control.[2] The populace that Cheney has just celebrated for its capacity to oppose and curtail disaffected academics is itself in need of control. The apparent democratic appeal of Cheney's populism is thus vitiated; in its place is a politics of suspicion toward democracy.

II

I return to my starting point—the long passage from Maya Angelou that concludes the first part of Cheney's report. I find this moment more deeply compelling than the corresponding climax at the end of part three when Cheney cites Matthew Arnold. My questions are: what purpose does the Angelou quotation serve in Cheney's report? and is Cheney's use of Angelou justified by Angelou's work as a whole?

Cheney's lengthy quotation of Angelou has a twofold function: it is meant both to bolster Cheney's opposition to political readings and to validate Cheney's defense of a traditional canon. The first purpose is signaled by the preface with which Cheney frames the excerpt from Angelou: "What gives them [the humanities] their abiding worth are truths that pass beyond time and circumstance; truths that, transcending accidents of class, race, and gender, speak to us all" (p. 14). Cheney's earlier concession to political analysis—"The key questions are thought to be about gender, race, and class. . . . These are, of course, legitimate questions" (p. 12)—proves to be a throwaway gesture. The substance of the concession is subsequently withdrawn and canceled by the way the term "accidents" trivializes and dismisses the conceptual significance of gender, race, and class.

For Cheney, Angelou's ability to make Shakespeare's Sonnet 29 speak her own situation as a black woman shows that gender, race, and class do not really matter, are irrelevant. But neither the sonnet itself nor Angelou's use of it support Cheney's point of view. The different class positions of the poet and the highborn young man are central, not incidental, to the sonnets because they articulate a social dynamic that works against simple transcendence. The poet's expressions of love do not triumphantly dissolve the class barrier; rather, the class difference helps to underscore the love's wishfulness and pathos. The couplet of Sonnet 29—"For thy sweet love rememb'red such wealth brings / That then I scorn to change my state with kings"—may assertively announce the power of love; but the couplet of Sonnet 87 employs the imagery of class hierarchy to insist with equal authority on the opposite: "Thus have I had thee as a dream doth flatter, / In sleep a king, but waking no such matter." Moreover, contrary to Cheney's interpretation, Angelou herself does not set aside class. Her identification with Shakespeare here is a statement about the lower-class position of many black women.

The special value of Angelou for Cheney's reinvigoration of the traditional canon involves the proposition that, if the emergence of black women writers threatens the established canon, then the most powerful response will be to have a black woman in her own voice endorse that canon and, further, to ratify it as a nonracial, nongendered tradition. To have Shakespeare quoted by Angelou and the two together quoted by Cheney constructs an impressive linear effect. This lining up of authors symbolically enacts a unified tradition, but the question remains of how well Angelou fits.

Cheney's conception of the canon blurs and conflates a key distinction between access and content, as though access to a certain set of works guarantees their communication of a self-evident, fixed meaning. When Cheney insists that "students should be knowledgeable about texts" (p. 12), she assumes that the outcome of this process will be a certain form of knowledge. To be knowledgeable means to possess a specific content that falls within a specified range. But acquaintance and content are two separate steps: one can accept the point about the need to engage traditional authors, yet disagree with the particular interpretations Cheney wishes to derive from them. Angelou's identification with Shakespeare primarily signifies a belief in access. "I suggest to you that an entire species depends upon keeping the arts alive and accessible. It is imperative that the arts are accessible and not other, not elite but available to everybody," she stresses in her 1985 address (p. 12). It does not follow that Angelou's vision of Shakespeare coincides with Cheney's. Angelou is unwilling to be limited to black culture and claims her right to the entire spectrum of cultural heritage. But this does not imply her denial of black culture as a distinct tradition, nor does it constitute an endorsement of the restricted concept of tradition advanced by Cheney.

When we put Angelou back in context—her own context—we see that the context of Cheney's report and the context of Angelou's work do not, in significant respects, match up. Taken in isolation, in the context with which Cheney surrounds it, Angelou's evocation of the moment when she overcomes her grandmother's stipulation that she choose black authors and satisfies her love for Shakespeare can be read as a triumph over the grandmother's provincial and separatist attitudes and as a one-way development of educational liberation. But this impression cannot be sustained when the passage is returned to its original context in Angelou's 1985 address. For in the address as a whole there can be no doubt that the representation of the grandmother has an overwhelmingly positive resonance. The grandmother is not a narrow, blocking figure but a source of support and survival.

In particular, Angelou's grandmother serves as a resource by embodying the specific Afro-American tradition of church music and ritual:

> So I started a song Momma [the grandmother] sang every Sunday. Now, it never occurred to me when she sang this song that it would be important to me, but of course I recorded it. . . . In Morocco all alone on the stage I sang her song. . . . It is important to remember that the first blacks were brought to this country in 1619. . . . How did we survive except by art.
> (pp. 8–10)

This passage counterbalances the Shakespearean one that Cheney chooses; the voice made possible by the grandmother's words is even stronger than the voice enabled by Shakespeare's language.

The cultural and political authority for Angelou of black religious expression is reinforced by the larger context of her five-volume autobiography.[3] Her allegiance to her religious heritage contributes to the dissolution of her interracial marriage when her husband opposes it, as she recounts in *Singin' and Swingin' and Gettin' Merry Like Christmas:*

> I tucked away the memory of my great-grandmother (who had been a slave), who told me of praying silently under old wash pots, and of secret meetings deep in the woods to praise God . . .
> I planned a secret crawl through neighborhood churches . . .
> The spirituals and gospel songs were sweeter than sugar. I wanted to keep my mouth full of them and the sounds of my people singing fell like sweet oil in my ears . . .
> After watching the multicolored people in church dressed in their gay Sunday finery and praising their Maker with loud voices and sensual movements, Tosh and my house looked very pale. Van Gogh and Klee posters which would please me a day later seemed irrelevant.
>
> (pp. 28–29)

The tension marked here between the Afro-American church and Western art implies an experience of multiple traditions instead of a single great tradition. Angelou's desire to embrace both traditions does not eliminate the multiplicity; no easy amalgamation or synthesis is possible.

The conflict between alternate traditions is dramatized in Angelou's account in *I Know Why the Caged Bird Sings* of her eighth-grade graduation from a segregated black school. The mood of the ceremony is destroyed by a representative from the white world: "Owens and the Brown Bomber were great heroes in our world, but what school official in the white goddom of Little Rock had the right to decide that those two men must be our only heroes?" (p. 151). What rescues the moment is not the planned allusion to Shakespearean heroism, but rather the spontaneous affirmation of a specifically Afro-American perspective:

> There was a shuffling and rustling about me, then Henry Reed was giving his valedictory address, "To Be or Not to Be". . . .
> . . . The English teacher had helped him to create a sermon winging through Hamlet's soliloquy. . . .
> I had been listening and silently rebutting each sentence with my eyes closed; then there was a hush, which in an audience warns that something unplanned is happening. I looked up and saw Henry Reed, the conservative, the proper, the A student, turn his back to the audience and turn to us (the proud graduating class of 1940) and sing, nearly speaking,
>
> > "Lift ev'ry voice and sing
> > Till earth and heaven ring
> > Ring with the harmonies of Liberty . . ."
>
> It was the poem written by James Weldon Johnson. It was the music composed by J. Rosamond Johnson. It was the Negro national anthem.
>
> (pp. 154–55)

Angelou concludes without reference to Shakespeare: "Oh, Black known and unknown poets, how often have your auctioned pains sustained us? . . . we survive in exact relationship to the dedication of our poets (include preachers, musicians and blues singers)" (p. 156). Three poems—"Lift Ev'ry Voice and Sing," Johnson's "O Black and Unknown Bards," to which Angelou obliquely alludes, and Paul Laurence Dunbar's "Sympathy," from which Angelou takes the title of her book—combine to emphasize the equation of poetry with singing. Through this motif Angelou joins three elements that will define her own career: religious music, entertainment, and writing.

Twenty years later in New York City, in 1960, when Angelou organizes *Cabaret for Freedom,* a theatrical presentation to benefit Martin Luther King's Southern Christian Leadership Conference, James Weldon Johnson's lyric again plays a key role. As Angelou portrays it in *The Heart of a Woman,* the initial effort calls forth Shakespearean inspiration: "'Well, hell, you start with Act I, Scene I, same way Shakespeare started'" (p. 65). But the Shakespearean model is sharply qualified: "We needed a story which had the complexity of *Hamlet* and the pertinence of *A Raisin in the Sun*" (p. 63). In the end, pertinence lacking in Shakespeare is achieved through the invocation of black literary tradition: "The entire cast stood in a straight line and sang 'Lift every voice and sing . . . '" (p. 68). Angelou affirms this tradition not only in her account of the Harlem Writers Guild (pp. 37–43), but also in the title, drawn from Georgia Douglas Johnson's poem, that frames the entire volume.[4]

Seen from the perspective of Angelou's work as a whole, Cheney's rendering of Angelou's Shakespearean passage in the NEH report has the effect of blunting, even of eliminating, the force of multiple traditions. Where Angelou's work presents dual traditions in tension, Cheney promotes a canon that is unified and harmonious. Canon formation is a political issue because there is a direct correlation between one's image of the canon and one's image of society. Cheney's version of the canon carries with it a vision of social harmony. Her cultural assumptions imply political assumptions since her canon asks us to act as though the "just society" (p. 3) she evokes is already achieved. By contrast, Angelou does not adopt the premature, self-congratulatory view of an American society whose major conflicts have been substantially moderated and resolved. Appealing instead to James Baldwin's phrase "these yet to be united states" (1985 address, p. 11), she implies that the 1960s she so vividly recalls in *The Heart of a Woman* are not over, that the issues raised in the sixties are still outstanding.

III

In the choice between the two models of a unitary canon or conflicting multiple traditions, Angelou's work—contrary to Cheney—does not lend support to the first over the second. The complexity that Cheney's selective presentation leaves out includes Angelou's problematic reliance on Shakespeare as one of the two most important authors who "formed my writing ambition."[5] In her discussion of the Angelou-Shakespeare connection, Christine Froula notes how precarious the voice is—because of the identification with Lucrece—to which Angelou's love of Shakespeare gives access in the case of *The Rape of Lucrece:* "But if Shakespeare's poem redeems Maya from her hysterical silence, it is also a lover that she embraces at her peril."[6]

In another instance, in *Singin' and Swingin' and Gettin' Merry Like Christmas,* Angelou's enthusiasm for Shakespeare seems excessive because of the way it uncritically enacts the realization of a fantasy of upward mobility. Arriving in Verona with the touring company of *Porgy and Bess,* Angelou exults: "I was so excited at the incredible turn of events which had brought me from a past of rejection, of slammed doors and blind alleys, of dead-end streets and culs-de-sac, . . . into a town made famous by one of the world's greatest writers" (pp. 140–41). But after this excitement over *Romeo and Juliet,* the arrival in Venice brings no mention of *Othello.* When on a return visit to Venice, two volumes later in *All God's Children Need Traveling Shoes,* Angelou imagines herself as "a sister to Othello," she does so with a deliberate reduction of awareness: "For a short while I let my Black American history sink beneath the surface of the city's sluggish water" (p. 175). As Angelou's Jewish companion in Berlin had remarked, " 'Neither you nor I can afford to be so innocent' " (p. 173).

If Angelou's appeal to Shakespeare consists of an unstable mixture of innocence and critical perspective, then Gloria Naylor and Adrienne Rich, the writers to be considered in the following two chapters, can be seen as conducting a more sustained and systematic negotiation with Shakespeare's work. While Angelou's response to Shakespeare involves unresolved ambivalence, Naylor and Rich pursue more active, unambiguous courses of revision. Their work enacts a definite pattern of development from dependence to an independence marked by the distinctive experience of stepping outside a Shakespearean framework. Through this move, the work of Naylor and Rich suggests a new formulation of the relationship between established and minority traditions, in which the former is evaluated from the perspective of the latter rather than the reverse.

7

Shakespeare's Changing Status
in the Novels of Gloria Naylor

The attempt to rewrite the Renaissance has been a major strand in criticism in the 1980s. At least four renaissances are being vigorously reinterpreted. The current reconsideration of the English and European Renaissance of the sixteenth and seventeenth centuries is exemplified by the collection *Rewriting the Renaissance,* whose title articulates a much wider effort.[1] Three American versions of renaissance are also being reconstructed. F. O. Matthiessen's classic *American Renaissance* has been challenged by a series of critics.[2] Gloria T. Hull's study reassesses the Harlem Renaissance.[3] In conversation with Gloria Naylor, Toni Morrison applies the term *renaissance* to contemporary black women writers: "It's a real renaissance. You know, we have spoken of renaissance before. But this one is ours, not somebody else's."[4] Yet work by critic Hazel V. Carby (discussed later in this chapter) suggests that this most recent renaissance is being rewritten even as Morrison formulates it.

My specific concern here is points of contact between the first and fourth of these renaissances as represented by Gloria Naylor's use of Shakespeare. *Othello* continues to be the primary focus for the discussion of race and racism in Shakespeare; Karen Newman's essay on the play demonstrates the extremely valuable results that can be produced from such a focus.[5] Shakespeareans, however, should not be limited to instances of black characters; responses to Shakespeare by a later black writer such as Gloria Naylor are also relevant. Canon studies that cross period divisions provide another avenue for considering Shakespeare's work in relation to questions of race.

I

Gloria Naylor's series of novels, eventually to be a quartet, is linked by a set of internal cross-references to characters and places.[6] Shakespeare, however, provides a second set of connections, for he figures in all three novels to date, and the range and depth of Shakespearean allusions have increased in Naylor's most recent novel, *Mama Day*. My starting point is a question: what is Shakespeare doing here? or why does Naylor so consistently evoke the Shakespearean reference point?

As an epitome of the literary master and as a representative of the main line of the inherited literary tradition, Shakespeare provides Naylor with a counterpoint to the emergent tradition of contemporary black women writers. The presence of Shakespeare allows Naylor to explore the relation between these two traditions, which she experiences not only as distinct but also as split, divided, opposed: "The writers I had been taught to love were either male or white. And who was I to argue that Ellison, Austen, Dickens, the Brontës, Baldwin and Faulkner weren't masters? They were and are. But inside there was still the faintest whisper: Was there no one telling my story?" ("Conversation," p. 568). Because of the absence of her story, it was "a long road from gathering the authority within myself to believe that I could actually be a writer" (p. 568). In Naylor's development, this authority comes crucially from her immediate predecessor Toni Morrison: "But for me, where was the *authority* for me to enter this forbidden terrain? But then finally you were being taught to me" (p. 575).

The perception of two traditions—one that omits black women, one that focuses on them—creates for Naylor an irreducible gap. The new tradition produces stories that are " 'different but equal' " (Mills, p. 17), with the stress falling on both terms. They are equal and not minor or second-rate, but they are also still different. Naylor resists the pressure of the logic that if they are truly equal, then they cannot be fundamentally different since all works of the first rank are judged by a single standard and thereby incorporated into a single canon.

Naylor's energies are directed rather toward preserving and dramatizing the signal differences between the dual traditions of which Shakespeare and Morrison are emblematic. Naylor's bond with Morrison as the originator of an alternate, non-Shakespearean tradition makes Morrison a more important resource than Shakespeare; Morrison provides an identity and a voice, which Shakespeare is powerless to do. Yet Naylor's primary allegiance to Morrison does not lead to the exclusion of Shakespeare. If, sustained by Morrison, Naylor need not approach Shakespeare with disabling reverence, neither does she simply reject him, as her evident attraction to Shakespearean language testifies. Naylor's involvement and negotiations with Shakespeare occur in an intermediate zone that conveys a delicate tension in Naylor's double perspective on Shakespeare: she appreciates Shakespeare while at the same time she is determined critically to rewrite him.

Naylor's attention to Shakespeare serves to raise the question of Shakespeare's changed status when seen from the vantage point of the emergent tradition in which Naylor is a participant. By putting into play and testing both positive and critical attitudes toward Shakespeare, Naylor's work dramatizes with particular fullness the conflict between established and emergent traditions.

II

In Naylor's first novel, *The Women of Brewster Place*, the Shakespearean moment is located in the "Cora Lee" story, the fifth of seven sections. The moment exemplifies the delicacy of tone with which Naylor approaches Shakespeare: her humor is too finely textured—too sympathetic and poignant—to be merely satirical.

Cora Lee, overwhelmed by her sole responsibility for her children, takes refuge from her burden in a heavy dose of TV soaps. This pattern is temporarily disrupted when she and the children are invited to a black production of *A Midsummer Night's Dream*. Shakespeare as cultural event inspires in Cora Lee an unprecedented outburst of energetic determination:

"It would be good for them. They need things like Shakespeare and all that" (p. 121), "They would sit still and get this Shakespeare thing if she had to break their backs" (p. 124). The specific incentive is defined by Cora Lee's association of Shakespeare with school, career aspiration, and upward mobility: "Junior high; high school; college—none of them stayed little forever. And then on to good jobs in insurance companies and the post office, even doctors or lawyers" (p. 126).

Naylor matches the comedy of *A Midsummer Night's Dream* with her own mischievous comic mood. She builds up the Shakespearean motif of the dream by linking Bottom's and Puck's references to dreaming (p. 126) with allusions to Mercutio's set piece on Queen Mab (p. 107, epigraph for "Cora Lee" section) and Prospero's "We are such stuff as dreams are made on" (p. 121). Using this Shakespearean background, Naylor plays off two meanings of dream—genuine hope and futile fantasy—against each other in the immediate context of black urban poverty. Though Mercutio's apparently genial speech comes from an early moment in *Romeo and Juliet* before the tragic current has taken hold, Naylor does not ultimately block out the tragic implications of Cora Lee's situation. The "night of wonders" (p. 127) that Shakespearean comedy creates for Cora Lee proves to be only an interlude. The evidence of "hopeful echoes" she finds upon her return home are summarily canceled: "Then she turned and firmly folded her evening like gold and lavender gauze deep within the creases of her dreams" (p. 127).

The discrepancy between hopeful dreaming and dead-end finality is abruptly brought into focus by her child's questioning: "'Mama,' Sammy pulled on her arm, 'Shakespeare's black?'" (p. 127). Naylor's gentle ironies become painful ones as she directly poses the issue of the relevance of Shakespeare's pastoral to black urban landscape. We are forced to acknowledge not only that Shakespeare is white but also that, even when "'brought . . . up to date'" (p. 119), his translation into a black cultural idiom is neither automatically assured nor unambiguously benign. Moving up from the low culture of white-produced TV soaps to the high culture of black-produced Shakespeare no longer seems an answer.

The problematic aspects of Shakespearean inspiration are intertwined with the paradoxical position of Kiswana Browne, who issues the invitation to Cora Lee to attend the Shakespeare play produced by her boyfriend Abshu. Unlike the others who "came because they had no choice and would remain for the same reason" (p. 4), Kiswana, having rejected her middle-class family situation in Linden Hills, is the one woman in Brewster Place who is there by choice. Kiswana's renunciation is subsequently vindicated by Naylor's own condemnation of Linden Hills in her second novel. Yet there is pointed irony in Kiswana's being the intermediary who arouses in Cora Lee a Shakespearean dream of upward educational mobility when Kiswana herself has already deliberately rejected it, having dropped out of college: "'Those bourgie schools were counterrevolutionary'" (p. 83); "'What good would I be after four or five years of a lot of white brainwashing in some phony, prestige institution, huh?'" (p. 84). When she does take courses again at a community college, Shakespeare is not in her curriculum (p. 161).

Kiswana's appeal to come to the performance of *A Midsummer Night's Dream* is her second invitation to Cora Lee; the first is a request that she attend the meeting of a tenants' association that Kiswana is organizing (pp. 115–16). Naylor does not so much reject Kiswana's political commitment as show its limits. Kiswana, too, is compromised by the double meaning of dreams as hope and as lack of realism: "She placed her dreams on the back of the bird and fantasized that it would glide forever . . . she watched with a sigh as the bird beat its wings in awkward, frantic movements. . . . This brought her back to earth" (p. 75).

When the well-attended meeting in Kiswana's apartment is disrupted over an objection to the participation of Lorraine, a lesbian, Kiswana is unable to respond effectively. Her belated apology still expresses this inadequacy: "'I should have said something—after all, it was my house—but things just sort of got out of hand so quickly, I'm sorry, I . . . '" (p. 160).

Kiswana's politics fail to include the political issue of lesbian relationships. Even in Mattie's dream sequence at the end of the novel, Kiswana is represented as hesitant to acknowledge the consequences of the hostility to Lorraine's lesbian identity. Confronted with bloodstained bricks that body forth both Lorraine's violent rape and her retaliatory murder of the defenseless man who befriends but ultimately cannot protect her against male aggression, Kiswana initially responds with denial:

> [Ciel] tried to pass a brick to Kiswana, who looked as if she had stepped into a nightmare.
> "There's no blood on those bricks!" Kiswana grabbed Ciel by the arm. "You know there's no blood—it's raining. It's just raining!"
> Ciel pressed the brick into Kiswana's hand and forced her fingers to curl around it. "Does it matter? Does it really matter?"
> Kiswana looked down at the wet stone and her rain-soaked braids leaked onto the surface, spreading the dark stain. She wept and ran to throw the brick spotted with her blood out into the avenue.
>
> (pp. 186–87)

Kiswana's weeping during this act of symbolic identification marks the final separation from the comic note struck by *A Midsummer Night's Dream*. The "Cora Lee" section containing the Shakespearean episode is strategically placed because of its sharp juxtaposition with the section that follows on "The Two," the lesbian couple. The humor, shifting to a different register, now serves as a medium for releasing and partially transforming suspicion and uncertainty about lesbian sexuality. The attack on Lorraine at the block meeting is defused through humor, but it is a strained, ambivalent humor that conveys tentative acceptance without completely dispelling the underlying discomfort and anxiety:

> The laughter that burst out of their lungs was such a relief that eyes were watery. The room laid back its head and howled in gratitude to Ben for allowing it to breath again.

> Sophie's rantings could not be heard above the wheezing, coughing, and backslapping that now went on.
>   Lorraine left the apartment.
>
> (p. 146)

The humor escalates in the wildly comic moment when Lorraine's lover Theresa puts on an angry display with food for the benefit of a disapproving voyeur (pp. 158–59):

> Theresa's sides were starting to ache from laughing, and she sat down in one of the kitchen chairs. Lorraine pushed the bowl a little further down the table from her, and this set them off again. Theresa laughed and rocked in the chair until tears were rolling down her cheeks. Then she crossed that fine line between laughter and tears and started to sob.
>
> (p. 159)

The phrase used to express the way humor gives access to hurt aptly characterizes Naylor's harsher comic action: in moving from "Cora Lee" to "The Two," the novel has "crossed the fine line between laughter and tears."

This crossing can be described as a shift from Shakespeare's rendering of the dream motif to that of Langston Hughes in "What happens to a dream deferred?," the politically charged poem that Naylor uses as the epigraph for the novel as a whole. Naylor's break with the evanescent atmosphere of *A Midsummer Night's Dream* is particularly appropriate because the play's design undermines female bonds: the intimate connection between Hermia and Helena is severed by the marital demands imposed by comic form.[7] Setting aside a comic pattern that cannot be accommodated to her focus on female bonds, Naylor answers Hughes's final line *"Or does it explode?"* with her own word "exploded" (p. 188). Naylor's explosion dismantles the wall that maintains Brewster Place as an isolated ghetto. By contrast, the removal of the wall in *A Midsummer Night's Dream* occurs within the concluding play-within-a-play, a carefully circumscribed entertainment that observes firm class distinctions between the lower-class artisans who perform and the aristocratic audience whom they serve to amuse.

Naylor's fantasy is fiercer, enabling a glimpse of black female action across differences in class and sexuality. Middle-class Kiswana, moving beyond her earlier evasiveness about Lorraine's lesbian identity (p. 160), participates in a protest she did not plan that honors Lorraine's sacrifice. Theresa, Lorraine's partner, joins in: "She grabbed the bricks from Cora and threw one into the avenue" (pp. 187–88). Naylor makes clear that this unified action occurs in imagination only, not in reality, by articulating it as Mattie's dream preceding the actual block party. But the dream vision is so intensely imagined that the daylight reality which succeeds cannot displace it; this achievement belongs to Naylor's, not Shakespeare's, imagination.

III

In *Linden Hills*, Naylor's second novel, the main reference point from Western literary tradition appears to be Dante's *Inferno* (Mills, p. 17). However, in a penultimate moment, the two black friends, Lester and Willie, the latter a struggling poet, discuss Shakespeare. The terms have modulated from the humorously innocent query "'Shakespeare's black?'" in *The Women of Brewster Place* to the more pressing issue of "'why black folks ain't produced a Shakespeare'" (*Linden Hills*, p. 282).

In these first two novels, the dominant typography is the splitting of black urban landscape into separate poor and middle-class areas. The novels' views of Shakespeare are correlated with this internal class division. From the perspective of Brewster Place, Shakespeare belongs to Linden Hills and the rising middle-class expectations associated with that privileged space: at the play, Cora "looked around and didn't recognize anyone from Brewster so the blacks here probably came from Linden Hills" (*The Women of Brewster Hills*, p. 124). But, on closer inspection in *Linden Hills*, Shakespeare is not to be found there either, as the exchange between Willie and Lester testifies:

"You'd think of all the places in the world, this neighborhood
had a chance of giving us at least one black Shakespeare."
   "But Linden Hills ain't about that, Willie. You should know
that by now."

(p. 283)

Shakespeare's location with respect to black society remains
elusive and hence the shift from the relatively playful tone in
the first novel's representation of Shakespeare to the more
frustrated note in the second.

The phrase "one black Shakespeare" expresses the highest
artistic desire as the replication of the Shakespearean model.
But to shape one's desire in this way may be to create a
self-defeating dependence; Shakespeare comes to symbolize
a quest for black recognition that is unattainable within the
narrow terms of imitation suggested by the uncomfortable
echo effect that ties Willie's name to Will Shakespeare's. Naylor's third novel will move outside this framework through a
decisive turn to a wider geographical exploration. The earlier
counterpoint between poor and middle-class is subsumed by
a larger structure of tensions between Northern urban and
Southern rural that gradually emerges into prominence over
the course of the three novels.[8] The increasing emphasis on
the North-South contrast leads, I shall argue, to a different
kind of engagement with Shakespeare because the Southern
terrain of *Mama Day* makes possible a literary mapping
wherein Shakespeare can be not only emulated but also out-
maneuvered.

The Women of Brewster Place dramatizes its Southern origins
through Mattie Michael, whose story both begins in the
South and begins the novel. Though left behind in the move
northward, the South has a powerful residual presence because a crucial part of the network of female bonds is formed
there: Mattie's friendship with Etta Mae Johnson (section 2) is
established before their arrival in New York as is Mattie's
relationship with Ciel (section 4). Partly because of this
Southern connection, Mattie can be seen as a prototype of
Mama Day in Naylor's third novel. While lacking Mama
Day's specific knowledge of magic, Mattie nonetheless has a

maternal force and communal authority that parallel Mama Day's. Mattie's care of Ciel after the death of Ciel's child is analogous to Mama Day's concern for Cocoa: "The black mammoth gripped so firmly that the slightest increase of pressure would have cracked the girl's spine. But she rocked" (*The Women of Brewster Place*, p. 103).

Mattie differs from Mama Day in two crucial respects: she remains permanently in the North with no prospect of returning to the home base in the South she has been forced to leave; and her reunion with Ciel is fulfilled only in a dream ("Mattie pressed Ciel into her full bosom and rocked her slowly" [p. 177]). But Mattie's dream organizes the women of Brewster Place in a manner that anticipates Mama Day's more potent art. In so doing, Mattie holds out the possibility of a black alternative to the Shakespearean imagination, an alternative to be realized when Naylor's Mama Day supplants rather than duplicates Shakespeare's Prospero.

The central line of development from Mattie to Mama Day can be traced in *Linden Hills* through the figure of Roberta Johnson, who, as grandmother to Laurel Dumont, is " 'the closest thing to a natural mother you got' " (p. 223). Remaining firmly based in the rural South, the grandmother sponsors the Berkeley education that separates them: "Because all Roberta knew was that she had cashed in her life insurance to send a child she had named Laurel Johnson to the state of California, and it sent her back a stranger" (pp. 226–27). Laurel's engulfment in the "emptiness" (p. 238) of middle-class achievement places her beyond the grandmother's power to rescue her:

> "Why did you come, Laurel?"
> There was a long pause, and then her voice was barely a whisper. "When people are in trouble, don't they go home?"
> Roberta covered her clenched hands gently. "But this ain't your home, child."
>
> (p. 231)

Yet in reversing the one-way northward migration, Laurel's attempt to reconnect with a Southern rural landscape in *Lin-*

den Hills prefigures Cocoa's return from New York City to the South in *Mama Day*.

The resource from which Laurel has been cut off involves tradition: "She was taking in the sight of an old woman, the sound of old stories, and the smells of an old tradition with nothing inside her to connect up to them" (p. 239). Roberta evokes the saving power of this native tradition by opposing it to the European art to which Laurel is habituated:

> "You can hear the hurt in Bessie or Billie and I just kinda wish that I'd come here and found you playing their stuff, 'cause that man you seem to like so much—that Mahler—his music says that he ain't made peace with his pain, child. And if you gonna go on, that's what you gotta do."
>
> (p. 235)

The motif of conflicting Afro-American and Western traditions extends, by implication, to the vexed homage Willie pays to Shakespeare as formulated in the need for "'one black Shakespeare'" (p. 283). Shakespeare, like Mahler, may be the wrong place to seek artistic salvation.

IV

Mama Day picks up where *Linden Hills* leaves off by greatly intensifying both the North-South cultural contrast and the Shakespearean motif. Before turning to *Mama Day's* treatment of the latter, I want to examine the former through a comparison of *Mama Day* with Paule Marshall's *Praisesong for the Widow*.[9] The correspondences between the two novels suggest a common pattern with four steps.

The first step in this sequence is the protracted struggle to achieve middle-class security. This driving upward mobility is recounted in Part II of *Praisesong for the Widow* in the story of the Johnsons' move from Halsey Street in Brooklyn to North White Plains. The counterpart to Jerome Johnson's rise as an accountant is George's successful New York–based engineering career in *Mama Day*. For Kiswana Browne in *The Women of Brewster Place*, the ultimate proof of "middle-class amnesia" (p. 85) is the existence of black Republicans, a condition she vows to avoid: " 'But I'll never be a Republican' " (p. 88). George in *Mama Day*, viewing his Republican affiliation as a necessary component of his business success, experiences only occasional regret: "Meeting his type always made me ashamed to be a Republican" (p. 56).

A second phase begins with symptoms of malaise after the hard-won attainment of middle-class status, with a growing awareness of the emptiness of arrival. Avey Johnson's perception of being at an impasse propels Marshall's novel forward. George's more muted dissatisfaction with the limitations of his constricted identity is implicitly expressed by his desire to reach out and to incorporate Cocoa's very different background:

> And I wondered if it was too late, if seven years in New York had been just enough for you to lose that, like you were trying to lose your southern accent. . . . That's why I wanted you to call me George. There isn't a southerner alive who could bring that name in under two syllables.
>
> (p. 33)

This turning point leads to a third stage, the counter-project of recovering what has been lost in middle-class achievement. The project takes the particular geographic form of leaving behind New York City in order to reclaim a living connection with a self-contained Southern black culture symbolized by an island community. In the case of *Praisesong for the Widow*, the specific locale is Tatum Island, where, as a child, Avey Johnson visited her great-aunt Cuney, who is responsible for Avey's name Avatara (p. 42).[10] Avey regains her connection with this heritage by literally enacting the meaning in her name—incarnation—in the ritual dance during the festival on the Caribbean island of Carriacou. Not only are Tatum and Carriacou both directly connected with the African origins of their black inhabitants, but also Avey's participation in the Carriacou festival is matched point for point with her recollections of Tatum.

In *Mama Day*, George too "crosses over" (pp. 165, 177) onto the Southern island of Willow Springs, a move which for him is equivalent to "entering another world" (p. 175) and which for Naylor marks the boundary of the novel's second half. Both for Avey Johnson and for George, the new realm is governed by a set of beliefs that demand faith and challenge skepticism. Avey manages the process with relative ease: "she had awakened with it [her mind] like a slate that had been wiped clean, a *tabula rasa* upon which a whole new history could be written" (p. 151). George's test of belief is more involuntary and more stressful: "How could I believe?" (p. 288).

Mama Day denies, or fulfills more stringently, the affirmative answer *Praisesong for the Widow* gives to Avey's question:

> Would it have been possible to have done both? That is, to have wrested, as they had done over all those years, the means needed to rescue them from Halsey Street and to see the children through, while preserving, safeguarding, treasuring those things that had come down to them over the generations, which had defined them in a particular way. . . . They could have done both, it suddenly seemed to her.
>
> (p. 139)

In Marshall's novel, the tragedy—the death of Avey's husband—has already occurred, leaving the novel free to concentrate on transcendence for Avey. *Mama Day*, however, dramatizes the tragic cost through its focus on George's crisis and sacrificial death.

Yet this difference between the two novels becomes less pronounced when the fourth stage of resolution is considered. Whatever George's deficiencies, the novel more than makes up for his inability to believe with its own decisive investment in the character of Mama Day. Despite Naylor's rejection of happy endings ("Grown women aren't supposed to believe in Prince Charmings and happily-ever-afters. Real life isn't about that" [p.119]), *Mama Day* conveys a strongly positive sense of completion through Mama Day's epilogue. With Mama Day's help, Cocoa finds the peace that eludes Laurel in *Linden Hills:* Cocoa's is "a face that's been given the meaning of peace" (p. 312). Although the transmission of heritage passes through the female line from Mama Day to Cocoa, George is included in this resolution. In spite of his failure, George initiates and shares the peace: "there was total peace" (p. 302). As Mama Day predicts, his bond with Cocoa is maintained after his death through her ongoing communication with him: "whatever roads take her from here, they'll always lead back to you" (p. 308).

A similarity between Marshall's and Naylor's respective endings is reinforced by the way their recovery of the distant past is accompanied by studied neglect of more recent political history. Avey's change in *Praisesong for the Widow* is measured symbolically by the reversal of her initial refusal to sell the White Plains house that she and her husband had struggled to acquire (p. 26):

> Sell the house in North White Plains as Marion had been urging her to do for years and use the money to build in Tatum.
> It would be a vacation house, and once she retired she would live part of the year there. . . .
> And Marion could bring some of the children from her school. . . . The place could serve as a summer camp.
> (p. 256)

By this decision, Avey responds to the "mission" bequeathed by her great-aunt Cuney (p. 42); at the same time, this triumph is partly undercut by the way her language suggests a real estate transaction.

The resolution is romanticized because it is a substitute for a direct confrontation with the images of political conflict in the sixties that Avey has "conveniently forgotten" (p. 31):

> Hadn't she lived through most of the sixties and early seventies as if Watts and Selma and the tanks and Stoner guns in the streets of Detroit somehow did not pertain to her, denying her rage, and carefully effacing any dream that might have come to her during the night by the time she awoke the next morning.
> (p. 140)

This spirit of denial remains in force; Avey's plan does not undo the repression of her anxiety over political struggle.[11] A similar dynamic is at work in *Mama Day*, where preoccupation with the deep time of the ancestral past squeezes out contemporary political issues from which Willow Springs is portrayed as fundamentally immune. The sixties are by-passed, treated peripherally as high comedy in the tale of outwitting the abrasive white deputy (pp. 79–81).

Both Marshall's Tatum and Naylor's Willow Springs take on an aspect of pastoral refuge that makes them subject to Hazel V. Carby's analysis of black folk tradition as a romantic avoidance of the present political crisis whose primary focus is urban.[12] In Carby's persuasive view, recent literary criticism has privileged the folk line as the authentic tradition, excluding or minimizing the other, equally authentic black urban mode and thereby participating in the evasion to which folk genres are prone. Like *Praisesong for the Widow*, *Mama Day* abandons New York City without regret: "It was a relief to leave for good" (p. 305). I want to acknowledge the force of Carby's powerful critique, but at the same time to argue that *Mama Day* is not simply escapist because it enacts another drama—the cultural political struggle with the Shakespearean past. Though Naylor's presentation will not permit disbelief in Mama Day, her skepticism remains active in relation to Shakespeare.

Much in *King Lear* and *The Tempest*, the two principal plays evoked in *Mama Day*, seems merely to aid and abet the sentimental pastoral tendencies in the novel. Both plays assume the salubrious value of pastoral space—the exposed heath in Lear's case, the magically controlled island in Prospero's. Both plays employ the rhythm of the tempest followed by the restorative calm after the storm; in Naylor's final line, "the waters were still" (p. 312). Moreover, the generic progression from *King Lear* as tragedy to *The Tempest* as late romance serves to reinforce a romanticized version of pastoral.

These congruencies between Shakespeare and *Mama Day* do not tell the whole story, however. Naylor's sustained engagement with Shakespeare cannot be explained by the image of Shakespeare as an exclusively positive resource, nor is Naylor's action limited to the harmonious adaptation and recapitulation of Shakespearean motifs. Rather, the effect of *Mama Day's* exploration of Shakespearean heritage is critically to revise and decenter it.

V

Naylor's reassessment of Shakespeare in *Mama Day* is carried out on two levels. On the first, George's attachment to *King Lear* is probed; on the second, more pervasive level, associations between Willow Springs and *The Tempest* are tested. This twofold approach is correlated with the novel's overall geographic movement from North to South since George's *Lear* is situated in the former while *The Tempest*'s connections are with the latter.

George's adoption of Shakespeare serves as a badge of his upward mobility. His successive editions of *King Lear* both mark the increasing value of the play as a material object and cultural status symbol and also measure the progress of his relationship with Cocoa. He begins with a "worn copy" (p. 60) that he prefers to Cocoa and ends with "the calfskin and gold-leafed copy" (p. 304) that Cocoa gives him as a birthday present. *King Lear* specifically provides the medium for negotiating George's seduction of Cocoa: "The games people play. I wasn't coming to your apartment the following Tuesday night to talk about *King Lear*" (p. 104).

The chief point of emotional connection to the play is George's identification with Edmund: "It had a special poignancy for me, reading about the rage of a bastard son" (p. 106). Edmund's soliloquy—"Now, gods, stand up for bastards"—speaks to George's desire to make it against the odds. George smugly notes Cocoa's naive reading, though he withholds his commentary so as not to impede the seduction:

> And you were so glad I'd turned you on to this. It showed you how hard the playwright tried to convey that men had the same feelings as women. No, that was not true. No way. Along with *The Taming of the Shrew,* this had to be Shakespeare's most sexist treatment of women—but far be it

from me to contradict anything you had to say. I didn't want
to waste any more time than necessary for you to work yourself up to untying the strings on that red halter.

(p. 106)

But George's own misinterpretation is just as bad, for Shakespeare does not stand up for bastards any more than for
women. Edmund is defeated by Edgar in the end, and George
chooses to neglect his fate.

George's relatively superficial attachment to Shakespeare
comes nowhere close to his passionate commitment to football. If Shakespeare's images of women are restrictive, football
excludes women entirely. In Cocoa's detached view of football's male bonding: "They line up, bend down, and all of a sudden they're in a pile, smelling each other's behinds" (p. 126).
Since Naylor herself shares Cocoa's resistance to George's love
of football,[13] one might say that Naylor has paid George back
by imposing on him her own fascination with Shakespeare.
After the tempest hits Willow Springs, she puts into George's
mouth a phrase derived from Prospero's revels speech: "this
was the stuff of dreams" (p. 258). But George's understanding
of the cue proves inadequate. While his attitude toward football approaches the religious ("And I'm not talking in meta-
phors—it could create miracles" [p. 124]), his response to
Mama Day conspicuously denies that this attitude could apply
to her female arena: " 'Well, you're talking in a lot of meta-
phors' " (p. 294). Ultimately his approach to Willow Springs
remains on the same order as his treatment of "the symbolism" (pp. 105–6) of *King Lear*.

The novel's second Shakespearean strand, the interplay
between *The Tempest* and Naylor's representation of the Southern island of Willow Springs, involves a much more active
encounter with Shakespeare. Naylor rewrites the exchange
between Prospero and Caliban concerning ownership, in effect honoring Caliban's accusation—"This island's mine, by
Sycorax my mother, / Which thou tak'st from me"—and re-
instating his legitimate, female-derived possession. The black
islanders of Willow Springs oppose the trend in island development that would reduce them to Caliban-like servility:

Hadn't we seen it happen back in the '80s on St. Helena, Daufuskie, and St. John's? And before that in the '60s on Hilton Head? . . . And the only dark faces you see now in them "vacation paradises" is the ones cleaning the toilets and cutting the grass. . . . Weren't gonna happen in Willow Springs. 'Cause if Mama Day say no, everybody say no.

(p. 6)

Their attitude toward real estate contrasts sharply with that represented by the black developer Luther Nedeed in *Linden Hills;* where Nedeed imitates the white model, Willow Springs rejects it. Nedeed's obsessive concern with the empty ceremony of a traditional family Christmas is replaced in *Mama Day* by the non-Christian observance of the winter solstice that signifies cultural independence: "old Reverend Hooper couldn't stop Candle Walk night. . . . Any fool knows Christmas is December twenty-fifth—that ain't never caught on too much here. And Candle Walk is always the night of the twenty-second" (p. 108).

Naylor's depiction of Willow Springs' resistance to white corporate and cultural control parallels her own resistance to Shakespearean colonization of her art. However, although Naylor teasingly alludes to Caliban—"some slave on a Caribbean island" Cocoa recalls "from her high school Shakespeare" (p. 64), the main line of Naylor's resistance lies elsewhere. As a recent survey shows, twentieth-century attempts to revise *The Tempest* have concentrated on reversing the Prospero-Caliban relationship by imagining a newly empowered Caliban.[14] Naylor's special contribution is her focus on women characters, a focus that adds a reconfiguration of genders to the issues of race and class associated with Caliban. Largely ignoring Caliban, Naylor's subversive strategy is to create a black female equivalent to Prospero.

The force of Naylor's project is implied by the central character's double name: both Miranda and Mama Day. If the former suggests the tie to Shakespeare, the latter breaks it by indicating the possibility of escape from Shakespearean entrapment in the subservient daughter role. Not only do the age and experience of Naylor's Miranda contrast with the youth and innocence of Shakespeare's Miranda but also Mama Day's scope encompasses and outdoes Prospero himself. In 1999 at the novel's close, Mama Day, having been born in 1895, is 104 years old and even then her epilogue is not quite ready to seek release: "and when she's tied up the twentieth century, she'll take a little peek into the other side—for pure devilment and curiosity—and then leave for a rest that she deserves" (p. 312). The hyperbole of her age establishes that Mama Day is more than able to compete with Prospero, whose "Every third thought shall be my grave" seems pinched and feeble next to the splendor of her approach to death.

Naylor not only has Mama Day usurp Prospero's role, but also redefines that role by altering the prerogatives that go with it. The moral structure of *The Tempest* is carried over into *Mama Day* only in a residual way. Ruby, for example, is an embodiment of evil against whom Mama Day is allowed a Prospero-like spectacular punitive display (pp. 270, 273). However, Naylor's main stress is on the differences between Prospero's and Mama Day's magical powers. The storm at the outset of *The Tempest* is Prospero's concoction, as he reveals with paternal reassurance and pride in act 1, scene 2. By contrast, Mama Day is powerless to prevent the storm's destruction of Little Caesar, the child whom she had helped Bernice to produce. As Mama Day reflects, "she ain't never tried to get *over* nature" (p. 262). While Prospero may belatedly accept the limits of his magic, Mama Day is mindful of her limitations from the beginning.

The contrast between Prospero and Mama Day is especially sharp with respect to gender politics. Though the relationship between Mama Day and her father Jean-Paul is portrayed as a positive resource, it is nonetheless subordinate to the primary emphasis on strong female bonds—bonds that Miranda's isolation makes impossible in *The Tempest*. Mama Day's central drama concerns the recovery of connections with three women: Sapphira, the slave woman who originated the Day line; Ophelia, Mama Day's mother who, distraught over the death of her daughter Peace, drowned herself; and Cocoa, her grandniece, who has left Willow Springs and now works in New York City.

Like Mama Day, Cocoa has a double name that operates to deny Shakespearean expectations. Cocoa is named Ophelia after her great-grandmother, whose death by water recalls the destiny of Shakespeare's Ophelia in the male-dominated world of *Hamlet*. Cocoa's alternate name aids the process of exorcising the burden both of her great-grandmother's demise and of the potential Shakespearean connotations. Mama Day's comment about tradition can be applied to the novel's general stance toward patriarchal political structures in *Hamlet*, *King Lear*, or *The Tempest*: " 'Tradition is fine, but you gotta know when to stop being a fool'" (p. 307).

It is true that in its own way *Mama Day* is as determined as any Shakespearean comedy in its marital and reproductive drive. Like Prospero, Mama Day orchestrates generational continuity: "I plan to keep on living till I can rock one of yours on my knee" (p. 35). This parallel does not mean, however, that Mama Day derives after all from a Shakespearean analogue. Mama Day is shaped rather by the figure of the black mother as artist described by writers such as Paule Marshall, Alice Walker, and June Jordan,[15] and it is within this distinct tradition that the Mama Day–Cocoa relationship has to be considered.

In Paule Marshall's *Praisesong for the Widow*, the unattributed poetic phrase "my sweetest lepers" (pp. 16, 256) comes from Gwendolyn Brooks's "the children of the poor," whose first line chillingly observes: "People who have no children can be hard."[16] This assertion has a resonance with Toni Morrison's *Tar Baby* (1981), where the unattached and childless Jadine is presented not as an opportunity but as a problem.[17] In the 1985 conversation with Naylor, Morrison comments: "That's another one of those unreal, I think also fraudulent, conflicts between women who want to be mothers and women who don't. Why should there be any conflict with that? You could, first of all, do both" (p. 573). But Morrison's idea of choice modulates into the imperative of doing both: "No one should be asked to make a choice between a home and a career. Why not have both? It's all possible" (p. 575).

Morrison's comments suggest some of the emotional charge behind the novel's procreational pressure, a pressure exemplified by the quilt Cocoa receives from Mama Day and her sister: "I also knew they hadn't gone through that kind of labor just for me. . . . They had sewed for *my* grandchildren to be conceived under this quilt" (p. 147). Cocoa begins as a potential Jadine, but through Mama Day's intervention ends by carrying on the family line, on which the inheritance of land and the survival of Willow Springs depend. The novel's conclusion leaves no room for doubt about Cocoa's commitment to Mama Day's legacy. Yet their bond is not completely idealized; a slight prickliness and tension flicker around the edges. Cocoa's original departure from the island signals her need for psychological separation; she vigorously rejects George's notion of settling in Willow Springs (p. 220); even when she relocates, she maintains some distance by living in Charleston instead of returning to the island itself.

We have in the end to see Naylor's work in relation to two different contexts, both of which are important for a full view. Naylor's departures from Shakespeare—especially her rejection of the absences and restrictions imposed by Shakespearean images of women—are substantial.[18] By countering Shakespeare, Naylor demonstrates the degree to which Shakespeare does not author us, the extent to which that role has irreversibly passed to others. New problems indeed arise, but they are not Shakespeare's problems nor does his work contain the materials needed for exploring all the possible options.

VI

The conclusion of this analysis of Naylor's use of Shakespeare is that Shakespeare's cultural reach is diminished, not extended. Shakespeare's work can no longer be conceived as an infinitely expanding literary umbrella, the ultimate primary source capable of commenting on all subsequent developments no matter how far historically removed. Faced with apparently limitless possibilities for interpretation, Shakespeareans have tended to romanticize their critical quandary by investing it with an existential myth of Shakespeare's inexhaustibility, by means of which Shakespeare already anticipates every possible future situation or response. This notion of Shakespearean anticipation amounts to a denial of history, of change, and of our own agency.

Naylor's work provides a valuable test case for how we are going to formulate a multicultural approach to literary studies. Naylor's interest in Shakespeare neither translates into kinship nor supports a model of continuity; the main note is rather one of conflict and difference. As Gloria T. Hull remarks, "Black women poets are not 'Shakespeare's sisters.' In fact, they seem to be siblings of no one but themselves."[19] *Mama Day* owes less to Shakespeare than to a separate tradition of black women writers. Shakespeare does not assimilate Naylor; Naylor assimilates Shakespeare.

The result is that we must give up the assumption that the literary curriculum revolves around Shakespeare. The habits of a Shakespeare-centered universe may inspire ever more elaborate and farfetched attempts at "saving the appearances" comparable to the calculations devised to defend a geocentric system against the encroachments of a heliocentric view. The cultural act of naming newly discovered moons—most recently those of Uranus—after Shakespearean characters may seem to provide confirmation of old patterns; new moons cannot talk back and disconfirm. But new authors like Gloria Naylor can. Her fictions encourage us to direct our energies toward investigations of Shakespeare's place in a reconstellated cultural situation in which his work, while still significant, is no longer the all-defining center of things.

8

Adrienne Rich's Re-Vision
of Shakespeare

I begin with two interrelated questions. The first concerns
Rich's focus on her father: how does her presentation of the
father-daughter relationship change, and what is the significance of these changes for her work as a whole? Second, what
is the place of Shakespeare in Rich's development? The two
questions converge, for example, in the poem "After Dark,"
with its explicit allusion to *King Lear:* what are the long-term
repercussions of the parallel evoked here between Cordelia
and Lear and Rich and her father?

In outline, the father-daughter motif in Rich's work can be
viewed in three distinct phases.[1] The early work, consisting
of the first four volumes of poetry and culminating in "After
Dark" in *Necessities of Life,* portrays a troubled fusion with the
father. Drastic separation from the father, dramatized as the
precondition for establishing an independent self, occurs in
the great middle phase conducted both in prose—sharply
etched versions of the father appear in "When We Dead
Awaken: Writing as Re-Vision" (first published in 1971) and
in *Of Woman Born* (begun in 1972)—and in poetry from *Leaflets*
to *A Wild Patience Has Taken Me This Far.* A third phase is
suggested by the essay "Split at the Root" (1982) and the
poem *Sources* (separately published in 1983), which witness
the surprising and moving reemergence of the father.

After devoting a section to each of these three phases in
turn, I then concentrate on the issue of how we are to characterize Rich's recent attention to her father. This point of
interpretation, I shall argue, is crucial to the question of how
the term *re-vision* from her essay "When We Dead Awaken:

Writing as Re-Vision" applies to Rich's relation to Shake-speare. It is also crucial to the ancillary question of what Rich's work means for Shakespeareans.

I

Rich's first volume of poetry, *A Change of World,* contains hints both of the father's presence and of Shakespeare's. *King Lear* stands behind the opening poem "Storm Warnings," aiding our recognition of external weather as a metaphor for internal emotional distress. Though Lear is cast out un-housed on the open heath while the speaker of "Storm Warnings" withdraws into a confined domestic enclosure, both are tormented by exposure to acute vulnerability. The "weather in the heart" anticipated by the speaker is akin to Lear's "tempest in my mind." "Change" (line 15) in "Storm Warnings" is experienced as a negative force that threatens to over-whelm one's fragile psychological defenses; the brooding, haunted sensation of "troubled regions" is powerfully ren-dered but is left vague, as though the content might be too dreadful to be further specified.

"What Ghosts Can Say," another poem that draws on Shakespeare, points to the original family context as the source of generic feelings of fear and guilt. The surface tone of this literary exercise in translating *Hamlet* into native Amer-ican idiom is whimsical and witty, but the underlying filial terror—the poem's "serious business"—is convincingly com-municated. The image of "his father's ghost" remains fixed in Harry Wylie's mind because he can recover no specific reason for the paternal violation ("As when he beat the boy's un-covered thighs") he so vividly recalls:

> But why the actual punishment had fallen,
> For what offense of boyhood, he could try
> For years and not unearth. What ghosts can say—
> Even the ghosts of fathers—comes obscurely.
> What if the terror stays without the meaning?

The resulting anxiety is inherent in the relation to the father and is therefore inaccessible to an explanation based on particular causation. The fictitious son serves as a screen that allows Rich indirectly to register the pressure of her own experience as a daughter who has been subjected to the father's oppressiveness, the precise nature of which she cannot yet "unearth."[2]

Equally oblique is the familial reference in the volume's title, *A Change of World*, which tacitly marks Rich's move from the family home in Baltimore to the college world of Radcliffe, where the book was completed in her senior year. In contrast to the later title *The Will to Change*, *A Change of World* generally gives the term a passive inflection: the change of location is not a significant change because it proves impossible to escape the internalized sense of family-based doom she carries with her. However, one poem, "Stepping Backward," tentatively strives to "Have out our true identity" by fashioning a clear alternative to inherited familial modes of relationship. Rich posits "the grace of lovers" for whom being fully "human" means to acknowledge "That imperfection has a certain tang."[3] This perspective enables Rich to shift her weather metaphor and to imagine with relish rather than anxiety its various moods: "We must at last renounce that ultimate blue / And take a walk in other kinds of weather." Rejecting "Plato's ghost," Rich finds "imperfection's school" in Shakespeare: the lovers who "know each other, crack and flaw" express their knowledge in terms that come from the exchange near the end of *Love's Labour's Lost:*

> BEROWNE. My love to thee is sound, sans crack or flaw.
> ROSALINE. Sans "sans," I pray you.
>
> (5.2.415–16)

Seizing on the qualities whose continuing denial makes the men in the play unqualified to love, Rich envisions the fulfillment which the play's women are forced to postpone. The poem's final line, elaborating the Shakespearean phrase, pays affectionate tribute to the beloved's "flaws that make you both yourself and human."

This hopeful note, however, is canceled in Rich's next volume, *The Diamond Cutters*, by a poem like "Autumn Equinox," which intimates that the new relationship is a recapitulation of, rather than a departure from, the parental relationship. The brief portrait of the directing father tacitly touches Rich's own experience:

> Father would have me clever, sometimes said
> He'd let me train for medicine, like a son,
> To come into his practice.

But marriage to another "man of intellect" like her father proves no alternative for the female speaker.[4] "Wearing the lace my mother wore before me," she goes to her doom: "While aunts around us nodded like the Fates / That nemesis was accomplished." In retrospect, "after fifty," the woman reviews her disillusionment—"'I thought that life was different than it is'"—a perception from which she has to shield her husband by suppression: "'Go back to sleep—I won't be so again.'" "Defiance" is quickly dissipated in the gesture of changing the parlor curtains. The only authentic defiance is heard in another marriage poem, "The Perennial Answer," in which the woman is freed only by her husband's death: "but at last I was alone / In an existence finally my own."

Rich's attainment of "an existence finally my own" can be achieved only by confronting her family of origin, as "Landscape of the Star" testifies. Rich openly expresses her alienation from the family, the firmness of her rejection of parental expectations underlined by the refusal of the ready-made reconciliation figured by the prodigal son:

> I walk, a foreigner,
> Upon this night that calls all travellers home,
> The prodigal forgiven, and the breach
> Mended for this one feast. Yet all are strange
> To their own ends, and their beginnings now
> Cannot contain them. Once-familiar speech
> Babbles in wayward dialect of a dream.
>
> Our gifts shall bring us home: not to beginnings
> Nor always to the destination named
> Upon our setting-forth. Our gifts compel,
> Master our ways and lead us in the end
> Where we are most ourselves. . . .

Trusting in "the solemn journey" as her "only residence," Rich effectively asserts her separation and difference from the family home. Yet the split between "our gifts" and "us," making the latter an object acted upon by the former, suggests an internal estrangement that hinders the assumption of full responsibility for her active agency as a first-person subject.

In subsequent volumes, Rich continues to survey the home territory which she wishes to leave behind. "Juvenalia" in *Snapshots of a Daughter-in-Law* and "After Dark" in *Necessities of Life* more directly than heretofore concentrate on the daughter's relation to the father. In "Juvenalia" Rich poses the problem from which she is unable to extricate herself. The poet pronounces damning self-criticism of her still immature poetry, her juvenalia, because her falsely "sedulous lines" directed at her first audience—her father ("for you above all to read")—in return for praise prevent her from writing out the fairy tales that "ebb like blood through my head" but remain under a taboo, literally "Unspeakable." Her restiveness signals simmering resentment against the father whose enticing collection of books is made available under conditions of "duress." Yet the muted nature of the anger against her father can be seen by comparison with the forthright rage expressed toward the mother in the opening section of "Snapshots of a Daughter-in-Law." The mother, having falsified her artistic promise as a pianist, just as Rich herself is now in danger of betraying her potential, provides no model: "Your mind now, mouldering like wedding-cake, / heavy with useless experience . . ." Separation from her is presented as clear-cut: "Nervy, glowering, your daughter / . . . grows another way." This other way includes the prospect of "smashing the mould straight off," a prospect hinted by her sardonic citation and bitter rejection of the song from *Much Ado About Nothing* beginning "Sigh no more, ladies." We are enjoined to supply the missing next line: "Men were deceivers ever" (2.3.62–63).

Imitating Eliot's notes on the sources and echoing his use of Baudelaire's line, Rich's "Snapshots of a Daughter-in-Law" is reminiscent of *The Waste Land*. Nevertheless, Rich's poem is not constrained by her dependence on this influence: her spirit, her method, and her conclusion are significantly different. The fulfillment which Rich envisions in her final lines—"delivered / palpable / ours"—contrasts with the more tentative and resigned "These fragments have I shored against my ruins." Rich is marshaling a different tradition— Emily Dickinson, Mary Wollstonecraft, Simone de Beauvoir— that will eventually enable her more completely to break out of the Eliot "mould." Even when Eliot and Rich use a common source, the effect moves in opposite directions. Eliot's appeal to *Antony and Cleopatra* in the opening line of the "Game of Chess" section evokes the past to deflate the present. This "mythical method," as he describes it in his review of Joyce's *Ulysses*, involves "a continuous parallel between contemporaneity and antiquity" in which the former is negatively cast as "the immense panorama of futility and anarchy which is contemporary history."[5] By contrast, the satirical force of Rich's use of *Much Ado About Nothing* implies a critique of the past that holds the potential for positive change in the present.

However, Rich remains enmeshed in the father's project for her partly because his library offers direct access to the art which she desires. The seditious potential in the Ibsen titles remains inert—the way out figured by *A Doll's House* is not taken; nor is the image of waking up in *When We Dead Awaken*, to whose subversive meaning Rich will later appeal in her essay and poem of that title, anything but suppressed in "Juvenalia." In a concluding throwaway gesture, Rich veers away from the father-daughter tension, projecting onto the books themselves all the unasked questions: "Behind the two of us, thirsty spines / quiver in semi-shadow, huge leaves uncurl and thicken." An ominous feeling now invests these dominating objects, after their vibrant celebration in the poem's opening lines: "Your Ibsen volumes, violet-spined, / each flaking its gold arabesque!" But there is no exit because the issues evoked are not engaged and the full-circle closure enacts her entrapment.

One way to approach the constraints that appear to hold Rich back here is to look beyond Ibsen and to propose a Shakespearean subtext. Rich's identification of her father with his library—an image so strong that it appears impossible to have one without the other—has an analogue in Prospero, for whom "my library / Was dukedom large enough" (1.2.109–10) and whose books are transported with him and his daughter into their exile on the island (166–68). For Rich, the father's library is not only the location of his books, but also the scene of his educational project for his daughter: "My father's library I felt as the source and site of his power" (*On Lies, Secrets, and Silence*, p. 200).[6] Held in check by the daughter role, Rich experiences her father's books as the medium of his control; the prescribed innocence of her role that confines her to juvenalia leaves her incapable of an open opposition to the father's literary kingdom. The power of the psychological and artistic stasis here can be measured by the force of the release needed to overcome it. Not until three volumes later in "The Burning of Paper Instead of Children," a poem occasioned and inspired by her own child's act of burning a book, does Rich fully dramatize a release from the oppressive sense of books as physical objects and as embodiments of inherited wisdom. The need for release can be traced to the image of the father's library, with whose recollection the poem begins: "Back there: the library. . . ." Though Rich cites Artaud's injunction to *"burn the texts,"* we can also recall Caliban's emphatic warning: "Burn but his books."

When Rich echoes *The Tempest* (4.1.148) in "After Dark," in *The Necessities of Life,* the emotional focus is on the daughter's ongoing attachment to her dying father: "Alive now, root to crown, I'd give / — oh,—something—not to know / our struggles now are ended." This line presents in microcosm the problem of revision, for though Rich's substitution of "struggles" for "revels" acknowledges the conflict with her father, the overall pull is toward denial of separation; hence the Shakespearean motif of an idealized father-daughter relationship prevails. The same stifled revision is writ large in Rich's appeal to *King Lear* as a vehicle for articulating her

grief. Rich changes the preposition in Lear's line to Cordelia
(4.7.8)—"Now let's away from prison"—as though to reverse
the direction of the deathward move that encompasses the
loyal daughter. But the minor modification is no proof against
the play's overwhelming image of the daughter's submission
to her father's needs, a submission figured by the vividly
rendered fantasy of reunion with the father in symbiotic
death: "and you embalmed beside me."[7] Despite its token
revisionist gestures, the poem reaffirms and perpetuates the
authority of *King Lear's* father-daughter dynamic, in which
the daughter's love constitutes self-sacrifice.[8] Adapting Lear's
language (4.7.10–11), Rich as daughter accepts her prescribed
part: "I'll sit with you there and tease you / for wisdom, if you
like. . . ." The compliant, self-sacrificial impulse of taking as
received wisdom the parental inheritance which she needs
critically to assess is compounded by the absence of forgiveness on the father's part, the forgiveness proffered by Lear to
secure Cordelia's submission.

The hollowness of the reconciliation enacted is suggested
by the juxtaposition of "After Dark" with Rich's later reflection on her father's lack of reciprocation: "I wanted him to
cherish and approve of me, not as he had when I was a child,
but as the woman I was, who had her own mind and had
made her own choices. This, I finally realized, was not to be;
Arnold demanded absolute loyalty, absolute submission to
his will" ("Split at the Root," p. 116). Her father and
Shakespeare, the representative of the literary heritage she
had received through her father, prevent Rich from an earlier
articulation of this perspective and thus betray her into granting this submission in "After Dark"; both inhibit more than
they assist exploration of the identity Rich prematurely claims
for herself in "After Dark."

II

In *Leaflets*—Rich's fifth volume of poetry, which marks the
opening of a second phase in her work—Rich directs an explosive attack against the constraints of the given cultural

tradition: "I was trying to drive a tradition up against the wall"; "I can't live at the hems of that tradition— / will I last to try the beginning of the next?" The attempt to construct a new tradition specifically involves the need to imagine points of view other than those sanctioned by Shakespeare: "Someone has always been desperate, now it's our turn— / we who were free to weep for Othello and laugh at Caliban."[9] But it is in part her own desperate and failed attempt to stay within the bounds of identification with Cordelia that drives this shift in perspective, this refusal to abide by Shakespearean-shaped expectations.

Two mourning poems in *The Will to Change* suggest in a transitional way what it might mean to recast the tradition. "The Stelae," written after her father's death in 1968, politely observes decorum, but its composure exudes a strength and self-confidence missing from "After Dark" five years earlier. The poet gently alters the terms of his bequest by imagining that she could inherit something he did not intend to give: "It's the stelae on the walls I want. . . . / You offer other objects." Because they are not books written in the father's language but stone slabs "incised with signs / you have never deciphered," the stelae are beyond his control and hence hold out the possibility of a new start.

The other poem, referring to her decision to end her marriage, is necessarily more stark in its insistence on a revised tradition.[10] The use of Donne's title, "A Valediction Forbidding Mourning," and the rejection of the content of his poem mark in a simple but effective way the promise of an alternative tradition. Not only does Rich's poem bear witness to an irreversible separation from her husband in contrast to the temporary separation of the lovers confident of reunion in Donne's, but also its challenge is more fundamental because Rich, giving a sharp twist to the idea of "forbidding mourning," deliberately chooses not to mourn. "To do something very common, in my own way" she asserts in the final line, as though determined to act according to the voice in "Snapshots of a Daughter-in-Law" that urged—*"Save yourself; others you cannot save."* This commitment to self signals a rejection not just of the circumstances of Donne's poem, but also of its assumption about male-female relationship.[11] Wilbur Sanders, commenting on the term "home" in Donne's poem, emphasizes its "domestic" quality.[12] Beyond the ending of one particular relationship, Rich's poem records the dissolution of this whole domestic mode.

The retrospective poem "From a Survivor" in *Diving into the Wreck*, where one meaning of the wreck whose damage she has to explore is the destruction of her marriage, confirms Rich's independent stance. The loss is recorded—"you are wastefully dead / who might have made the leap / we talked, too late, of making"—but the death is defined as a waste in which she has no further investment. The emphasis falls instead on her own survival, her future growth. The direction of that growth is implied by the opening two poems which form a contrasting pair. "Trying to Talk with a Man" has behind it the force of a long series of poems concerning Rich's struggle with her father and her husband, and hence serves as a summation of this whole line of development. In "When We Dead Awaken," Rich's newly awakened consciousness turns to the possibility of female bonds as the central relationship:

> Even you, fellow-creature, sister,
> sitting across from me, dark with love,
> working like me to pick apart
> working with me to remake
> this trailing knitted thing, this cloth of darkness,
> this woman's garment, trying to save the skein.

The line "this trailing knitted thing, this cloth of darkness" obliquely echoes Prospero's "own[ing]" of Caliban: "this thing of darkness I / Acknowledge mine" (5.1.275–76).[13] But Rich has disassociated the image from its hierarchal connotations in the Shakespearean context and redirected its meaning toward the acknowledgment of female sexuality, darkness now referred to "dark with love." The transfer of loyalties to women inaugurates Rich's vast project of rewriting the family romance, recovering the mother, and establishing a lesbian identity.[14] As the image of dismantling ("pick apart") and reconstructing ("remake") suggests, the notion of rewriting the literary tradition is at the heart of Rich's effort. As Rich puts it in a subsequent prose counterpart to this lyrical evocation: "For the lesbian poet it means rejecting the entire convention of love-poetry and undertaking to create a new tradition. She is forced by the conditions under which she loves, and the conditions in which all women attempt to survive, to ask questions that did not occur to a Donne or a Yeats" (*On Lies, Secrets, and Silence*, p. 252).

The importance of Rich's version of "A Valediction Forbidding Mourning" is that it begins to demonstrate what it could mean, as Rich puts it in "When We Dead Awaken: Writing as Re-Vision," "to do without authorities" (p. 45). In the prose work to which Rich now devotes a major portion of her energy, Rich's father and Shakespeare appear as intertwined familial and literary authorities whom she can do without. Rich's personal survival of the demise of her marriage gives her a strength—an inner authority—from which she can generalize: "Re-vision—the act of looking back, of seeing with fresh eyes, of entering an old text from a new critical direction—is for women more than a chapter in cultural history: it is an act of survival" (p. 35). Rich indicates her survival of the intense bond with her father as her first teacher and audience: "The obverse side of this, of course, was that I tried for a long time to please him, or rather, not to displease him" (pp. 38–39). In the same essay she also puts Shakespeare behind her, noting his limitations as a resource: "We know more than Jane Austen or Shakespeare knew: more than Jane Austen because our lives are more complex, more than Shakespeare because we know more about the lives of women" (p. 49).

Similarly, in *Of Woman Born*, Rich specifies both her father and Shakespeare as obstacles she has had to overcome to achieve the different perspective from which to break the hold of the old tradition and to start a new. Rich's title draws on the language of *Macbeth* (4.1.80, 5.8.13), but she does not share the play's fascination with the possibility of a man who is not of woman born, nor is she sympathetic to the exception the play makes for Macduff. The suggestion that her stance has Shakespeare's warrant does not suffice, for Rich's study of motherhood and gender relations has a depth that makes it substantively different from any critical perspective we may attribute to Shakespeare. Rich makes clear that her quest is not continuous with Shakespeare's: "The loss of the daughter to the mother, the mother to the daughter, is the essential female tragedy. We acknowledge Lear (father-daughter split), Hamlet (son and mother) . . . as great embodiments of the human tragedy; but there is no presently enduring recognition of mother-daughter passion and rapture" (p. 237). When Rich goes on immediately to celebrate the Demeter-Persephone relationship embodied in the Eleusinian mysteries, Shakespeareans may want to claim that Rich has unwittingly neglected her debt and adherence to the old tradition. But the Hermione-Perdita reunion at the close of *The Winter's Tale* does not speak to the reconfiguration that Rich addresses here.[15] It is not simply that Rich reinstates the mother-daughter connection to serve as the basis for lesbian sexuality—a development not present in Shakespeare. It is also that *The Winter's Tale* restores to Leontes his central position as paternal authority, while, for Rich, an essential element in the definition of the "self-chosen woman" is that she is "the woman who refuses to obey, who has said 'no' to the fathers" (*On Lies, Secrets, and Silence*, p. 202). *The Winter's Tale* does not say "no" to the fathers but concentrates on reforming patriarchy and assimilating women with a boundless capacity to forgive into the revised image of benign patriarchy.

By contrast, Rich presents father-centered and mother-centered worlds as counterpointed sets of values, as two different psychological and political systems between which one must choose. The drive to seek the mother requires the withdrawal of allegiance to the father, a change announced in "Reforming the Crystal" from *Poems Selected and New, 1950–1974:*

> If I remind you of my father's favorite daughter,
> look again. The woman
> I needed to call my mother
> was silenced before I was born.

When the reformulation of the family is completed in "Sibling Mysteries" in *The Dream of a Common Language* and Rich, through the bond with her sister, reimagines the connection to her mother, the father is displaced: "then one whole night / our father upstairs dying / we burned our childhood, reams of paper. . . ." Gone is the Cordelia- and Miranda-like solicitousness and suffusion in "After Dark."

The feminist vision which Rich articulates in *Of Woman Born* and which receives poetic fulfillment in *The Dream of a Common Language* is further consolidated in the next volume, *A Wild Patience Has Taken Me This Far*. The father occasionally appears, but only on the periphery. The emotional charge is still there, readily surfacing when new occasions "turn up the jet of my anger," but the father-daughter episode appears to function largely as a baseline, as testimony to a process that she has completed and resolved:

> my Jewish father writing me
> letters of seventeen pages
> finely inscribed harangues
> > ("For Ethel Rosenberg")

> Yet smoldering to the end with frustrate life
> ideas nobody listened to, least of all my father
> > ("Grandmothers," 1)

> All through World War Two the forbidden word
> *Jewish* was barely uttered in your son's house
> > ("Grandmothers," 2)

> and absolute loyalty was never in my line
> once having left it in my father's house
> > ("Rift")

III

The sudden reemergence of the father as a central figure in Rich's recent work—"Split at the Root" (1982) and *Sources* (1983)—represents a striking and unforeseen development. Rich's statement in "Resisting Amnesia: History and Personal Life (1983)," however, offers a compelling reason for the continued interest in her father:

The desire to be twice-born is, I believe, in part a longing to escape the burdens, complications, and contradictions of continuity. . . . Too much of ourselves must be deleted when we erase our personal histories and abruptly dissociate ourselves from who we have been. We become less dimensional than we really are.

. . . We may know no other way to separate from parents, sisters, brothers, lovers, husbands except awkwardly and violently, so great are the pain and anger. But to deny that the connection ever existed, to pretend that we have moved on a direct, single-minded track—that is to subtract from ourselves the fullness of what we are.

(*Blood, Bread, and Poetry*, pp. 143–44)

One can locate the poetic work behind this prose summation in the juxtaposition of "Toward the Solstice" in *The Dream of a Common Language* with "Integrity" in the next volume, *A Wild Patience Has Taken Me This Far*. The first poem formulates both the desire to be free of the family preoccupations that haunt her ("I can feel utterly ghosted in this house") and the inability to find a definitive, concluding gesture that would give the desired "release." The poet seeks "to ease the hold of the past / upon the rest of my life / and ease my hold on the past" by means of a "separation"

> between myself and the long-gone
> tenants of this house,
> between myself and my childhood,
> and the childhood of my children. . . .

But the pressure for closure ends in an impasse: "and my hand still suspended / as if above a letter / I long and dread to close." The mood of suspension and irresolution stems from the frustration of this longing:

> A decade of cutting away
> dead flesh, cauterizing
> old scars ripped open over and over
> and still it is not enough

"Integrity" reverses the action of "cutting away" and "cauterizing" in favor of an inclusiveness that affirmatively recasts the image of fragmentary selves—"I am trying to hold in one steady glance / all the parts of my life"—in "Toward the Solstice." "Release" is now redefined as release into wholeness: *"Nothing but myself? . . . My selves. /* After so long, this answer."

> Anger and tenderness: my selves.
> And now I can believe they breathe in me
> as angels, not polarities.
> Anger and tenderness: the spider's genius
> To spin and weave in the same action
> from her own body, anywhere—
> even from a broken web.

This resolution makes possible the emotional timbre of Rich's new approach to her father in *Sources*, where she readmits the hold of the past and acknowledges the family home as a permanent feature of her psychic landscape.

The immediate cause for the turn to her father as a source is Rich's new focus on her divided religious heritage ("neither Gentile nor Jew" she had put it twenty years earlier) and, in particular, her concern to come to terms with the Jewish identity that she has only by thinking back through her father, despite his attempts to erase his Jewish origins. Here, too, the intertwined influences of her father and Shakespeare have to be disentangled. In "Split at the Root," Rich comments on her childhood role as Portia, a part in which she was coached by her father: "he tells me to convey, with my voice, more scorn and contempt with the word 'Jew.'" Portia's resounding defeat of the patriarchal figure Shylock validates female power, but also legitimizes anti-Semitism as its vehicle. "Like every other Shakespearean heroine," Rich concludes, "she proved a treacherous model" (pp. 104–5).

Rich's recovery of her Jewish identity leads in *Sources* to a more modulated and sympathetic view of her father: "I saw the power and arrogance of the male as your true watermark; I did not see beneath it the suffering of the Jew." Yet the poignant attention to her father is not a reversion to the suffusion in sympathy dictated by the Cordelia-like pose in "After Dark."[16] Rich goes on, "It is only now, under a powerful, womanly lens, that I can decipher your suffering and deny no part of my own"; there is no retraction of her criticism of her father and no denial or softening of the requirements of her identity. When Rich ends the poem by repeating the words "powerful" and "womanly," these terms draw strength from their earlier use in the specific context of the relationship with her father. The long history of her struggle in that relationship is thus affirmed in full rather than moderated: only by maintaining this struggle could Rich preserve her "powerful, womanly lens."

This account of three stages in Rich's poetic development establishes a context from which I can now go on to consider the larger implications of *Sources* for the direction of Rich's work as a whole and for the spirit of her revision of Shakespeare. It is possible to view *Sources* as the long-delayed realization of the "generosity" Helen Vendler called for after *Diving into the Wreck* in 1973,[17] thereby aligning *Sources* with the Shakespearean precedent of the final turn to the late romances. Though I am moved by the new tenderness in Rich's regard for her father and husband, I think it is inaccurate to read *Sources* simply as a poem of reconciliation.[18]

What would be lost in a line of interpretation based on Vendler's equation of "generosity" with "self-forgetfulness" is Rich's ongoing commitment to "the eye of the outsider" (*Blood, Bread, and Poetry*, p. 3). Rich's critique of the father-daughter relationship continues to serve as the personal reference point for her general analysis of the dangers of a tokenism that "acts to blur her outsider's eye, which could be her real source of power and vision. Losing her outsider's vision, she loses the insight which both binds her to other women and affirms her in herself" (p. 6). In my reading of *Sources*, the outsider's eye remains strongly present, the political perspective strongly in force.

Ultimately, interpretation involves the status of politics in Rich's work.[19] Rich defeats the easy formula that equates the political with the reductive because her political explorations are enormously complicated.[20] Her views are not static but changing, and they are becoming more complex rather than less. For Rich, re-vision applies not only to the received literary tradition, but also to her own politics: "What writing and politics have most in common, perhaps, is that both are creative processes requiring many false starts and strange go-rounds, many hard choices" (*Blood, Bread, and Poetry*, p. xi). A footnote in the new edition of *Of Woman Born* marks one such revision: "There has been a feminist temptation to replace a 'primary contradiction' of class with a 'primary contradiction' of sex. A majority of the women in the world, however, experience their lives as the intersection of class, sex and race" (p. 112). This enlarged international perspective, fostered by the sharpened awareness of her national "location" that results from Rich's visit to Nicaragua, receives increasing attention. The essays from 1983 on in *Blood, Bread, and Poetry* probe Rich's concern that Virginia Woolf's statement—"as a woman I have no country. . . . As a woman my country is the whole world" (pp. 162, 183, 211)—can be used as a shortcut to a "false transcendence" (p. 183). Rich's reconsideration of Marxist analysis leads to a view of global economy that is consistent with Gayatri Spivak's insistence on the international division of labor as antidote to a universalizing tendency in Western feminism.[21]

The specific focus of this chapter on the father-daughter relationship can now be placed in its larger context as one element in the process of exploring the whole range of multiple selves, along with the multi-cultural social conflicts they reveal:

> The woman who seeks the experiential grounding of identity politics realizes that as Jew, white, woman, lesbian, middle-class, she herself has a complex identity. Further, that her very citizenship, which gives her both grief and privilege, is part of her identity: her U.S. passport, in this world, is part of her body, and she lives under a very specific patriarchy.
>
> (*Blood, Bread, and Poetry*, p. xii)

The reassessment of differences among women makes Rich newly attuned to her own array of differences, including the Jewish identity that revives the connection with her father and enables the new view of him. The changed father-daughter dynamic in *Sources* cannot be separated from this overall project, nor can it be portrayed as a purely psychological development within a self-enclosed individual relationship.

The relevance of the larger vision for *Sources* is enacted in "Split at the Root," the essay that specifically focuses on her father, when the three concluding paragraphs movingly evoke the motif of multiple selves in its entirety. This action is political and not merely personal because it involves "enlarging the range of accountability": "There is no purity and, in our lifetimes, no end to this process" (p. 123).

IV

In conclusion, I return to the question of Rich's relation to Shakespeare, of Shakespeare's relation to Rich, as these relations are negotiated in the transition from "After Dark" to *Sources*. Women's forgiveness is so central to the articulation of what one can find moving in *King Lear* and *The Winter's Tale* that it can become fixed in our minds as an inviolable element of father-daughter relations.[22] The prospect of the father's redemption in *Sources* is bound to arouse all our Shakespearean expectations with an intensity that will not tolerate disappointment. Yet the weight of the tradition cannot override the difference that detailed analysis reveals. The assimilation of Rich to Shakespeare is blocked. *Sources* does not recapitulate the Lear-Cordelia paradigm. Rather Rich breaks its hold, and her departure justifies in a positive way the anxious bravado of her earlier protest that "The old masters, the old sources, / haven't a clue what we're about" ("In the Evening," *Leaflets*).

The study of Rich is relevant for Shakespeareans because our knowledge of the new tradition embodied in her poetry provides a new frame of reference that changes our relation to Shakespeare. Rich's opening up of new possibilities—new feelings and values—makes us realize in a concrete, experiential way that Shakespeare does not encompass everything, is not universal. Her exploration of the father-daughter motif exemplifies how our perceptions of Shakespeare are altered.

Coming from Rich, we see *King Lear* with fresh eyes, with a new awareness of what Shakespeare can and cannot do. *King Lear* is dramatized primarily from Lear's point of view; consequently, as Janet Adelman remarks, the play loses touch with Cordelia's inwardness.[23] Whether or not Shakespeare is seen as critical of Lear, Shakespeare cannot give us Cordelia's point of view.

Cordelia's story cannot adequately be told in Shakespearean terms. Rich rewrites Cordelia's "silence" by taking the daughter's point of view, thus making Shakespeare's limits understood and actively felt as limitations. This perspective prevents our slipping into total identification with Lear; compassion for Lear is qualified, partially withdrawn. Our new awareness of alternative modes for conceiving the father-daughter relationship may be temporarily bracketed for the sake of historical investigation, but this awareness can never be eradicated, left completely out of account.[24] Shakespeare can no longer be treated as an absolute, unframed standard as though his art were fully adequate to the range of thought and feeling possible for us in the present.

It is easy to caricature Rich's remark that we know more than Shakespeare by treating it as a shortsighted claim to be more liberated than Shakespeare. The only reasonable alternative then seems to resume a posture of humility and to reaffirm Shakespeare's supreme artistic greatness. Such reverence, however, can become an avoidance mechanism by which issues of historical difference are circumvented. Feminist critics can acknowledge the lasting power of Shakespeare's verbal and dramatic brilliance without acceding to the pretense that his values are permanent or above criticism. Shakespeare's artistic greatness is not in question, only his use as the ultimate, inviolable arbiter of experience. His work provides not a body of timeless, inexhaustible, or unmodifiable knowledge, but rather a historical baseline that helps us to measure our difference.

My understanding of feminist practice includes reorganizing our sense of the literary canon so as to validate elements of contemporary literature, to temper some of the claims made for Shakespeare, and to create space to move back and forth between these two discontinuous worlds. The negotiations that a critic conducts between past and present should involve full recognition of each and not require diminished awareness of the present or arbitrary constraints on our contemporary imagination. Attentiveness to the present is not a solution, a salvation, or an escape: the present contains its own intractable difficulties. It is an evasion to act as though Shakespeare's work provided a cultural field so capacious that it adequately addresses the lives that we are living now, to see our lives for the purposes of historical investigation as mere distortions rather than the positive resources they are. Full-strength feminist criticism of Shakespeare can be made to appear negative when it is cut off from its larger context, its contribution to the feminist revaluation of the tradition as a whole. The constructive spirit of the project of re-vision can emerge fully only if we reject narrow period specialization as the exclusive definition of what comprises the professionally legitimate, and acknowledge responsibility to the entire range of cultural heritage, including the present.

Not all revisions are the same in degree and scope. We should not expect women writers from diverse historical contexts to be fundamentally the same; there is no one single model of revision applicable to all situations. Rich's revision of Shakespeare, for example, differs markedly from Virginia Woolf's. In "When We Dead Awaken: Writing as Re-Vision," Rich's critical perspective extends not only to Shakespeare but also to Woolf, and in particular to Woolf's problematic accommodation with literary tradition: "I think we need to go through that anger, and we will betray our own reality, if we try, as Virginia Woolf was trying, for an objectivity, a detachment, that would make us sound more like . . . Shakespeare" (pp. 48–49).[25] Rich's poem "A Primary Ground" in *Diving into the Wreck* adds the anger absent from *To the Lighthouse*, while her subsequent rejection of androgyny breaks with the principal means by which Woolf connects with Shakespeare.[26] I bring out these differences because I think they are major and because an overemphasis on continuity blurs distinctions that should be sharply etched if we are to experience the full force of Rich's particular version of revision.

In my view, Rich's work has a special role within the general effort to reformulate the literary tradition because of her historical positioning. The sharpness and depth of her move outside Shakespearean precedent seem to me to be distinctively new and to be possible only because of particular political and cultural developments, including contemporary feminism, in her—and our—historical moment. The afterword will explore the present historical moment through a consideration of the difficult shifts in pronoun forms (from "me" to "her" to "our") in the previous sentence.

Afterword: Identity Politics, Multicultural Society

The coordination of the two parts of this book can now be summarized: the conclusion of Part 2 is that in key instances contemporary twentieth-century literature engages in a re-vision that moves outside a Shakespearean framework; Part 1 shows that a related re-vision is presently occurring within Shakespeare studies proper. The two activities are thus parts of the same overall project of revaluation. A crucial issue, however, is the precise extent of the change associated with the idea of re-vision.

Re-vision can be represented in two distinct ways—a conciliatory mode that urges moderation and balance or an oppositional mode that insists on a more uncompromising critical perspective. The first mode tends to mitigate conflict and to maintain the continuity of Shakespeare's cultural role. Challenges are acknowledged and valued, but temporized: new departures are seen as modifications that confirm rather than disrupt the primary image of Shakespeare's positive influence. The second, the oppositional, mode does not deny but qualifies Shakespeare's greatness. Yet the qualification is so substantial as to reconstitute the tradition and to alter Shakespeare's status as the dominant artistic force. The result is that Shakespeare can no longer be conceived as defining and controlling the overall shape and direction of the literary canon. This study supports the second approach. What is controversial about this position is the function of the categories of race and gender in its argument. I shall explore the controversy by returning to the questions concerning the ideological status of author and of critic that I raised in the Introduction.

A repeated objection to rigorous feminist reassessment of Shakespeare is that Shakespeare is being dismissed on the grounds that he happens to be a white male author. The objection is a misrepresentation. First, Shakespeare is not being rejected wholesale. Second, the author's race and gender are not being treated merely as external characteristics. These categories do not have fixed meanings that can be mechanically read off from the author's identity as though works came pre-coded, already read. Rather, the immediate focus is on works, not authors. The meanings of the works cannot be known in advance; assumptions, perceptions, and values with regard to race and gender are established in the specific context of detailed interpretation of particular works. Misrepresenting the complex inductive approach of feminist criticism as a simplistic deductive one frames the argument as a choice between a caricature and a traditionalist transcendent view in which the authorial qualifiers of race and gender are irrelevant or of marginal interest.

One reason for the pressure on the white-male couplet is the powerful emergence of black women authors whose existence calls attention to the equivalent terms of white and male, thus making highly visible what could previously be left unsaid. Efforts to cancel the new self-consciousness about race and gender identity by arguing that, when artistically successful, black women writers can be universal too are unconvincing. What needs explanation is the overreaction to critical consciousness of the race and gender of authors, as though merely to specify them is enough to cause the entire pantheon of white male writers to collapse. The exaggerated sense of threat has a subtext: if white male authors are vulnerable, then white male critics are exposed as well. Explicit attention to a critic's identity can be more directly threatening than consideration of an author's. White male critics, who have been able to take their identity credentials for granted, suddenly find themselves in the uncomfortable position of being subject to disqualification, of having a wrong or devalued identity that signifies potential exclusion.

To this point I have for the most part appealed to our own historical moment in the first-person plural, as though contemporary critics could be treated as an undifferentiated collective body. However, "ourselves" in the title of this book refers not simply to a generalized, homogeneous "we," but rather to our diverse plural identities. I want now to amplify the critical notations—"the critic exists in history" and " 'localization' is an idea we need to apply to ourselves"—invoked as guiding mottoes on the opening page of this study. Both formulations are limited because too abstract; they require much greater specificity. In particular, I want to address my own specific situation as a white male critic.[1] In the present context, this cultural location has two aspects: my relation as a specifically white male critic to Shakespeare on the one hand, and, on the other, to contemporary twentieth-century writers, exemplified by the black women writers previously discussed. I speak for my particular self here; I recognize that the paths traversed by, for example, white male critics and black female critics in moving from Shakespeare to contemporary black women writers (or the reverse) are not necessarily congruent and may involve a different set of negotiations with different social consequences.

The Shakespearean part of my project involves undoing the automatic, apparently given, equation between Shakespeare as white male author and myself as white male critic. The subject position of white male is not monolithic or fixed, though it is not totally fluid either. My aim is to expand the possibilities for differentiation within the white male subject position, with a view to redefining my male identity. A new masculinity cannot simply be announced, however; it must be worked through. Outright rejection of Shakespeare would short-circuit this process and make revaluation impossible. Deep cultural change requires that men as well as women go through the lengthy, intimate process of articulating the differences that separate them from Shakespeare. Serious criticism of Shakespeare's limitations is apt to be stigmatized as an exercise in blaming. But in my view the value of critically establishing authorial flaws is that the critic can thereby locate his or her own cultural responsibilities. While I see Shakespeare as an indispensable part of this effort, I do not think it can be conducted exclusively in relation to Shakespeare. I

plan neither to abandon nor to be confined to the Shakespearean field.

In my own case, the tangible awareness of a wider field
came, at the start of my first teaching position in 1976, from
my desire to change the departmental introductory literature
course to include black and women writers. Through this
practical experience of curricular reform, I wrote an article on
Alice Walker in the summer of 1977.[2] The personal and professional significance of the article is not only that it was my
first publication but also that the encounter with Walker was
crucial in helping me to find my voice. Having a base and an
allegiance outside Shakespeare studies gave me the emotional
strength to write critically about Shakespeare from a male
feminist perspective. Though I have since published primarily
as a Shakespearean, I have maintained the pattern of working
both in Renaissance and in contemporary twentieth-century
literature. The purpose of this book is to bring the two activities together.

What, then, is my relation as a white male critic to the
black women writers whom I have studied? Here I am working toward an alternative to the two versions I reject as unsatisfactory: absolute disqualification as a critic because of my
white male identity or total freedom to move across the cultural board without impediments. The first option too readily
serves as an avoidance mechanism by which white critics
excuse themselves from acquaintance with black literature
because they are unqualified by virtue of identity. This response lends itself to separate academic spheres, in which
black literature is ceded to black critics while white critics
retain a monopoly on the interpretation of the mainstream
classic white writers, who really count most in the overall
scheme. Such curricular divisions exemplify the general condition diagnosed by Gerald Graff.[3]

My approach depends on bringing together the concepts
of common culture and identity politics and on realizing
the tensions between them. A major energizing force behind
the move to build a greatly expanded and revised canon is the
excitement and insight gained from participation in the full

range of social experience represented by the entire literary spectrum. I use the phrase *common culture* to evoke this sense of participation as access and responsibility to all of our culture's literary production. In this sense, *common* does not do away with difference but rather calls attention to it. For we are differently positioned with respect to our common culture, and these different locations are defined in part by the politics of our identities. However, I must stress that I present this approach as a way of entering the problem rather than as a cure-all; it does not magically resolve the concerns about appropriation but rather puts them into play.

I

Perhaps the most difficult conceptual issue that attends the prospect of opening up the canon is what becomes of the idea of a common culture. I should say at once that I do not intend to give up this idea; rather, my inquiry considers three versions of common culture, each of which gives a different construction to the term *common*. The first, the strict traditionalist version, produces a unified culture by restricting it to a narrow base. This shortcut to common culture is invalid because it does not face the field as a whole. It denies diversity by excluding it; emergent literature need not be taken seriously because it is defined as outside the realm of objects accorded full academic treatment. This back-to-the-classics mentality makes a virtue out of ignorance by pretending that the literary ferment following the social upheaval in the 1960s either did not happen or has no lasting significance.

Diane Ravitch's modified traditionalist position is far more inclusive and complicated. Ravitch acknowledges the validity and necessity of the term *multicultural* in dealing with American culture.[4] Yet Ravitch goes on to distinguish between good ("pluralistic") and bad ("particularistic") forms of multiculturalism, the basis of the distinction being the presence or absence of the concept of universalism: "The conflict between pluralism and particularism turns on the issue of universalism" (p. 342). In my view, Ravitch too quickly sets up particularism as a scapegoat. More important, I question Ravitch's belief that the idea of common culture must be based on universalism. Ravitch's appeal to this concept works as a hedge against multiculturalism; universalism preserves a notion of transcendence that curtails and vitiates the full force of cultural difference. We must proceed with a sharper sense of the cultural differentiation within the present historical moment that prevents the present from being constituted as a single unit. My goal is to formulate a model of culture that is both strongly multicultural and common, yet does not resort to universalism to mediate between the two.

The problem is how to maintain some form of the idea of common culture—culture held in common—without eviscerating, compromising, or downplaying the idea of difference. My alternative to Ravitch's concept of universalism is the concept of identity politics, which refers to the categories of race, gender, and class by which we name difference. Thus, when the ideal of common culture is counterbalanced by giving equal weight to the principle of identity politics, the verb *counterbalanced* means that the two terms are not so much reconciled as held in productive tension. If, by virtue of the ideal of common culture, I have access to the entire range of literature, this access is not unrestricted, as though all barriers dissolve in the magical realm of literature. Rather, the access that literature gives heightens the reader's own cultural difference. When, for example, I read a work by a black woman author, I do not enter into a transcendent human interaction, but instead become more aware of my whiteness and maleness, social categories that shape my being. The deep heart's core of literary experience involves the engagement with one's cultural specificity, including its political ramifications. While the notion of universality sidesteps the task of acknowledging and assessing cultural difference, identity politics enables us to begin this task.

Applying the principle of universalism to readers as well as to authors, the traditionalist approach produces a self-validating, circular relation between common reader and common culture; as the echo effect suggests, the word "common" never comes into question because it is automatically guaranteed. The problem with traditionalist logic is that it confuses two separate issues: the principle of equal access to the realm of culture regardless of race or gender is transposed into the notion that we therefore become raceless, genderless readers. But racial and gender identity does not simply vanish in the act of reading. The point here is not to create absolute, impermeable barriers, but to insist that readers' positioning by identity needs to be taken into account if we are to attain a convincing image of a common American culture. I am suggesting not that white readers are unable to read black literature, but that this is a cross-cultural process that should be thought through in all its complexities instead of being taken for granted. Nor, in acknowledging my identity as a white male critic, am I declaring that the two coordinates of white and male are in some essentialist way fixed and predetermined, as though there were one and only one white male reading of every text. Rather, this acknowledgment opens up these terms for exploration as historical contingencies that affect our reading in ways that not only vary but also can actively be changed. Insofar as the terms of identity form obstacles, we need to take their intellectual measure, not deny and avoid them.

In his vociferous attack on feminist criticism, Peter Shaw's response to the loss of privileged identity is a bitterly satirical reductio ad absurdum; if he is disqualified, then everyone is disqualified, even those whose identities seem most impeccable:

> Gayatri Chakravorty Spivak's uneasiness suggests that, to be safe from recrimination, a feminist critic at the present moment would need to have not only Third World credentials like her own (or credentials as a black or "Chicana" woman), but also be a lesbian, and preferably a Marxist or at least a *soi-disant* radical at the same time. Ordinary feminist literary critics can too easily be assailed as heterosexist, homophobic, racist, or guilty of "cultural imperialism". . . .
> The sexually and politically ideal writer, it can be concluded, like the ideal critic, can never be found.[5]

Behind Shaw's attempt to prove that the categories of race and gender introduce standards so stringent as to be unworkable, one can hear anxiety about his own safety: "to be safe from recrimination." The implicit rationale of the argument is a quest for immunity. To my mind Shaw misses the point. Neither safety nor purity is the goal: both are figments.

I find Shaw's defensive posture unproductive. The effort to develop a more constructive alternative, however, must engage rather than deny the anxieties manifested in Shaw's rhetoric. The desire for protection is prompted by a confused double fear that needs to be disentangled. One fear stems from anticipation of the emotional and intellectual pain that would accompany a full exploration of a multicultural model of tradition. This fear is realistic; the painfulness involved in a sustained encounter with the historical exclusions that have indelibly shaped our social institutions is genuine and un-avoidable. Less warranted is a second fear founded on the expectation that a stringent multicultural investigation will inevitably exclude critics—especially white males—whose identity profiles reflect the dominant power structures. We are all qualified to research the categories of race and gender and their varied, complicated literary manifestations: the ra-cial and gender composition of our individual identities is one of the resources by which each of us can conduct this re-search. We cannot avoid the vulnerability to which this pro-cess of self-examination commits us. But our vulnerability provides one basis for a critical reassessment of our culture whose long-term consequences can be positive.

My use of the term *identity politics* is derived from Adrienne Rich.[6] This concept is not a self-evident good, but an in-tensely debated area. Work by Hazel V. Carby, Jenny Bourne, and June Jordan offers salient critiques of identity politics as a critical method, to which I am also indebted.[7] Yet, though the criticisms are valid, I would argue that Rich has increas-ingly taken them into account and accordingly modified her procedures. The concept of identity politics is therefore still usable, provided that one remains aware of the difficulties. My own pursuit of identity politics draws on Stuart Hall's approach to ethnicity:

I am also well aware that the politics of anti-racism has often constructed itself in terms of a contestation of "multi-ethnicity" or "multi-culturalism". . . .

. . . The fact that this grounding of ethnicity in difference was deployed, in the discourse of racism, as a means of disavowing the realities of racism and repression does not mean that we can permit the term to be permanently colonized. That appropriation will have to be contested, the term disarticulated from its position in the discourse of "multi-culturalism" and transcoded, just as we previously had to recuperate the term "black", from its place in a system of negative equivalences.[8]

Much hinges on how wide the range of the term *politics* in identity politics is construed. In particular, two dangers must be guarded against. First, identity politics is not a matter of reader-response criticism understood as individual psychological explorations with no reference to the social constituents of identity. The identity in view is rather the self as shaped by larger historical and political forces. Second, identity politics does not endorse an exclusively literary and curricular politics through which canon revision becomes an end in itself. Canon revision does not in and of itself promote multicultural diversity; the outcome depends on the principles by which the new canon is organized and interpreted. If disconnected from the wider social context and treated as an insular operation, canon revision is liable to substitute solving problems in the curriculum for solving problems in society and thereby to promote false harmony. Revision of the literary canon is a legitimate space for the exploration and negotiation of cultural difference, but only if its potential is not overestimated and the link to larger social change strongly maintained.[9]

II

The contemporary renaissance of minority literatures allows us to resituate Shakespeare's Renaissance in a wider field. The relation between the two renaissances is then figured as a triangulation, the two points providing a powerful resource for articulating crucial issues in our own cultural period. Viewed from one renaissance, Shakespeare's position may seem guaranteed; viewed from the other renaissance, his canonical status is no longer taken for granted but subjected to intensive critical scrutiny.

Some may find this revaluation an unpalatable prospect to be resisted at all costs as mere "Shakespeare bashing," whose end result will be "to put literature out of business."[10] However, Shakespeare criticism is not going out of business. It has been reestablished on a new basis, and this basis is constructive. Shakespeare becomes a resource in a different sense as a richly complex reference point within the larger project of cultural change we are undergoing with respect to race, gender, and class. The current critique of Shakespeare involves a partial transfer of cultural energy in which Shakespeare's language still matters but is not the last word. If Shakespeare is no longer construed as having the final say against the power of emergent voices, then the new critical perspective on Shakespeare is a welcome, positive development.

Notes

INTRODUCTION

1. Louis A. Montrose, "Professing the Renaissance: The Poetics and Politics of Culture," in *The New Historicism*, ed. H. Aram Veeser (New York: Routledge, 1989), p. 24. The phrase "the critic exists in history" also occurs in Montrose's previous essay, "The Elizabethan Subject and the Spenserian Text," in *Literary Theory/Renaissance Texts*, ed. Patricia Parker and David Quint (Baltimore: Johns Hopkins University Press, 1986), p. 305. The later essay builds on and revises material from the opening and closing sections of the earlier essay. I wish to make clear that my own polemical intervention—"Rewriting the Renaissance, Rewriting Ourselves," *Shakespeare Quarterly* 38 (1987): 327–37—was addressed to Montrose's earlier version, as was the commentary on Montrose in my review in *Medieval and Renaissance Drama in England* 4 (1989): 282–89.

2. Leah S. Marcus, *Puzzling Shakespeare: Local Reading and Its Discontents* (Berkeley and Los Angeles: University of California Press, 1988), p. 36. In a review of Marcus's superb book, in *Modern Philology* 88 (1990): 70–73, I explain my reservations about her execution of this dimension of her study.

3. Adrienne Rich, "Ten Years Later: A New Introduction," in *Of Woman Born: Motherhood as Experience and Institution* (New York: Norton, 1986), p. xxiii; *Blood, Bread, and Poetry: Selected Prose, 1979–1985* (New York: Norton, 1986), pp. xii, 218.

4. Adrienne Rich, "When We Dead Awaken: Writing as Re-Vision (1971)," in *On Lies, Secrets, and Silence: Selected Prose, 1966–1978* (New York: Norton, 1979), pp. 33–49.

5. In "Scholarship, Theory, and More New Readings: Shakespeare for the 1990s," in *Shakespeare Study Today: The Horace Howard Furness Memorial Lectures*, ed. Georgianna Ziegler (New York: AMS Press, 1986), pp. 127–51, Jean E. Howard explains why—contrary to Richard Levin's call for an end to new readings—she favors more: "A reading of a Shakespeare play is an occasion for a complex contemporary interaction with a classic text; it is inevitably an occasion for creation by which the critic acknowledges his [or her] own place in history" (p. 138). In a subsequent, related essay, "The New His-

toricism in Renaissance Studies," *English Literary Renaissance* 16 (1986): 13–43, Howard makes clear that our historically inflected readings are not the result of deliberate distortion or avoidable skewing: "The goal of such a dialogue [between past and present] is not, certainly, the willful reproduction of the present in the mirror of the past, but involves steady acknowledgement that the past is not transparent and that the pursuit of history is neither objective nor disinterested" (p. 23; also see p. 43).

6. An indication of the wider public resonance of academic disputes is the reception accorded the revision of the western civilization course at Stanford University, a revision that attracted the attention both of the Reagan appointee William Bennett and of the presidential candidate Jesse Jackson. Bennett's speech at Stanford is reported in *The New York Times* (April 19, 1988), p. A18, with editorial commentary on April 20 and May 2; Jackson's response to Stanford student demonstrators is described in Steven C. Phillips's "When Words Collide: Reading, Writing, and Revolution," *Voice Literary Supplement* 71 (January/February 1989): 31.

7. Since I too am a white male critic, the posture and positioning of the white male image in the *New York Times* article symbolize a problem for my study. One measure of success will be the degree to which I can avoid the danger of reproducing this image in my own work. While I realize that changes in subject position depend on factors more complicated than statements of good will or adjustments of style, I do want to register my disaffiliation from the particular version of the white male critic presented by the *Times* article.

8. The term *(de)canonized* in Robert Weimann's incisive essay "Shakespeare (De)Canonized: Conflicting Uses of 'Authority' and 'Representation'" (*New Literary History* 20 [1988]: 65–81) suggests that decanonizing is ambiguously and inextricably linked with canonizing. Weimann refuses "to subscribe to either the traditional naturalizing mode of canonization or, for that matter, a deconstructionist position which, beyond all considerations of the cultural uses and values of Shakespeare, presumes to rewrite literary history outside the dialectic of continuity and discontinuity" (p. 67). Weimann instead pursues a third alternative:

> Talking about Shakespeare we are faced with the widely acknowledged centrality of his text, which makes it impossible to think of his writings as altogether subsumed under conditions of either canonization or decanonization. . . . The difficulty, then, is not so much to perceive how and to what extent Shakespeare has been used to help establish certain criteria of canonization, but to be aware of the historicity of such criteria in relation to the needs and possibilities of our time and our own selves.
>
> (pp. 73–74)

9. The full citations are as follows: *Representing Shakespeare: New Psychoanalytic Essays*, ed. Murray M. Schwartz and Coppélia Kahn (Baltimore: Johns Hopkins University Press, 1980); *The Woman's Part: Feminist Criticism of Shakespeare*, ed. Carolyn Ruth Swift Lenz, Gayle Greene, and Carol Thomas Neely (Urbana: University of Illinois Press, 1980); Stephen Greenblatt, *Renaissance Self-Fashioning: From More to Shakespeare* (Chicago: University of Chicago Press, 1980); *Political Shakespeare: New Essays in Cultural Materialism*, ed. Jonathan Dollimore and Alan Sinfield (Manchester: Manchester University Press, 1985).

10. Steven Mullaney, *The Place of the Stage: License, Play, and Power in Renaissance England* (Chicago: University of Chicago Press, 1988), pp. x–xi.

11. Since the insistence on the validity of labels applies to my own work, my claim to a feminist perspective is immediately subject to qualification as "male feminist." I acknowledge this term and accept its difficulties, to which I return in the Afterword.

12. Adrienne Rich, "Toward a More Feminist Criticism (1981)," in *Blood, Bread, and Poetry*, pp. 85–99.

13. Neely's essay "Feminist Criticism in Motion" appears in *For Alma Mater: Theory and Practice in Feminist Criticism*, ed. Paula A. Treichler, Cheris Kramarae, and Beth Stafford (Urbana: University of Illinois Press, 1985), pp. 69–90. My list of the original group of American feminist Shakespeare critics includes Janet Adelman, Shirley Nelson Garner, Gayle Greene, Coppélia Kahn, Carol Thomas Neely, Marianne Novy, Madelon (Gohlke) Sprengnether, and Carolyn Ruth Swift (Lenz). My own kinship with this group can be suggested by my essays on *As You Like It* and *The Winter's Tale*, written in 1979–80 and contemporaneous with *The Woman's Part*, and by my inclusion in the two special issues of *Women's Studies* 9, 1–2 (1981–82) that Greene and Swift edited in conjunction with *The Woman's Part*. For a brief account of early feminist criticism of Shakespeare through 1985, see my entry in *The Women's Studies Encyclopedia*, vol. 2: *Literature, Arts, and Learning*, ed. Helen Tierney (Westport, Conn.: Greenwood Press, 1990), pp. 314–18.

14. My affiliation with psychoanalytic criticism began with graduate work on Freud with C. L. Barber and Norman O. Brown at the University of California, Santa Cruz in 1970–71 and is reflected in the fact that the subject of my first book review was *Representing Shakespeare: New Psychoanalytic Essays*; see "Shakespeare's 'Family-Centered Art,'" *Canto: Review of the Arts* 4 (1981): 148–55. My more recent reviews express a necessary double response to psychoanalytic criticism. My review of *The (M)other Tongue: Essays in Feminist Psychoanalytic Interpretation*, in *Hurricane Alice: A Feminist Review* 3, 1 (Fall 1985): 6–7, points out problems with the feminist-psycho-

analytic tie and argues for a stronger feminist criticism of psychoanalysis. On the other hand, my discussion of Stephen Greenblatt's contribution to *Literary Theory/Renaissance Texts*, in *Medieval and Renaissance Drama in England* 4 (1989): 282–89, rejects a wholesale bracketing of psychoanalytic criticism and argues for its inclusion as a relevant subordinate component.

15. I have expressed my reservations about new historicism in two articles—"Rewriting the Renaissance, Rewriting Ourselves," *Shakespeare Quarterly* 38 (1987): 327–37, and a review of Leonard Tennenhouse's *Power on Display*, in *Shakespeare Quarterly* 39 (1988): 508–12—as well as in my participation in the forum "Feminism Versus New Historicism" at the 1988 Shakespeare Association meeting in Boston. Against this criticism should be balanced the indebtedness indicated in my essay on *The Merry Wives of Windsor* in *Shakespeare Reproduced: The Text in History and Ideology*, ed. Jean E. Howard and Marion F. O'Connor (London: Methuen, 1987), pp. 116–40.

16. Because of the differences between cultural materialism and new historicism, I disagree with Carol Neely's conflation of the two as "cult-historicists" in her article "Constructing the Subject: Feminist Practice and the New Renaissance Discourses," *English Literary Renaissance* 18 (1988): 5–18. In my view, these differences are important from a specifically feminist standpoint even when cultural materialists themselves fail to make the application to feminist criticism. My own account of cultural materialism is given in the review of *Political Shakespeare* in *Shakespeare Quarterly* 37 (1986): 251–55. In personal terms, this review enabled me to recover and to update my work with Stuart Hall at the Centre for Contemporary Cultural Studies, University of Birmingham, England, in 1967–68.

17. Citations are to Louis Montrose's introductory essay, pp. 1–16, and Harry Berger's afterword, pp. 453–73, in Harry Berger, *Revisionary Play: Studies in the Spenserian Dynamics* (Berkeley and Los Angeles: University of California Press, 1988). A related essay is Berger's "'Kidnapped Romance': Discourse in *The Faerie Queene*," in *Unfolded Tales: Essays on Renaissance Romance*, ed. George M. Logan and Gordan Teskey (Ithaca: Cornell University Press, 1989). I should say at the outset that Harry Berger has been and continues to be a model for my work in the sense specified by Montrose (pp. 1, 16).

18. I discuss the disruption of the author-critic bond in "Shakespeare and the 'Author-Function,'" in *Shakespeare's "Rough Magic": Renaissance Essays in Honor of C. L. Barber*, ed. Peter Erickson and Coppélia Kahn (Newark: University of Delaware Press, 1985), pp. 245–55. Berger's separation of narrator and author in Spenser's nondramatic poetry can be readily transposed to the distinction between character and author in the case of drama, as indicated by Berger's statement that "criticism of Shakespeare is actually Shake-

speare's criticism of Prospero" ("Miraculous Harp: A Reading of Shakespeare's *Tempest*," in Berger's *Second World and Green World: Studies in Renaissance Fiction-Making* [Berkeley and Los Angeles: University of California Press, 1988], p. 149, n. 3).

However, a critical stance cannot be evaluated merely in terms of its explicit theoretical positions, for Berger's actual practice is more complicated than his theory. Though he provides no account at the theoretical level, Berger's informality of voice and style nevertheless communicates a strong sense of the critic's personal location; in probing characters' "darker purposes," Berger can often be understood as exploring his own. Berger's self-presentation is much more forthright and much less guarded than, for example, that of Richard Levin in "Hazlitt on *Henry V*, and the Appropriation of Shakespeare," *Shakespeare Quarterly* 35 (1984): 134–41, which evades the self-disclosure it recommends to others: "It seems perfectly fair, therefore, to ask them to state some of these differences in attitude" (p. 141). The ways in which Levin's own attitudes differ from those he constructs for Shakespeare are neither specified nor engaged.

19. Stuart Hall's writing on ideology includes "Re-Thinking the 'Base-and-Superstructure' Metaphor," *Papers on Class, Hegemony and Party*, ed. Jon Bloomfield (London: Lawrence and Wishart, 1977), pp. 43–72; "Culture, the Media and the 'Ideological Effect,'" *Mass Communication and Society*, ed. James Curran, Michael Gurevitch, and Janet Woollacott (London: Edward Arnold, 1977), pp. 315–48; "The Hinterland of Science: Ideology and the 'Sociology of Knowledge,'" in Centre for Contemporary Cultural Studies, *On Ideology* (London: Hutchinson, 1978), pp. 9–32; "Some Problems with the Ideology/Subject Couplet," *Ideology and Consciousness*, no. 3 (1978): 113–21; "Race, Articulation and Societies Structured in Dominance," in *Sociological Theories: Race and Colonialism* (Paris, UNESCO, 1980), pp. 305–45; "The Whites of Their Eyes: Racist Ideologies and the Media," in *Silver Linings: Some Strategies for the Eighties*, ed. George Bridges and Rosalind Brunt (London: Lawrence and Wishart, 1981), pp. 28–52; "Notes on Deconstructing the 'Popular,'" in *People's History and Socialist Theory*, ed. Raphael Samuel (London: Routledge and Kegan Paul, 1981), pp. 227–40; "The Rediscovery of 'Ideology': Return of the Repressed in Media Studies," in *Culture, Society and the Media*, ed. Michael Gurevitch, Tony Bennett, James Curran, and Janet Woollacott (London: Methuen, 1982), pp. 56–90; *Ideology and the Modern World* (Melbourne: La Trobe University, 1983); "The Problem of Ideology—Marxism without Guarantees," in *Marx: A Hundred Years On*, ed. Betty Matthews (London: Lawrence and Wishart, 1983), pp. 57–85; "The Narrative Construction of Reality: An Interview with Stuart Hall," *Southern Review* (Adelaide) 17 (1984): 3–17; "Signification, Representation, Ideology: Althusser and the

Post-Structuralist Debates," *Critical Studies in Mass Communication* 2 (1985): 91–114; "Introduction" (with James Donald) and "Variants of Liberalism," in *Politics and Ideology*, ed. James Donald and Stuart Hall (Milton Keynes: Open University Press, 1986), pp. ix–xx and 34–69; "Gramsci's Relevance for the Study of Race and Ethnicity," *Journal of Communication Inquiry* 10, 2 (Summer 1986): 5–27; "The Toad in the Garden: Thatcherism among the Theorists," in *Marxism and the Interpretation of Culture*, ed. Cary Nelson and Lawrence Grossberg (Urbana: University of Illinois Press, 1988), pp. 58–73; *The Hard Road to Renewal: Thatcherism and the Crisis of the Left* (London: Verso, 1988); "The Emergence of Cultural Studies and the Crisis of the Humanities," *October* 53 (Summer 1990): 11–23.

Two books in preparation will in the future provide more convenient access to Hall's work: *Reproducing Ideologies*, a two-volume collection of essays, and *Cultural Studies*, based on a series of lectures given at the University of Illinois in 1983. Hazel V. Carby is compiling a comprehensive bibliography of Hall's publications.

20. Stuart Hall, "In Defense of Theory," in *People's History and Socialist Theory*, ed. Raphael Samuel (London: Routledge and Kegan Paul, 1981), pp. 378–85. See also the comments on Thompson in Hall's "Althusser and the Post-Structuralist Debates" (1985), pp. 96–97, and "The Toad in the Garden" (1988), p. 35.

21. In *Marxism and Literature* (Oxford: Oxford University Press, 1977) Raymond Williams discusses *ideology* (pp. 55–71) and *structure of feeling* (pp. 128–35) in separate places and with sharply contrasting sympathies. The senses of *ideology* in *Keywords: A Vocabulary of Culture and Society* (2d ed.; New York: Oxford University Press, 1985), pp. 153–57, continue the generally negative stance toward this term, while in *Politics and Letters* (London: New Left Books, 1979) Williams defends the concept of experience, using it as a virtual synonym for structure of feeling (pp. 158–74). As defined by Williams, ideology is seen as too formal and narrow to take in the experiential subtleties he intends by structures of feeling: " 'Feeling' is chosen to emphasize a distinction from the more formal concepts of 'world-view' or 'ideology' " (*Marxism and Literature*, p. 132). But ideology need not be thus restricted; the concept can be both enlarged and made more supple and thus be attuned to the levels of experience that Williams thinks must necessarily elude it.

22. Stuart Hall, "Cultural Studies: Two Paradigms," *Media, Culture and Society*, no. 2 (1980): 57–72; quotations from pp. 64, 69. In "The Williams Interviews," a review of Williams's *Politics and Letters* (1979), in *Screen Education*, no. 34 (1980): 94–104, Hall makes clear that his strictures are not limited to Williams's early writing but apply to *Marxism and Literature* and subsequent work: see especially Hall's comments on Williams's use of the term *experience* on p. 101.

Hall's review has now been reprinted in *Raymond Williams: Critical Perspectives*, ed. Terry Eagleton (Boston: Northeastern University Press, 1989), pp. 54–66.

23. Stuart Hall, "The Toad in the Garden" (1988), pp. 47–48. Hall characteristically uses Gramsci as a counterpoint who shows Althusser's deficiencies and provides an alternate resource. Of particular interest is Hall's use of Gramsci as a "test of historical concreteness": "Gramsci gave me an alternative to the antihistorical thrust of Althusserianism. I deeply resented Althusser's conflation of historicism with the historical. Historicism is a particular way of looking at history; but the historical is quite different" (p. 69). On the British reception of Gramsci's work, see David Forgacs, "Gramsci and Marxism in Britain," *New Left Review* 176 (July/August 1989): 70–88.

24. "Althusser attempts to redress the functionalist balance of this essay in a footnote on ideology as 'struggle'—but, so far as the theoretical structure of his argument was concerned, this eleventh-hour revision was merely 'gestural'" ("Cultural Studies and the Centre: Some Problematics and Problems," in Centre for Contemporary Cultural Studies, *Culture, Media, Language: Working Papers in Cultural Studies, 1972–79* [London: Hutchinson, 1980], pp. 15–47; quotation from p. 35). Also see "The Toad in the Garden" (1988), p. 48.

25. Stuart Hall, "Althusser and the Post-Structuralist Debates" (1985), pp. 104, 112. In addition, see Hall's discussion of articulation (pp. 53–55) in "On Postmodernism and Articulation: An Interview with Stuart Hall," *Journal of Communication Inquiry* 10, 2 (Summer 1986): 45–60.

CHAPTER 1

1. Shakespeare's conversion from patriarchal to antipatriarchal stance is asserted in Claire McEachern's "Fathering Herself: A Source Study of Shakespeare's Feminism," *Shakespeare Quarterly* 39 (1988): 269–90. McEachern rightly opposes an interpretation that sees all of Shakespeare's work merely as the expression of an extreme, unchanging patriarchal attitude; yet she too easily appeals to a vocabulary (*interrogates, rebellious, subversive*) that is radical sounding but vague and unqualified. A third option—a flexible, subtle, sensitive approach to patriarchal values—could account for Shakespeare's complexity relative to his sources and allow space for his revisions, while also acknowledging the continuation of patriarchal structures in modified forms. McEachern's insistence on Shakespeare's feminism makes it difficult to analyze the exact status of Shakespeare's complexity and avoids the question of the precise degree of his change. McEachern also tends to make patriarchy disappear through a narrow focus on blatantly repressive fathers, but

"the end of paternal control" (p. 273) is not the same as the end of patriarchy. A figure like Egeus in *A Midsummer Night's Dream* is a readily displaced straw man; yet as assessments of the play by Louis Adrian Montrose and Shirley Nelson Garner have shown, a larger patriarchal value system remains in place; often the more serious issue is not the father but rather the patriarchal husband who supplants him. Finally, McEachern's parallel between Shakespeare's opposition to the literary fathers of his sources and daughters' opposition to fathers in the plays presupposes a cross-gender identification between Shakespeare and the daughters that elides male-female differences which should be under examination. In her review of Carol Thomas Neely in *Shakespeare Studies* 20 (1988): 306–11, McEachern candidly characterizes Neely's feminist approach as "defeatist" (p. 309). I do not find Neely's spirited account at all defeatist, and I think the perception of defeatism is linked to an implicit belief that the inspiration and authorization for feminist criticism are legitimate only to the extent that we can see Shakespeare himself as feminist. However, such a belief is unwarranted. Shakespeare is not our only hope, our only source of empowerment; the historical dialectic between his past and our present that makes us aware of Shakespeare's limitations is a positive gain.

2. The distinction between violent and benign forms of patriarchy is made in the chapter on *As You Like It* in *Patriarchal Structures in Shakespeare's Drama* (Berkeley and Los Angeles: University of California Press, 1985), p. 32. The term *benign patriarchy* has a critical force similar to that of Kathleen McLuskie's concept of a "humanized patriarchy in which power and status remained with men but under which women's subordination was mitigated by men's paternalistic concern for women's comfort and happiness" (*Renaissance Dramatists* [Atlantic Highlands, N.J.: Humanities Press, 1989], p. 35). My reading of *As You Like It* was intended as an analysis of this specific play, not as a generalization about comedy or a formula that applied to all Shakespearean drama; agonized, exposed patriarchy, for example, has a different register and dynamic from the confidently benevolent.

3. Louis Adrian Montrose, " 'Shaping Fantasies': Figurations of Gender and Power in Elizabethan Culture," *Representations* 1 (Spring 1983): 61–94; Leah S. Marcus, "Elizabeth," in *Puzzling Shakespeare: Local Reading and Its Discontents* (Berkeley and Los Angeles: University of California Press, 1988), pp. 51–105; Gabriele Bernhard Jackson, "Topical Ideology: Witches, Amazons, and Shakespeare's Joan of Arc," *English Literary Renaissance* 18 (1988): 40–65. Behind Montrose's work stands Stephen Greenblatt's study of Ralegh's relations with Elizabeth in *Sir Walter Ralegh: The Renaissance Man and His Roles* (New Haven: Yale University Press, 1973), parts of which are di-

rectly carried over into the discussion of Elizabeth in *Renaissance Self-Fashioning: From More to Shakespeare* (Chicago: University of Chicago Press, 1980). To these two landmarks I would add a third, Greenblatt's trenchant review of Roy Strong's *The Cult of Elizabeth* in *Renaissance Quarterly* 31 (1978): 642–44. While Strong's work is extremely informative and indispensable, Greenblatt properly draws a contrast between a genial iconographical approach and a more sharply analytical assessment. Strong's belated attempt to accommodate the latter is reflected in his title change for the revised version of *Splendour at Court: Renaissance Spectacle and Illusion* (London: Weidenfeld and Nicolson, 1973); the new title, *Art and Power: Renaissance Festivals, 1450–1650* (Woodbridge, Suffolk: Boydell Press, 1984), picks up the key new historicist term, *power*.

4. The term *cult of Elizabeth* is Roy Strong's: *The Cult of Elizabeth: Elizabethan Portraiture and Pageantry* (London: Thames and Hudson, 1977). More recent work on Elizabeth includes Elizabeth W. Pomeroy, *Reading the Portraits of Queen Elizabeth I* (Hamden, Conn.: Archon Books, 1989); Philippa Berry, *Of Chastity and Power: Elizabethan Literature and the Unmarried Queen* (London: Routledge, 1989); Andrew Belsey and Catherine Belsey, "Icons of Divinity: Portraits of Elizabeth I," in *Renaissance Bodies: The Human Figure in English Culture c. 1540–1660*, ed. Lucy Gent and Nigel Llewellyn (London: Reaktion Books, 1990), pp. 11–35; and *Reading Elizabeth I*, ed. Leah S. Marcus and Mary Beth Rose (Chicago: University of Chicago Press, forthcoming). Constance Jordan's extraordinarily comprehensive study, *Renaissance Feminism: Literary Texts and Political Models* (Ithaca: Cornell University Press, 1990), includes a section entitled "Women's Rule: The Tudor Queens" (pp. 116–33). I am grateful to Professor Jordan for allowing me to see her book in page proofs.

5. In *Elizabeth I: A Feminist Perspective* (Oxford: Berg, 1988), Susan Bassnett summarily dismisses the argument of Allison Heisch's "Queen Elizabeth I and the Persistence of Patriarchy," *Feminist Review* 4 (1980): 45–75. Bassnett comments:

> Most recently, yet another version of Elizabeth has appeared, a narrow feminist perspective that accuses her of not having done enough for other women, in much the same terms as Margaret Thatcher might be accused today, but with the difference, of course, that feminist ideology conceived in such terms did not exist in the sixteenth century. Elizabeth would have perceived women as biologically different from men, as occupying different social roles, her notion of the relative positions of men and women in society would have been a Renaissance view, quite unlike that of the twentieth century.
>
> (p. 5)

But the issue is not one of accusation or blame. Rather, the historical difference granted, the value of Heisch's perspective is precisely the way it so sharply highlights that difference as to forestall unqualified sentimental celebrations of Elizabeth's power.

6. Roy Strong, *Portraits of Queen Elizabeth I* (Oxford: Oxford University Press, 1963).

7. Russell Fraser, *Young Shakespeare* (New York: Columbia University, 1988), pp. 9–10. In this view, the mediating term is *England's greatness*, to which Elizabeth and Shakespeare equally and similarly testify: "Universal Shakespeare is first of all Stratford's son, singing the praises of doughty English, e.g. the 'band of brothers' we hear about in *Henry V*" (p. 29).

8. In "A New History for Shakespeare and His Time," *Shakespeare Quarterly* 39 (1988): 441–64, Leeds Barroll critically examines one incident, the staging of *Richard II* prior to the Essex rebellion, in which the three figures of Elizabeth, Essex, and Shakespeare appear to converge. Barroll concludes, however, by acknowledging a distinction between Shakespearean drama's direct topical intervention in court politics and the "more general truth" of its "production and reproduction of power relations" (p. 463). My emphasis here is on the latter, and my starting point is the work of Mervyn James, which Barroll does not cite. Moreover, I would eschew one of the motives Barroll finds for the construction of the Essex-Shakespeare connection as "a narrative promoted by a nineteenth-century aristocratic ideology that constantly sought to raise Shakespeare to the status of confidant with the peerage" (p. 443). However distant and culturally mediated Shakespeare's response to Essex, its class implications are much more multiple and conflicting, and cannot sustain the single interpretation of aristocratic identification.

9. Recent work on the theater's institutional position includes Steven Mullaney, *The Place of the Stage: License, Play, and Power in Renaissance England* (Chicago: University of Chicago Press, 1988)— whose approach is clarified in his reviews of Walter Cohen in *Shakespeare Quarterly* 37 (1986): 512–16 and of Michael Bristol in *Renaissance Quarterly* 40 (1987): 575–78; Annabel Patterson, "'The Very Age and Body of the Time His Form and Pressure': Rehistoricizing Shakespeare's Theater," *New Literary History* 20 (1988): 83–104; Robert Weimann, "Bifold Authority in Shakespeare's Theatre," *Shakespeare Quarterly* 39 (1988): 401–17.

10. Jean E. Howard, "Old Wine, New Bottles," *Shakespeare Quarterly* 35 (1984): 234–37; Carol Thomas Neely, "Constructing the Subject: Feminist Practice and the New Renaissance Discourses," *English Literary Renaissance* 18 (1988): 5–18, especially p. 8. Neely makes a telling correlation between a focus on upper-class or upwardly mobile males and the enactment of an empty "yuppie criticism" (p. 14). The embedded new historicist metaphor of academics as com-

petitive courtiers is instructive up to a point, but it turns into an overinvestment in narrow careerism when alertness to the political dimensions of professional scholarly ambition and advancement becomes an end in itself, unaccompanied by the clear articulation of larger social responsibilities that go with academic success. When such articulation is present, however, it meets with anxious calls for a more easy-going professionalism exemplified by the final sentence of Stanley Fish's "Commentary: The Young and the Restless," in *The New Historicism*, ed. H. Aram Veeser (New York: Routledge, 1989), pp. 303–16.

11. Jean E. Howard, "Crossdressing, the Theatre, and Gender Struggle in Early Modern England," *Shakespeare Quarterly* 39 (1988): 418–44; quoted phrase from p. 418.

12. Since much of the work on Renaissance women writers is in progress or forthcoming, I list here only a few examples: Margaret W. Ferguson, "A Room Not Their Own: Renaissance Women as Readers and Writers," in *The Comparative Perspective on Literature: Approaches to Theory and Practice*, ed. Clayton Koelb and Susan Noakes (Ithaca: Cornell University Press, 1988), pp. 93–116; Ann Rosalind Jones, *The Currency of Eros: Women's Love Lyric in Europe, 1560–1620* (Bloomington: Indiana University Press, 1990); *The Renaissance Englishwoman in Print: Counterbalancing the Canon*, ed. Anne M. Haselkorn and Betty S. Travitsky (Amherst: University of Massachusetts Press, 1990); Margaret J. M. Ezell, "The Myth of Judith Shakespeare: Creating the Canon of Women's Literature," *New Literary History* 21 (1990): 579–92; and Margaret W. Ferguson, "Running On with Almost Public Voice: The Case of 'E. C.'," in *Tradition and the Talents of Women*, ed. Florence Howe (Urbana: University of Illinois Press, 1991), pp. 37–67. Papers include Carolyn Ruth Swift, "*Mariam:* Elizabeth Cary's Meditation on Personal Choice," Buffalo Symposium in Literature and Psychoanalysis, April 1989; Barbara Lewalski, "Rewriting Patriarchy and Patronage: Margaret Clifford, Ann Clifford and Aemilia Lanier," English Institute, August 1989; and work presented in the seminar "Renaissance Women as Readers and Writers" chaired by Margaret Ferguson and Ann Rosalind Jones, Shakespeare Association of America meeting, April 1990, and in the symposium "Attending to Women in Early Modern England," University of Maryland, November 1990. Lewalski's paper suggests that the breakthrough in women's authorship occurred in the Jacobean period in part because of Elizabeth's cultural domination during her reign. Elizabeth H. Hageman's two important bibliographies on women writers appeared in *English Literary Renaissance* 14 (1984): 409–25 and 18 (1988): 138–67. Hageman's bibliographies are updated in *Women in the Renaissance: Selections from English Literary Renaissance*, ed. Kirby Farrell, Elizabeth H.

Hageman, and Arthur F. Kinney (Amherst: University of Massachusetts Press, 1990).

13. François Rigolot, "Gender vs. Sex Difference in Louise Labé's Grammar of Love," and Ann Rosalind Jones, "City Women and Their Audiences: Louise Labé and Veronica Franco," in *Rewriting the Renaissance: The Discourses of Sexual Difference in Early Modern Europe*, ed. Margaret W. Ferguson, Maureen Quilligan, and Nancy J. Vickers (Chicago: University of Chicago Press, 1986), pp. 287–98 and 299–316.

14. In " 'None of Woman Born': Shakespeare, Women, and Revolution," *Shakespeare Jahrbuch* (Weimar) 124 (1988): 130–41, Walter Cohen argues that it should be "possible to hear, however dimly, dissident, radical women's voices" (p. 136) in Shakespeare's tragedies, reading them in retrospectively from a later historical moment if necessary. Cohen's analysis, which traces a dialectic between two basic patriarchal options he calls "extreme misogynistic" and "patriarchal humanist" (parallel to the violent/benevolent distinction in n. 2, above), appears to leave no room for an independent political perspective outside of Shakespeare's work. However, Cohen posits, without clearly explaining its source, a mechanism of distortion that transforms women's voices from positive to negative, a process which may be equivalent to what I refer to as the filtering effect of Shakespeare's works.

15. Kathleen McLuskie, *Renaissance Dramatists*, pp. 39–40, 226–27.

CHAPTER 2

1. J. Dover Wilson, *The Essential Shakespeare: A Biographical Adventure* (Cambridge: Cambridge University Press, 1932), p. 76.

2. My discussion of the poems is indebted to Coppélia Kahn's pioneering essays on them: "Self and Eros in *Venus and Adonis*," *Centennial Review* 20 (1976): 351–71, and "The Rape in Shakespeare's *Lucrece*," *Shakespeare Studies* 9 (1976): 45–72. These remain the best feminist psychoanalytic criticism on the poems and among the most trenchant in any mode. Kahn, however, does not link the poems, which is my aim here. The diverging critical methods of her two essays—the one on *Venus and Adonis* is primarily psychoanalytic, that on *The Rape of Lucrece* primarily feminist and sociological—suggest a lack of connection between the poems, and this split is reinforced by the inclusion of only one, not both, of the essays in her book *Man's Estate: Masculine Identity in Shakespeare* (Berkeley and Los Angeles: University of California Press, 1981). Kahn's most recent work, " 'Magic of bounty': *Timon of Athens*, Jacobean Patronage, and Maternal Power," *Shakespeare Quarterly* 38 (1987): 34–57, refers

briefly to Adonis (pp. 54–55) and is relevant to the present study because of Kahn's effort to combine feminist criticism and new historicism.

3. Elkin Calhoun Wilson, *England's Eliza* (Cambridge: Harvard University Press, 1939), p. 213. Edgar Wind, who discusses the synthesis of Venus and Diana in the Venus-Virgo motif in *Pagan Mysteries in the Renaissance* (New York: Norton, 1968), pp. 75–80, observes: "In view of the Italian sources of Elizabethan imagery, perhaps the question is not unjustified whether the worship of Queen Elizabeth as Diana was not also a cult of Venus in disguise." The painting, noted by Wind (p. 83), that illustrates Elizabeth's power to assimilate the qualities of three distinct goddesses, is analyzed in greater detail in Louis Adrian Montrose's "Gifts and Reasons: The Contexts of Peele's *Araygnement of Paris*," *English Literary History* 47 (1980): 433–61, especially pp. 445–47.

4. Akrigg's discussion of the two poems occurs on pp. 195–200 and 202–5 of *Shakespeare and the Earl of Southampton* (Cambridge: Harvard University Press, 1968).

5. See especially pp. 62–63 of Bradbrook's "Beasts and Gods: Greene's *Groats-worth of Witte* and the Social Purpose of *Venus and Adonis*," *Shakespeare Survey* 15 (1962): 62–72.

6. F. T. Prince, introduction to the New Arden edition of *The Poems* (London: Methuen, 1960), p. xxv.

7. Muriel Bradbrook, *Shakespeare and Elizabethan Poetry* (London: Chatto and Windus, 1951), pp. 115–16.

8. On political patronage, see Wallace T. MacCaffrey, "Place and Patronage in Elizabethan Politics," in *Elizabethan Government and Society: Essays Presented to Sir John Neale*, ed. S. T. Bindoff, J. Hurstfield, C. H. Williams (University of London: Athlone Press, 1961), pp. 95–126. On the relative "decentralization" of cultural patronage under Elizabeth, see R. Malcolm Smuts, *Court Culture and the Origins of a Royalist Tradition in Early Stuart England* (Philadelphia: University of Pennsylvania Press, 1987), pp. 16–18. On the role of Burghley, Elizabeth's most powerful minister, as patron, see Jan van Dorsten, "Literary Patronage in Elizabethan England: The Early Phase," in *Patronage in the Renaissance*, ed. Guy Fitch Lytle and Stephen Orgel (Princeton: Princeton University Press, 1981), pp. 194–99. As G. P. V. Akrigg notes in *Shakespeare and the Earl of Southampton*, Southampton receives his education under Burghley's direction as a ward at Cecil House and then under Burghley's sponsorship at St. John's College (pp. 23–30).

9. Sheila ffolliott, "Catherine de' Medici as Artemisia: Figuring the Powerful Widow," in *Rewriting the Renaissance: The Discourses of Sexual Difference in Early Modern Europe*, ed. Margaret W. Ferguson, Maureen Quilligan, and Nancy J. Vickers (Chicago: University of

Chicago Press, 1986), pp. 227–41. The overall organization of *Rewriting the Renaissance* stresses the concept of the exception by entitling the volume's final section, "The Works of Women: Some Exceptions to the Rule of Patriarchy," but ffolliott's essay, which is placed in this section, shows how problematic the status of the exception can be in some instances: "Houel in the *Histoire* seeks to rationalize female rulership by arguing the case of an exceptional woman ruler—that is, an exception to the general rule of women's inherent inferiority" (p. 233).

10. Allison Heisch, "Queen Elizabeth I and the Persistence of Patriarchy," *Feminist Review* 4 (1980): 45–56. For a similar argument, see Adrienne Rich's comment on Elizabeth in *On Lies, Secrets, and Silence: Selected Prose, 1966–78* (New York: Norton, 1979), pp. 10–11.

11. James E. Phillips, Jr., "The Background of Spenser's Attitude toward Women Rulers," *Huntington Library Quarterly* 5 (1941): 5–32.

12. Katherine Usher Henderson and Barbara F. McManus, *Half Humankind: Contexts and Texts of the Controversy about Women in England, 1540–1640* (Urbana: University of Illinois Press, 1985), pp. 12–13. For another account of Aylmer, see Constance Jordan's "Woman's Rule in Sixteenth-Century British Political Thought," *Renaissance Quarterly* 40 (1987): 421–51, which concludes: "Perhaps because of his reliance on the mysterious aspects of monarchic authority rather than on proofs of woman's worth, Aylmer's defense of women's rule did not challenge the fundamentally restrictive concept of womankind current in mid-sixteenth-century England" (p. 441).

In a related essay, "Feminism and the Humanists: The Case for Sir Thomas Elyot's *Defense of Good Women*," in *Rewriting the Renaissance*, pp. 242–58, Jordan argues that Elyot is subversive in relation to "neo-Aristotelian misogyny" (p. 248). But Jordan simultaneously acknowledges that Elyot's commitment to equality is vitiated by problematic elements that counteract the positive treatment of women: "These women logically prove the worth of their sex by denying it: a strange form of defense. While it questions sexual stereotypes, that some women can do men's work, it also seems to confirm gender-related values, that everything female is inferior" (p. 252). Elyot's Zenobia "duly conforms to the expectations of conservative readers by being modest, dutiful, temperate, patient, and obedient to her husband. Yet she is also unmistakably the product of a humanist imagination working (or playing) on the possibility that a woman can also attain a full measure of humanity" (p. 254). Elyot's compromised, equivocal position on female empowerment can thus be seen as always cutting two ways—toward a liberal challenge to orthodox views of women and toward continuing constriction of women in a revised form. The recuperation of female subordination is signaled by the overall result, which falls well short of the tran-scendence of patriarchal social structures and assumptions: "But the victory is Candidus' alone, for Zenobia, despite her virtue, remains the captive of the Emperor Aurelianus and among the conquered not the conquering" (p. 256).

13. Gordon J. Schochet, *Patriarchalism and Political Thought: The Authoritarian Family and Political Speculation and Attitudes Especially in Seventeenth-Century England* (Oxford: Basil Blackwell, 1975), p. 44.

14. R. W. K. Hinton, "Husbands, Fathers and Conquerors: 1. Filmer and the Logic of Patriarchalism," *Political Studies* 15 (1967): 291–300; quotation from p. 293.

15. Sir Thomas Smith, *De Republica Anglorum*, ed. Mary Dewar (Cambridge: Cambridge University Press, 1982), p. 60.

16. Mary Dewar, *Sir Thomas Smith: A Tudor Intellectual in Office* (University of London: Athlone Press, 1964), pp. 7, 172.

17. Both quotations are from *Rewriting the Renaissance:* Louis Adrian Montrose, "*A Midsummer Night's Dream* and the Shaping Fantasies of Elizabethan Culture: Gender, Power, Form," pp. 65–87, quotation from p. 81; and Peter Stallybrass, "Patriarchal Territories: The Body Enclosed," pp. 123–42, quotation from p. 132. Stallybrass refers directly to the key passage—*Faerie Queene*, 5.5.25—while Mon-trose discusses Book V on pp. 71, 78–79. The original version of Montrose's essay—*Representations* 2 (Spring 1983): 61–94—cites the actual passage (pp. 77–78). Additional useful commentary on this passage includes James E. Phillips, Jr., "The Woman Ruler in Spen-ser's *Faerie Queene*," *Huntington Library Quarterly* 5 (1941): 217; Ellen Cantarow, "A Wilderness of Opinions Confounded: Allegory and Ideology," *College English* 34 (1972): 234; Lillian S. Robinson, *Mon-strous Regiment: The Lady Knight in Sixteenth-Century Epic* (New York: Garland, 1985), pp. 334–35; Pamela Joseph Benson, "Rule, Virginia: Protestant Theories of Female Regiment in *The Faerie Queene*," *English Literary Renaissance* 15 (1985): 280; and Patricia Parker, "Suspended Instruments: Lyric and Power in the Bower of Bliss," in *Cannibals, Witches and Divorce: Estranging the Renaissance*, ed. Marjorie Garber (Baltimore: Johns Hopkins University Press, 1987), pp. 27–28. Also pertinent are Jonathan Goldberg's comments on Radigund and Brit-omart in *James I and the Politics of Literature* (Baltimore: Johns Hopkins University Press, 1983), p. 10, and Maureen Quilligan's account of Book V in "The Comedy of Female Authority in *The Faerie Queene*," *English Literary Renaissance* 17 (1987): 167–71. Quilligan's general the-sis, cited in the epigraph to Part 1, may serve as a summary statement.

18. David Norbrook, *Poetry and Politics in the English Renaissance* (London: Routledge and Kegan Paul, 1984), p. 119.

19. This account is drawn from Akrigg, *Shakespeare and the Earl of Southampton.*

20. A fine, detailed analysis of the Essex subculture is presented in Mervyn James's "At a Crossroads of the Political Culture: The Essex Revolt, 1601," in his *Society, Politics and Culture: Studies in Early Modern England* (Cambridge: Cambridge University Press, 1986), pp. 416–65. A useful supplement to James's essay is the commentary on Essex in John Guy's chapters "Political Culture" and "The Tudor *Fin de Siècle*," in his *Tudor England* (Oxford: Oxford University Press, 1988), pp. 408–58. Also valuable are the discussions of Essex in Richard C. McCoy's *The Rites of Knighthood: The Literature and Politics of Elizabethan Chivalry* (Berkeley and Los Angeles: University of California Press, 1989) and in Eric S. Mallin's "Emulous Factions and the Collapse of Chivalry: *Troilus and Cressida*," *Representations* 29 (Winter 1990): 145–79.

21. The connection between Venus and Elizabeth is made in section I of Kirby Farrell's chapter "Love, Death, and the Hunt in *Venus and Adonis*," in his *Play, Death, and Heroism in Shakespeare* (Chapel Hill: University of North Carolina Press, 1989), pp. 125–30.

22. For accounts of this moment, see Robert Lacey's *Robert, Earl of Essex* (New York: Atheneum, 1971), pp. 211–14, and Mervyn James's "At a Crossroads of the Political Culture: The Essex Revolt, 1601," p. 445.

23. William Empson suggests that when censorship is taken into account it is possible to hear a tacit, though cautious, republican element in the poem: "Southampton, who seemed fated to irritate the Queen, might well be inclined to cool thoughts about royalty; and Shakespeare would be wise to hesitate as to how far one might go" (introduction to the Signet edition of *Poems* [New York: New American Library, 1963], pp. xxiv–xxv).

24. F. T. Prince, introduction to the New Arden edition of *The Poems*, p. xxxiv.

25. The emotional intensity that can be aroused by an identification with Adonis is exemplified by Wayne Rebhorn's "Mother Venus: Temptation in Shakespeare's *Venus and Adonis*," *Shakespeare Studies* 11 (1978): 1–19. Rebhorn's essay makes a sharp critique of Venus and defense of Adonis based on the latter's right to the "freedom" (pp. 4, 5, 11) and "autonomy" (pp. 4, 9) that constitute "the adult male's world" (p. 16). Rebhorn's protest simply assumes these watchwords of adult manhood as givens that require no explanation. He does not critically examine the criteria for this "adult male world"; he neither asks whether Adonis has the capacity for it nor considers where in the poem such a life is possible. Does the hunt really provide the genuine alternative of adult manhood, or does it merely offer an escape route that confirms Adonis's immaturity? By avoiding these issues, Rebhorn recapitulates the poem's tendency to project Adonis's difficulties onto Venus. His romantic,

one-sided presentation of the heroic tradition that opposes Venus preserves male bias by its neglect of the problematic side of male heroism, by its refusal to acknowledge the legitimate modifications in this pure male freedom required by authentic relations with women.

26. This phrase is drawn from Natalie Zemon Davis's essay "Women on Top," in her *Society and Culture in Early Modern France* (Stanford: Stanford University Press, 1975), pp. 124–51.

27. C. L. Barber and Richard P. Wheeler, *The Whole Journey: Shakespeare's Power of Development* (Berkeley and Los Angeles: University of California Press, 1986), p. 147.

28. Akrigg discusses Southampton's "possible homosexuality" in *Shakespeare and the Earl of Southampton*, pp. 181–82, as does Russell Fraser in *Young Shakespeare* (New York: Columbia University Press, 1988), p. 178.

29. By contrast, Jonathan Crewe's concluding chapter on *The Rape of Lucrece* in *Trials of Authorship: Anterior Forms and Poetic Reconstruction from Wyatt to Shakespeare* (Berkeley and Los Angeles: University of California Press, 1990), pp. 140–63, finds that Shakespeare makes a largely positive and unobstructed identification with Lucrece because her subordination offers a sympathetic emblem for Shakespeare's subordinate position in patronage relations with Southampton: "Shakespeare's figure of Lucrece is Shakespeare's figure *as* Lucrece" (p. 161). However, Crewe qualifies this formulation by seeing Shakespeare's "participatory interest in Lucrece's struggle" as a "quasi-identificatory interest" (p. 160) that does not mean "establishing common cause or fully representing the sociopolitical interest of the woman as other, as if it were identical to his own interest" (p. 162). My approach emphasizes the divergencies between their respective interests, with the result that the poem's margin for "unforeclosed possibility in the rewriting of sociocultural scripts" is considerably smaller.

30. The action of the image of Brutus's "burying" echoes, but in a benign way, Tarquin's violent deposit: "She bears the load of lust he left behind" (734). However, the echo is pertinent because it suggests that, despite the difference between violent and benevolent approaches, the latter nonetheless contains its own form of callousness.

31. Both Kahn (n. 2) and Rebhorn (n. 25) have documented the network of references in the poem that establish Venus's maternal role.

32. In her essay "'The blazon of sweet beauty's best': Shakespeare's *Lucrece*"—in *Shakespeare and the Question of Theory*, ed. Patricia Parker and Geoffrey Hartman (London: Methuen, 1985), pp. 95–115—Nancy J. Vickers shows how the logic of the blazon in

praise of Lucrece's beauty reaches its conclusion in the final display of "her bleeding body thorough Rome" (line 1851; Vickers, p. 108). The image of the breast with the self-inflicted wound bespeaks the same logic, to whose authority Lucrece herself has been forced to accede. The extent to which Lucrece is drawn into this male competitive process is indicated by the way Lucrece directs her suicide against women, as Vickers notes: "Her dramatic refusal to live is, in part, a refusal to encourage wantonness in women" (p. 110). Linda C. Hults discusses Renaissance visual images of Lucrece's suicide in "Dürer's *Lucretia:* Speaking the Silence of Women," *Signs* 16, 2 (Winter 1991): 205–37. See also Mary D. Garrard's interpretation of the Lucretia motif in *Artemisia Gentileschi: The Image of the Female Hero in Italian Baroque Art* (Princeton: Princeton University Press, 1989), pp. 210–44, and Griselda Pollock's review of Garrard's book in *The Art Bulletin* 72 (1990): 499–505.

33. Stephen Greenblatt, *Sir Walter Ralegh: The Renaissance Man and His Roles* (New Haven: Yale University Press, 1973), p. 59.

34. The combined analysis of gender and class is exemplified by Susan Dwyer Amussen in "Gender, Family and the Social Order, 1560–1725," in *Order and Disorder in Early Modern England,* ed. Anthony Fletcher and John Stevenson (Cambridge: Cambridge University Press, 1985), pp. 196–217; and in her subsequent book, *An Ordered Society: Gender and Class in Early Modern England* (Oxford: Basil Blackwell, 1988). For a later historical period, see Leonore Davidoff and Catherine Hall, *Family Fortunes: Men and Women of the English Middle Class, 1780–1850* (Chicago: University of Chicago Press, 1987): "The principal argument rests on the assumption that gender and class always operate together, that consciousness of class always takes a gendered form" (p. 13).

35. Keith Wrightson refers to "an incipient class dimension" in his *English Society, 1580–1680* (New Brunswick, N.J.: Rutgers University Press, 1982), p. 65; his opening chapter is a survey entitled "Degrees of People" (pp. 17–38). Raymond Williams provides a linguistic history of the term *class* relative to the words *rank, order, estate* and *degree* in *Keywords: A Vocabulary of Culture and Society* (2d ed.; New York: Oxford University Press, 1985), pp. 60–69.

36. David Cressy, "Describing the Social Order of Elizabethan and Stuart England," *Literature and History* 3 (1976): 29–44; quotation from p. 29. On the class pressures created by social mobility, see "Courtesy Literature and Social Change," chapter 1 of Frank Whigham's *Ambition and Privilege: The Social Tropes of Elizabethan Courtesy Theory* (Berkeley and Los Angeles: University of California Press, 1984), pp. 1–31.

37. Steven Mullaney, *The Place of the Stage: License, Play, and Power in Renaissance England* (Chicago: University of Chicago Press, 1987),

pp. 141–42; David Scott Kastan provides a related discussion of theatrical representations of class in his essay "Is There a Class in This
Text?" (manuscript). For analyses of theater audiences, see "Shakespeare's Unprivileged Playgoers, 1576–1642," in Martin Butler's *Theatre and Crisis, 1632–1642* (Cambridge: Cambridge University Press,
1984), pp. 293–306, and "Social Composition," chapter 3 of Andrew
Gurr's *Playgoing in Shakespeare's London* (Cambridge: Cambridge University Press, 1987), pp. 49–79.

38. Walter Cohen, *Drama of a Nation: Public Theater in Renaissance
England and Spain* (Ithaca: Cornell University Press, 1985), pp. 183–
84.

CHAPTER 3

1. The date for *All's Well That Ends Well* is uncertain. G. K.
Hunter gives "a tentative dating" of 1603–4 in the New Arden edition of the play (London: Methuen, 1959), p. xxv; Anne Barton specifies 1602–3 in *The Riverside Shakespeare* (Boston: Houghton Mifflin,
1973), p. 502; David Bevington indicates a range of 1601–4 in his
Bantam edition (1988), p. 263. Given the uncertainty, it may be possible to view the play both in Elizabethan and in Jacobean terms. My
goal, however, is to place the play in its Elizabethan context.

2. G. P. V. Akrigg, *Shakespeare and the Earl of Southampton* (Cambridge: Harvard University Press, 1968), pp. 255–56.

3. S. Schoenbaum, *William Shakespeare: A Compact Documentary
Life* (New York: Oxford University Press, rev. ed. 1987), p. 179.
Schoenbaum similarly denies any significant connection between
Shakespeare and Essex. Reviewing the circumstance of the staging
of *Richard II* prior to Essex's revolt, Schoenbaum finds no involve-
ment on Shakespeare's part (*Documentary Life*, pp. 217–19; "Richard
II and the Realities of Power," *Shakespeare and Others* [Washington,
D.C.: Folger Shakespeare Library, 1985], pp. 86–90).

4. Mervyn James, "At a Crossroads of the Political Culture: The
Essex Revolt, 1601," *Society, Politics and Culture: Studies in Early Modern England* (Cambridge: Cambridge University Press, 1986), pp.
416–65. Also relevant is James's earlier essay on honor culture, "English Politics and the Concept of Honour, 1485–1642," pp. 308–415,
which shows how in response to "the facts of social mobility" a
redefinition of honor occurred that tended "to present honour, virtue and nobility as detachable from their anchorage in pedigree and
descent" (p. 375). The struggle between Helena and Bertram is in
part a conflict between new and old ideas of honor.

5. I do not discount the critical perspective on Henry V built into
the play, which I have discussed in " 'The fault / My father made':
The Anxious Pursuit of Heroic Fame in Shakespeare's *Henry V*,"

Modern Language Studies 10, 1 (Winter 1979–80): 10–25, and in chapter 2 of *Patriarchal Structures in Shakespeare's Drama* (Berkeley and Los Angeles: University of California Press, 1985), pp. 39–65. My concern here, however, is to emphasize the relative contrast between Henry V and Bertram.

6. There is a line of criticism—from Clifford Leech's "The Theme of Ambition in 'All's Well That Ends Well,'" *English Literary History* 21 (1954): 17–29, to Richard A. Levin's "*All's Well That Ends Well*, and 'All Seems Well,'" *Shakespeare Studies* 13 (1980): 131–44—that provides ample testimony to the perception of Helena's ambition and power. However, in the absence of a feminist perspective, the cultural significance of her ambition is lost and this criticism amounts to a restatement of male complaint. Feminist interest in the reversal of customary gender roles whereby Helena becomes the active pursuer rather than the pursued leads to a wholly different emphasis on Helena as the center of the play's action. See Carol Thomas Neely, chapter 2, "Power and Virginity in the Problem Comedies: *All's Well That Ends Well*," in her *Broken Nuptials in Shakespeare's Plays* (New Haven: Yale University Press, 1985), pp. 58–104; Carolyn Asp, "Subjectivity, Desire and Female Friendship in *All's Well That Ends Well*," *Literature and Psychology* 32, 4 (1986): 48–63; Lisa Jardine, "Cultural Confusion and Shakespeare's Learned Heroines: 'These are old paradoxes,'" *Shakespeare Quarterly* 38 (1987): 1–18; Susan Snyder, "*All's Well That Ends Well* and Shakespeare's Helens: Text and Subtext, Subject and Object," *English Literary Renaissance* 18 (1988): 66–77.

7. The expected comparison would be the one between Henry V and Elizabeth with which R. Malcolm Smuts begins his "Public Ceremony and Royal Charisma: The English Royal Entry in London, 1485–1642," in *The First Modern Society: Essays in English History in Honour of Lawrence Stone*, ed. A. L. Beier, David Cannadine, and James M. Rosenheim (Cambridge: Cambridge University Press, 1989), pp. 65–93:

> Thus when Henry V returned from Agincourt, the Lord Mayor and Aldermen in scarlet robes, and 300 mounted citizens dressed in coats of murrey (dark purple) with gold chains around their necks, rode out to meet him at Blackheath and accompanied him back to Westminster. More than a century and a half later, in 1584, Elizabeth returned from a progress to an essentially similar welcome.
>
> (pp. 68–69)

Shakespeare's reference to Essex disrupts the continuity by marking the difference between a male king's military campaign in Agincourt and Elizabeth's domestic progresses. Annabel Patterson's discussion of the fifth Chorus, which became available only after I had completed this chapter, overlaps with mine on several points: see "Back by Popular Demand: The Two Versions of *Henry V*," chapter 5 in *Shakespeare and the Popular Voice* (Cambridge: Basil Blackwell, 1989), pp. 71–92.

8. The political tensions between Elizabeth and Essex, which Mervyn James excludes from Shakespeare's presentation, are discussed in Jonathan Dollimore and Alan Sinfield, "History and Ideology: The Instance of *Henry V*," in *Alternative Shakespeares*, ed. John Drakakis (London: Methuen, 1985), pp. 206–27, especially p. 219.

9. Carol Thomas Neely develops the contrast between the efficacy of female solidarity and the emptiness of male bonds in *Broken Nuptials in Shakespeare's Plays*, pp. 74–78.

10. This motif also occurs, for example, in *As You Like It* when Duke Senior performs a similar act of recognition for Orlando. Senior reconstitutes the father-son bond by testifying both to the son's and to his own connection to the deceased father.

11. The age/youth conflict is also enacted in a simplified, one-sided form in the encounter between Lafew and Parolles (2.3.184–260), but the interaction between the king and Bertram is not reducible to this version. Nor is it accurate to portray Helena as siding with and supporting the older generation: her alliance with the older group serves her interests and values, not theirs.

12. In "Bed Tricks: On Marriage as the End of Comedy in *All's Well That Ends Well* and *Measure for Measure*," in *Shakespeare's Personality*, ed. Norman H. Holland, Sidney Homan, and Bernard J. Paris (Berkeley and Los Angeles: University of California Press, 1989), pp. 151–74, Janet Adelman discusses the psychological tension epitomized by the Venus/Diana motif in *All's Well* (pp. 160–61). I would add that an undercurrent of associations with Queen Elizabeth's female power accentuates this tension.

13. Susan Snyder, "*All's Well That Ends Well* and Shakespeare's Helens: Text and Subtext, Subject and Object," pp. 66–67. Of the four feminist critics cited in note 6, only Lisa Jardine finds Helena's power sharply diminished: "in the second half of the play, Helena acts out an *atonement* for her 'forwardness'" that implies a "ritual return to exemplary passivity" ("Cultural Confusion and Shakespeare's Learned Heroines: 'These are old paradoxes,'" p. 11). Jardine contrasts Helena with Portia of *The Merchant of Venice*: the latter "does not resolve the actively knowing heroine into passively tolerant wife" (p. 12). I agree with Jardine's basic point that the traditional marital terms of Helena's quest set limits to her exercise of power, but I want to complicate the comparison by suggesting that Portia's power is also qualified. Her dominance is ensured by her withdrawal to the private sphere of Belmont, her intervention in the social action of Venice having been temporary. Portia does not directly challenge the male

power structure invested in the position of the Duke of Venice and she leaves it intact. By contrast, Helena's actions place the already questionable authority of the King of France into further question. Moreover, while the compliant Bassanio presents very little opposition to Portia's designs, Bertram offers determined resistance to Helena's. From this standpoint, Helena appears the more powerful figure: she triumphs over greater opposition. Finally, because she lacks the upper-class status that Portia takes for granted, Helena has to traverse a greater social distance to reach the levers of power; by this measure, Helena alters the balance of power to a degree that Portia does not and her victory is consequently more socially disruptive. This view helps to account for the comparatively more strained ending of *All's Well That Ends Well*.

14. I present an alternative, critical account in chapter 5, "The Limitations of Reformed Masculinity in *The Winter's Tale*," in *Patriarchal Structures in Shakespeare's Drama*, pp. 148–72. In "T. S. Eliot and the Creation of a Symbolist Shakespeare"—*Twentieth Century Literature in Retrospect* (Harvard English Studies 2), ed. Reuben A. Brower (Cambridge: Harvard University Press, 1971), pp. 191–204—G. K. Hunter criticizes Eliot's treatment, influenced by G. Wilson Knight's *The Wheel of Fire* (1930), of the late romances. However, Hunter's own method recapitulates Eliot's view. Hence the romances demonstrate "the power of a new poetic vision," "allowing the recognition scene to be human without infringing the symbolic power of the event" (introduction to the New Arden edition of *All's Well That Ends Well*, p. lvi). Reading back from this view of the late romances projects an ideal of harmonious resolution that mitigates and distorts the experience of gender conflict in *All's Well That Ends Well*. Moreover, the ultimate assurance of Perdita's high birth in *The Winter's Tale* eliminates the problem of class difference that Helena presents so sharply.

15. Because of this doubling effect, I would rephrase Muriel Bradbrook's claim that "by making his social climber a woman, Shakespeare took a good deal of the sting out of the affair" ("Virtue Is the True Nobility: A Study of the Structure of *All's Well That Ends Well*," *The Review of English Studies* 1, n.s., no. 4 [October 1950]: 289–301, quotation from p. 297). Helena's combined lower-class and female status, on the contrary, increases the sting. Technically Helena's power is derived from her father's medical expertise, but her own female initiative quickly outstrips the paternal derivation. Moreover, Helena's spectacular success in curing the king is noteworthy because in England the male Royal College of Physicians in effect excluded women from the medical profession.

16. J. Dover Wilson, *The Essential Shakespeare: A Biographical Adventure* (Cambridge: Cambridge University Press, 1932), pp. 58–59.

17. In *The Whole Journey: Shakespeare's Power of Development* (Berkeley and Los Angeles: University of California Press, 1986), C. L. Barber and Richard P. Wheeler discuss *All's Well That Ends Well* on pp. 15–18, 161, 190–91, and 196; quotation from p. 17.

18. It is indicative of the ideological power of norms—and of Shakespeare's implication in them—that Petruchio's handling of Kate in *The Taming of the Shrew* can appear humorous and beneficial, while the reversal of gender roles results in a mood that is strained and unpleasant: the motif of the dominant woman and the resisting male forbids similar comic treatment. The potential tragic cast of Bertram's situation can be suggested by reference to Coriolanus, whose aristocratic military identity is broken not only by his mother's manipulations but also by vulnerability to a lower-class threat. The difference is that Bertram faces this double gender and class threat combined in the single person of Helena.

19. In "The Third Eye: An Essay on *All's Well That Ends Well*," in his *The Sovereign Flower* (London: Methuen, 1958), pp. 93–160, G. Wilson Knight assumes a trouble-free continuity between Helena and Shakespeare by positing a "creative bisexuality" (p. 156) that they share. Thus Shakespeare's androgynous capacity gives him a direct, unobstructed connection with women: "Shakespeare's women lovers may be said to have been created from the female element in his own soul" (p. 132). Opposing this line of approach, I argue against an authorial androgyny that enables Shakespeare to transcend gender conflict and in favor of his problematic involvement as a male author in the sexual political struggles he stages. It is symptomatic of Knight's thinking that he can so easily find the "new form of society where the female values will be in the ascendent," which he sees prefigured by the play, "darkly symbolized in the queenship of Shakespeare's age" (p. 160). This concluding bit of idealism ignores complicated questions about Elizabeth's status in a patriarchal culture and about Shakespeare's dramatization of this dilemma.

CHAPTER 4

1. Barber's commentary occurs in the middle section, "Piety, Outrage, and Theatrical Aggression in *Hamlet*," of chapter 8 in *The Whole Journey: Shakespeare's Power of Development* (Berkeley and Los Angeles: University of California Press, 1986), pp. 255–72; quotations are from the heart of Barber's argument on pp. 266–67.

For similar comments on *Hamlet*'s lack of ironic control, see pp. 50–51 and 157–58 of Barber's *Creating Elizabethan Tragedy: The Theater of Marlowe and Kyd* (Chicago: University of Chicago Press, 1988), to which Richard P. Wheeler contributes an introduction particularly valuable for its effort to place Barber's work in relation to new historicism.

2. The following discussion builds upon and assumes my previous analysis of the pattern of gender relations in *Hamlet*, in *Patriarchal Structures in Shakespeare's Drama* (Berkeley and Los Angeles: University of California Press, 1985), pp. 66–80. Since my present focus is strictly Elizabethan, I should note that my reservations about Shakespeare's treatment of gender extend to the Jacobean tragedies, as analyzed in my earlier book.

3. Harold Jenkins's New Arden edition (London: Methuen, 1982), p. 13, G. R. Hibbard's Oxford edition (Oxford: Oxford University Press, 1987), pp. 4–5, and David Bevington's Bantam edition (New York: Bantam Books, 1988), pp. xxx–xxxi and 151, concur in giving 1599–1601 as the range of dates for *Hamlet*.

4. In *The Essential Shakespeare: A Biographical Adventure* (Cambridge: Cambridge University Press, 1932), J. Dover Wilson states that, though "Hamlet is not Essex," "everything is there" in the play: "Shakespeare loved Essex. . . . Thus he not only shared in the general horror and grief at the earl's fall; he felt it in a personal fashion" (pp. 104–7). The opening chapter of David Bevington's *Tudor Drama and Politics: A Critical Approach to Topical Meaning* (Cambridge: Harvard University Press, 1968) makes specific reference to the equation of Essex with Hamlet (pp. 21–23). In "'Jack hath not Jill': Failed Courtship in Lyly and Shakespeare," *Shakespeare Survey* 42 (1989): 1–13, Bevington marks the shift from "the 'old' historicism" of "political allegory" to the "broader topical level" of new historicist concern with the symbolic effects of "an Eliza figure" (pp. 2, 5). The latter approach makes it possible to combine "political and psychological readings . . . if we imagine that Queen Elizabeth's flirtatious ways of holding her courtiers at bay simply exacerbated the dualizing Petrarchan sensibility that was already there in the courtly attitudes of the governing class" (p. 3).

5. Annabel Patterson, *Shakespeare and the Popular Voice* (Cambridge, Mass.: Basil Blackwell, 1989), p. 178, n. 7. For Patterson, the signs of Essex's cultural impact on *Hamlet* are twofold: the term "late innovation" (2.2.331) incorporates a specific reference to Essex's rebellion in 1601 (p. 27); and, more generally, the play's tone communicates a sense of "national crisis" (p. 11), "a *fin de siècle* malaise, which in England at the turn of the sixteenth century was exacerbated by two related events from which no one could avert his eyes: the Essex rebellion and the imminent death of Elizabeth" (pp. 93–94).

In *Hero and Saint: Shakespeare and the Graeco-Roman Tradition* (New York: Oxford University Press, 1971), Reuben A. Brower links Essex's revolt with Laertes's return (p. 304)—a threat powerfully conveyed by Laertes's violent entry into the king's presence: "The doors are broke" (4.5.11). But surely fear of popular revolt also fits Claudius's perception of Hamlet (4.3.2–7; 4.7.16–24).

6. Peter Stallybrass, "Time Space and Unity: The Symbolic Discourse of *The Faerie Queene*," in *Patriotism: The Making and Unmaking of British National Identity*, ed. Raphael Samuel (London: Routledge, 1989), vol. 3, pp. 199–214; quotation from p. 204. On gardens as part of the cult of Elizabeth, see Roy Strong, *The Renaissance Garden in England* (London: Thames and Hudson, 1979), pp. 45–49.

7. On the Ditchley portrait, see Roy Strong, *Gloriana: The Portraits of Queen Elizabeth I* (London: Thames and Hudson, 1987), pp. 134–41, and the brief comment on p. 55 of Richard Helgerson, "The Land Speaks: Cartography, Choreography, and Subversion in Renaissance England," *Representations* 16 (Fall 1986); 50–85.

8. Barber, *The Whole Journey*, p. 271.

9. Louis Adrian Montrose, "Of Gentlemen and Shepherds: The Politics of Elizabethan Pastoral Form," *English Literary History* 50 (1983): 415–59; quotation from p. 426.

10. In "Essex and the Art of Dying," *Huntington Library Quarterly* 13 (1950): 109–29, Beach Langston demonstrates that Essex's end was composed along the lines of *ars moriendi* convention and that Essex "died according to the book" (p. 128).

11. Essex's long poem "The Passion of a Discontented Mind" is discussed in Edward Doughtie's "The Earl of Essex and Occasions for Contemplative Verse," *English Literary Renaissance* 9 (1979): 355–63, and in Stephen W. May's edition of Essex's poetry in *Studies in Philology* 77, no. 5 (1980). What makes it plausible that Essex could compose the poem in such a compressed time frame is its conventional structure: under the right precipitating circumstances, the poem in a sense writes itself. The poem's penitential stance resonates with a similar motif in *Hamlet*: Gertrude's confession (3.4.89–91) recalls the poem's image of a spotted soul (line 23); Claudius's attempted repentance (3.3.97–98) parallels Essex's struggle (lines 161–62) as does Hamlet's partial repentance (3.4.175). The poem's mood is consonant with Hamlet's: both Essex and Hamlet are portrayed as experiencing an acute sensation of exposure and inadequacy. Hamlet's juxtaposition of "how like an angel" with "this quintessence of dust" (2.2.306–8) corresponds to Essex's outcry (lines 181–82). Like Hamlet, Essex wrestles with "The worme of conscience" (line 151); like Hamlet, Essex is driven by a self-torturing, self-lacerating emphasis on tears.

12. See Nancy Lee Beaty, *The Craft of Dying: A Study of the Literary Tradition of the Ars Moriendi in England* (New Haven: Yale University Press, 1970).

13. Harry Berger, "*Ars Moriendi* in Progress, or John of Gaunt

and the Practice of Strategic Dying," *Yale Journal of Criticism* 1 (1987): 39–65. Gaunt's death exemplifies the overlapping of *ars moriendi* and pastoral since his parting words include the peroration on England as garden (2.1.31–68).

14. Though courageous for its time, Carolyn Heilbrun's "The Character of Hamlet's Mother," *Shakespeare Quarterly* 8 (1957): 201–6, falls well short of a ringing defense. Rebecca Smith's later essay—"A Heart Cleft in Twain: The Dilemma of Shakespeare's Gertrude," in *The Woman's Part: Feminist Criticism of Shakespeare*, ed. Carolyn Ruth Swift Lenz, Gayle Greene, and Carol Thomas Neely (Urbana: University of Illinois Press, 1980), pp. 194–210—more candidly concedes that the best a characterological approach can achieve is to substitute one female stereotype for another: "However, if she were presented on stage and film as only her own words and deeds create her, Gertrude might become another stereotypical character: the nurturing, loving, careful mother and wife—malleable, submissive, totally dependent, and solicitous of others at the expense of herself. This is still a stereotype" (p. 207).

15. The text I use for Essex's device is taken from *The Letters and Life of Francis Bacon Including All His Occasional Works*, ed. James Spedding (London: Longman, Green, Longman, and Roberts, 1861), vol. 1, pp. 374–91; vol. 1 is numbered vol. 8 in the complete *Works of Francis Bacon*. In Appendix I, "Sources for the Accession Day Tilts," in his *Cult of Elizabeth: Elizabethan Portraiture and Pageantry* (London: Thames and Hudson, 1977), Roy Strong provides "a suggested order" of speeches (p. 209).

16. On Essex's role in the composition of the device, see Steven W. May's discussion of attribution (pp. 88–90).

17. On court entertainment in general, see Marie Axton, "The Tudor Mask and Elizabethan Court Drama," in *English Drama: Forms and Development, Essays in Honour of Muriel Clara Bradbrook*, ed. Marie Axton and Raymond Williams (Cambridge: Cambridge University Press, 1977), pp. 24–47; and *The Queen's Two Bodies: Drama and the Elizabethan Succession* (London: Royal Historical Society, 1977). For the specific context of Essex's 1595 device, see Roy Strong, "Fair England's Knights: The Accession Day Tournaments," in his *Cult of Elizabeth*, pp. 129–62.

18. This observation is recorded in Rowland Whyte's letter to Sir Robert Sydney, as quoted by David H. Horne in *The Life and Minor Works of George Peele* (New Haven: Yale University Press, 1952), p. 180. Peele's praise of Essex's device in *Anglorum Feriae* (1595) extends the enthusiastic acceptance Elizabeth herself denied. But Peele's simplified, compressed version of the device (lines 190–209 on pp. 270–71 of Horne's edition) eliminates the palpable tension conveyed by the device's self-assertive tone. In *George Peele* (Boston: Twayne,

1983), A. R. Braunmuller gives an account of Peele's poem (pp. 21–22).

19. Edgar Wind, *Pagan Mysteries in the Renaissance* (New York: Norton, 1968).

20. Rowland Whyte's letter cited in n. 18.

21. So far as Bacon's involvement in Essex's device is concerned, F. J. Levy's "Francis Bacon and the Style of Politics," *English Literary Renaissance* 16 (1986): 101–22, provides an interesting context. In Levy's account, during the 1590s Bacon's career went through a crisis, which was part of a larger "crisis in English politics" (p. 102): in 1593, Bacon was committed to the ideals of civic humanism and conscience; in 1597 he had completed the transition to an aphoristic, ambiguous "language of seeming" (p. 111). Coming in the middle of this period, the 1595 device belongs primarily to the earlier phase. The neoplatonic idealism goes with a forthright political humanism, and the device repeats and extends Bacon's previous outspokenness: "In essence, Bacon had set himself, and his private conscience, as equal to the Queen. That was what Elizabeth found unforgivable. She required royal servants, not equals" (p. 109).

22. As reported in the abstract (my only source) of her paper "Narcissus Interrupted: Specularity and Succession in Spenser's *Faerie Queene*," in *Spenser Newsletter* 21, 1 (Winter 1990): 16–17, Linda Gregerson makes the same point: "But Philautia's gender and iconography suggest that she is not simply a mirror of Essex's narcissism: she is 'implicitly equated with the Queen in her withholding humor.'" Roy Strong provides a possible visual image of Essex's Philautia in "Fair England's Knights: The Accession Day Tournaments," p. 145.

23. Robert Lacey, *Robert, Earl of Essex* (New York: Atheneum, 1971), pp. 241–42. Lacey's narrative is melodramatically inflated, but so is the imagination Hamlet projects.

24. The first quotation is from Harry Berger, "The Renaissance Imagination: Second World and Green World" (1965), in his *Second World and Green World: Studies in Renaissance Fiction-Making* (Berkeley and Los Angeles: University of California Press, 1988), p. 15. The second quotation is from Stephen Greenblatt, *Shakespearean Negotiations: The Circulation of Social Energy in Renaissance England* (Berkeley and Los Angeles: University of California Press, 1988), p. 8.

25. In *Hero and Saint*, Reuben Brower underlines Fortinbras's phrase "Like a soldier" (pp. 313–15), but the artifice of Hamlet's martial image promotes rather than undercuts the play's effect as fantasy, to which Hamlet's sense of role playing has all along contributed.

26. Ray Heffner, "Essex, the Ideal Courtier," *English Literary History* 1 (1934): 7–36.

27. E. P. Kuhl, "The Earl of Essex and Liberalism," *Philological Quarterly* 24 (1945): 187–90.

28. The text of this letter is given in Walter Bourchier Devereux, *Lives and Letters of the Devereux, Earls of Essex* (London: John Murray, 1853), vol. 1, pp. 499–502.

29. Richard C. McCoy's *The Rites of Knighthood: The Literature and Politics of Elizabethan Chivalry* (Berkeley and Los Angeles: University of California Press, 1989) provides a subtle account of Essex in chapter 4. Yet the book's overall framework situates Essex in a more positive political context than is warranted. The book begins and ends with the nodal point of Essex's rebellion (pp. 2, 157). The introduction locates a powerful source of subversion in Essex's chivalric challenge (pp. 3, 8), while the epilogue recuperates Essex in an extenuating, plangently upbeat historical sketch that issues in Milton. McCoy is reacting to the apparent disallowance of subversion in some new historicist criticism, but in my view finds an unconvincing—and certainly more problematic than he acknowledges—location for subversion in Essex's actions.

In related work, Annabel Patterson's account of Essex ends on the optimistic note of the future parliamentary extension of Essex's spirit (p. 92). Patterson's *Shakespeare and the Popular Voice* uses a populist version of Essex as one basis for constructing a radical Shakespeare that can serve as inspiration for the political needs of our own time. What is unusual about Patterson's approach is that she finds Shakespeare capable of breaking the historical time barrier, not because of his artistic transcendence, but because of his political acuity. I would argue, however, that the Essex-Shakespeare connection makes Shakespeare historically time-bound: the cultural congruency of Essex's political stance and Shakespeare's dramatic work shows the latter's serious and unattractive limitations. For a critique of Patterson's use of Essex, see my otherwise strongly appreciative review of her book in *Criticism* 32 (1990): 534–37. In *Drama of a Nation: Public Theater in Renaissance England and Spain* (Ithaca: Cornell University Press, 1985), Walter Cohen suggests a different, and in my view more balanced and accurate, assessment of the radical element in elite factional conflict: "The conspirators, motivated by a combination of thwarted ambition at court and financial distress, often accompanied their desperate political activity with various forms of religious heterodoxy. Although the tendency of these men was toward reaction, they were sufficiently unstable to dabble in radicalism of the left as well" (p. 289).

CHAPTER 5

1. Paule Marshall's "Brazil" is included in her collection of stories, *Soul Clap Hands and Sing* (New York: Atheneum, 1961), pp.

131–77; Rita Dove's "Shakespeare Say" is found in her second volume of poetry, *Museum* (Pittsburgh: Carnegie Mellon University Press, 1983), pp. 33–34.

2. This concern with the present should not automatically be construed as ahistorical. What I have in mind are the points of contact between past and present that are struck across, and revealing of, historical difference, which Stephen Greenblatt refers to as resonance ("The Resonance of Renaissance Poetry," *ADE Bulletin* 64 [May 1980]: 7–10). In his most recent statement on "Culture," in *Critical Terms for Literary Study,* ed. Frank Lentricchia and Thomas McLaughlin (Chicago: University of Chicago Press, 1990), pp. 225–32, Greenblatt portrays resonance in a necessarily doubled historical perspective, as the tension between a voice's accent and its fulfillment: we can hear "the voice of the displaced and oppressed" in "the accents of Caliban," but "Caliban, of course, does not triumph: it would take different artists from different cultures—the postcolonial Caribbean and African cultures of our own times—to rewrite Shakespeare's play and make good on Caliban's claim" (p. 232).

3. In the Prologue to *An Appetite for Poetry,* Frank Kermode cites the following works, given in their chronological order: chapters 7 and 8 of *The Art of Telling: Essays on Fiction* (Cambridge: Harvard University Press, 1983); *Forms of Attention* (Chicago: University of Chicago Press, 1985); "Canon and Period," in *History and Value* (Oxford: Clarendon Press, 1988); *An Appetite for Poetry* (Cambridge: Harvard University Press, 1989).

4. Kermode, *The Art of Telling,* p. 179.

5. Kermode, *Forms of Attention,* pp. 88–89.

6. Kermode, *An Appetite for Poetry,* p. 8.

7. Kermode, *An Appetite for Poetry,* pp. 25, 22. Kermode's remark about the Renault factory touches a sensitive nerve if one considers how it taps into the concern expressed in Alan Sinfield's *Literature, Politics, and Culture in Postwar Britain* (Berkeley and Los Angeles: University of California Press, 1989): "Human freedom has gained immeasurably from the books of Raymond Williams but, revisiting Pandy, I met Mrs. Smith, the retired postmistress who remembers him as a boy; she told me she has never read one of them" (p. 268). The difference, however, is that while Kermode presents the issue as an unanswerable debating point, Sinfield treats it as a problem for which a workable approach can be found in a "middle-class dissidence" that does not assume it speaks for the working class (p. 274). Furthermore, there is an undue literalism involved in a too narrow focus on actual readership; the social impact of cultural work is not limited to those who have read specific items.

8. Kermode, *History and Value,* p. 126.

9. Kermode, *History and Value*, p. 126.

10. Frank Kermode, "The Last Classic," *Yale Review* 78, 2 (Winter 1989): 147–65. This essay is included in *An Appetite for Poetry*.

11. Frank Kermode, *The Classic: Literary Images of Permanence and Change* (New York: Viking Press, 1975).

12. That there is nothing normative or inevitable about Kermode's stance can be seen by comparing "The Last Classic" with Cynthia Ozick's "T. S. Eliot at 101" (*The New Yorker* [Nov. 20, 1989]). Ozick and Hilton Kramer debate the meaning of her article in "Cynthia Ozick, T. S. Eliot and High Culture: An Exchange," *The New Criterion* 8, 8 (April 1990): 5–10. On the evidence of his review, "T. S. Eliot's Anti-Semitism," in *Commentary* 89, 3 (March 1990): 63–66, I would argue that even Hilton Kramer's approach to Eliot differs significantly from Kermode's.

13. On black women writers, see Kermode, *History and Value*, pp. 113–14.

14. Kermode refers to "subcanons" in *History and Value*, p. 126.

15. Kermode, *History and Value*, p. 114.

16. Raymond Williams, *The Long Revolution* (London: Chatto and Windus, 1961), pp. 50–53.

17. Francis Mulhern, *The Moment of "Scrutiny"* (London: NLB, 1979), pp. 154–57. Also see Mulhern's discussion of Leavis in "English Reading," in *Nation and Narration*, ed. Homi K. Bhabha (London: Routledge, 1990), pp. 250–64.

18. On Leavis's relation to Eliot, see Bernard Bergonzi, "Leavis and Eliot: The Long Road to Rejection," *Critical Quarterly* 26 (1984): 21–43, and Denis Donoghue, "Leavis on Eliot," in his *England, Their England: Commentaries on English Language and Literature* (New York: Knopf, 1988), pp. 332–50.

19. In *Politics and Letters: Interviews with New Left Review* (London: NLB, 1979), Williams observes: "I knew perfectly well who I was writing against: Eliot, Leavis and the whole of the cultural conservatism that had formed around them" (p. 112).

20. See the exchange between Eagleton and Williams on this issue in *Raymond Williams: Critical Perspectives*, ed. Terry Eagleton (Boston: Northeastern University Press, 1989), pp. 180–81.

21. This cultural distinction between the United States and England is consistent with Frank Kermode's pattern of citing American critics as the source of tendencies he finds troubling. Specific instances are Houston Baker in *History and Value*, Jonathan Culler in *An Appetite for Poetry*, and Richard Poirier and Harold Bloom in "The Last Classic." Kermode comments on the American-British difference in the interview in *Poetry, Narrative, History* (Cambridge, Mass.: Basil Blackwell, 1990), pp. 77–81.

22. Two recent attempts have been made to defend Matthiessen

against Trilling's critique included in *The Liberal Imagination* (1950): Jonathan Arac, "F. O. Matthiessen: Authorizing an American Renaissance," in *The American Renaissance Reconsidered: Selected Papers from the English Institute, 1982–83*, ed. Walter Benn Michaels and Donald Pease (Baltimore: Johns Hopkins University Press, 1985), pp. 110–11, n. 20; and William E. Cain, *F. O. Matthiessen and the Politics of Criticism* (Madison: University of Wisconsin Press, 1988), pp. 120–23.

23. The combined influence of Eliot and Matthiessen enters Shakespeare studies through the work of C. L. Barber, as documented in my essay, "In Memory of C. L. Barber: 'The man working in his works,'" in *Shakespeare's "Rough Magic": Renaissance Essays in Honor of C. L. Barber*, ed. Peter Erickson and Coppélia Kahn (Newark: University of Delaware Press, 1985), pp. 303–22.

24. My principal sources of information about Trilling and about *Partisan Review* are Mark Krupnick, *Lionel Trilling and the Fate of Cultural Criticism* (Evanston: Northwestern University Press, 1986), and Alan Wald, *The New York Intellectuals: The Rise and Decline of the Anti-Stalinist Left from the 1930s to the 1980s* (Chapel Hill: University of North Carolina Press, 1987). Also helpful is the compendium of material in "The New York Intellectuals and *Partisan Review*," in *Twentieth-Century Literary Criticism*, ed. Paula Kepos and Dennis Poupard, vol. 30 (Detroit: Gale, 1989), pp. 117–98.

25. Lionel Trilling, "'Elements That Are Wanted,'" *Partisan Review* 7 (1940): 367–79.

26. *The Experience of Literature: A Reader with Commentaries*, ed. Lionel Trilling (Garden City, N.Y.: Doubleday, 1967), pp. 938–43.

27. Diana Trilling provides firsthand testimony in "Lionel Trilling, a Jew at Columbia," *Commentary* 67, 3 (March 1979): 40–46. On assimilation, see Mark Krupnick's chapters 2 and 3 in *Lionel Trilling and the Fate of Cultural Criticism.*

28. Mark Krupnick's "Fiction as Criticism," in *Lionel Trilling and the Fate of Cultural Criticism*, pp. 79–89, and Alan Wald's "The New York Intellectuals in Fiction," in *The New York Intellectuals*, pp. 231–39.

29. Don E. Wayne, "Power, Politics, and the Shakespearean Text: Recent Criticism in England and the United States," in *Shakespeare Reproduced: The Text in History and Ideology*, ed. Jean E. Howard and Marion F. O'Connor (London: Methuen, 1987), pp. 47–67, particularly pp. 53–56. Cornel West's discussion of Trilling in "Minority Discourse and the Pitfalls of Canon Formation," *Yale Journal of Criticism* 1 (1987): 193–201, and in *The American Evasion of Philosophy: A Genealogy of Pragmatism* (Madison: University of Wisconsin Press, 1989), pp. 164–78, seems to me useful for extending Wayne's argument.

30. In the interview in Robert Moynihan's *A Recent Imagining*

(Hamden, Conn.: Archon Books, 1986), Hartman, after citing Lionel Trilling's difficulties at Columbia, remarks that "there existed at Yale until the 1960s what goes under the name of cultural anti-Semitism" (p. 85). Hartman's "The Longest Shadow," *Yale Review* 78 (1989): 485–96, specifies T. S. Eliot as epitomizing the environment that he "was working against" (p. 489).

31. Louis Montrose, "Introductory Essay," in Harry Berger, *Revisionary Play: Studies in the Spenserian Dynamics* (Berkeley and Los Angeles: University of California Press, 1988), pp. 8–9. Montrose's assessment receives confirmation from Frederick Crews's reference to the "ethnic obtuseness" of a Christian humanism linked to T. S. Eliot's "tonal influence" (*Skeptical Engagements* [New York: Oxford University Press, 1986], p. 211).

32. Harold Bloom, "Reflections on T. S. Eliot," *Raritan* 8, 2 (Fall 1988): 70–87. See also Bloom's spirited comment on Yale in the late fifties as "an Anglo-Catholic nightmare" in *Criticism in Society*, ed. Imre Salusinszky (New York: Methuen, 1987), p. 61.

33. Introduction to *William Shakespeare's The Merchant of Venice*, ed. Harold Bloom (New York: Chelsea House, 1986), p. 1.

34. Adrienne Rich, *Blood, Bread, and Poetry: Selected Prose, 1974–1985* (New York: Norton, 1986), pp. 104–5.

35. In "The Ideology of Canon-Formation: T. S. Eliot and Cleanth Brooks," *Critical Inquiry* 10 (1983): 173–98, John Guillory observes that Bloom "obviously and urgently rewrites 'Tradition and the Individual Talent,' which suggests to me that Eliot's work is still the Ur-text of critical ideology" (p. 198, n. 24). The connection to Eliot holds for Bloom but not, as I shall argue, for Rich.

36. T. S. Eliot, "Tradition and the Individual Talent," in *The Sacred Wood* (London: Methuen, 1920), pp. 42–53; Adrienne Rich, "When We Dead Awaken: Writing as Re-Vision," *On Lies, Secrets, and Silence: Selected Prose, 1966–1978* (New York: Norton, 1979), pp. 33–49.

37. *Adrienne Rich's Poetry*, ed. Barbara Charlesworth Gelpi and Albert Gelpi (New York: Norton, 1975), p. 204.

38. Rich, *Blood, Bread, and Poetry*, pp. x–xi.

39. "'Wholeness is No Trifling Matter': Some Fiction by Black Women," *New Women's Times Feminist Review*, no. 13 (December 1980/January 1981): 10–13, and no. 14 (February/March 1981): 12; quotation from second part of article.

40. Rich, "Ten Years Later: A New Introduction," in *Of Woman Born: Motherhood as Experience and Institution* (New York: Norton, 1986), pp. xxv–xxx.

41. "The Female and the Silence of a Man" appears in Jordan's *Naming Our Destiny: New and Selected Poems* (New York: Thunder's Mouth Press, 1989).

42. For a full survey of Jordan's poetry, see my articles: "June

Jordan," in *Dictionary of Literary Biography*, vol. 38: *Afro-American Writers after 1955: Dramatists and Prose Writers*, ed. Thadious M. Davis and Trudier Harris (Detroit: Gale, 1985), pp. 146–62; "The Love Poetry of June Jordan," *Callaloo*, no. 26 (Winter 1986): 221–34; and the review of the "North Star" section of new poems in *Naming Our Destiny*, in *Hurricane Alice: A Feminist Quarterly* 7, 1–2 (Winter/Spring 1990): 4–5.

43. Ursula K. LeGuin, *The Women's Review of Books* 6, 10–11 (July 1989): 26–27; Richard Poirier, *London Review of Books* 11, 19 (12 October 1989): 18–22.

CHAPTER 6

1. Cheney's quotation of Angelou occurs on pp. 14–15 of *Humanities in America: A Report to the President, the Congress, and the American People* (Washington, D.C.: National Endowment for the Humanities, September 1988). The original passage appears on pp. 4–5 of Angelou's "Journey to the Heartland" (address delivered at the National Association of Local Arts Agencies Convention, Cedar Rapids, Iowa, June 12, 1985) and is an amplification of Angelou's declaration of love for Shakespeare at the outset of the first volume of her autobiography, *I Know Why the Caged Bird Sings* (p. 10).

2. Raymond Williams's "A Hundred Years of Culture and Anarchy" (1970), in his *Problems in Materialism and Culture* (London: Verso, 1980), pp. 3–8, stresses this tension.

3. The five volumes of Maya Angelou's autobiographical sequence to date are: *I Know Why the Caged Bird Sings* (New York: Random House, 1970); *Gather Together in My Name* (New York: Random House, 1974); *Singin' and Swingin' and Gettin' Merry Like Christmas* (New York: Random House, 1976); *The Heart of a Woman* (New York: Random House, 1981); and *All God's Children Need Traveling Shoes* (New York: Random House, 1986).

4. Angelou's comment on the allusion in the title *The Heart of a Woman* appears in *Conversations with Maya Angelou*, ed. Jeffrey M. Elliot (Jackson: University Press of Mississippi, 1989), p. 117.

5. See Claudia Tate's interview of Angelou in *Black Women Writers at Work* (New York: Continuum, 1983), p. 11.

6. Christine Froula, "The Daughter's Seduction: Sexual Violence and Literary History," *Signs* 11 (1986): 621–44, quotation from p. 636. Using Alice Walker's *Color Purple* to provide a comparative perspective on Angelou, Froula remarks that Walker's work is "more powerful" because it involves a more fundamental cultural revision (p. 637). See also Marjorie Garber's discussion of Angelou in "Shakespeare as Fetish," *Shakespeare Quarterly* 41 (1990): 242–50.

CHAPTER 7

1. *Rewriting the Renaissance: The Discourses of Sexual Difference in Early Modern Europe*, ed. Margaret W. Ferguson, Maureen Quilligan, and Nancy J. Vickers (Chicago: University of Chicago Press, 1986).
2. Recent work on Matthiessen includes Jonathan Arac, "F. O. Matthiessen: Authorizing an American Renaissance," in *The American Renaissance Reconsidered: Selected Papers from the English Institute, 1982–83*, ed. Walter Benn Michaels and Donald E. Pease (Baltimore: Johns Hopkins University Press, 1985), pp. 90–112; Sacvan Bercovitch, "The Problem of Ideology in American Literary History," *Critical Inquiry* 12 (1986): 631–53; Donald E. Pease, "F. O. Matthiessen," in *Modern American Critics, 1920–1955*, ed. Gregory S. Jay (Detroit: Gale, 1988), pp. 138–48; William E. Cain, *F. O. Matthiessen and the Politics of Criticism* (Madison: University of Wisconsin Press, 1988).
3. Gloria T. Hull, *Color, Sex and Poetry: Three Women Writers of the Harlem Renaissance* (Bloomington: Indiana University Press, 1987). See also *Shadowed Dreams: Women's Poetry of the Harlem Renaissance*, ed. Maureen Honey (New Brunswick: Rutgers University Press, 1989).
4. Gloria Naylor and Toni Morrison, "A Conversation," *Southern Review* 21 (1985): 567–93, quotation from p. 589; hereafter cited as "Conversation." Morrison's use of the term *renaissance* is repeated in *Wild Women in the Whirlwind: Afra-American Culture and the Contemporary Literary Renaissance*, ed. Joanne M. Braxton and Andrée Nicola McLaughlin (New Brunswick: Rutgers University Press, 1990).
5. Karen Newman, "'And wash the Ethiop white': Femininity and the Monstrous in *Othello*," in *Shakespeare Reproduced: The Text in History and Ideology*, ed. Jean E. Howard and Marion F. O'Connor (New York: Methuen, 1987), pp. 141–62. Naylor glances only briefly at Othello in *Mama Day* (p. 64), where she finds other points of entry into Shakespeare more useful. In her passing reference to Othello in *The Temple of My Familiar* (San Diego: Harcourt Brace Jovanovich, 1989), Alice Walker emphasizes what Shakespeare's play omits: "'But did you never wonder why, in the little bit of the story the whites could not prevent Shakespeare, at least, from trying to tell . . . that there are only Moors (defined as men) and no Moor*esses*?'" (p. 195). In shifting her focus to the missing black female, Walker implicitly notes the play's limitations as an imaginative resource.
6. Naylor's first three novels are *The Women of Brewster Place* (New York: Viking Press, 1982); *Linden Hills* (New York: Ticknor and Fields, 1985); and *Mama Day* (New York: Ticknor and Fields, 1988). The fourth novel, *Bailey's Cafe*, is mentioned in Bronwyn Mills's interview article, "Gloria Naylor: Dreaming the Dream," *Sojourner* (May 1988): 17; hereafter cited as Mills.

7. A full analysis of this aspect of the play is given in Shirley Nelson Garner's "*A Midsummer Night's Dream:* 'Jack shall have Jill; / Nought shall go ill,'" *Women's Studies* 9, 1 (1981): 47–63.

8. The resonance of the Southern location is increased when its autobiographical dimension is added: though born in New York City, Naylor "returned to the town of Robinsonville, Mississippi, where her family originated, to research folk medicine for *Mama Day*" (Mills, p. 17).

9. Marshall's third novel, *Praisesong for the Widow* (New York: G. P. Putnam's Sons, 1983), precedes *Mama Day* by five years.

10. In her introduction to her 1967 short story "To Da-duh in Memoriam," in *Reena and Other Stories* (Old Westbury: Feminist Press, 1983), p. 95, Marshall links the character Aunt Cuney with Da-duh, Marshall's grandmother. The balance of forces between New York City and black island culture to the south is quite differently portrayed in the two cases. The granddaughter's triumph in the short story is reversed sixteen years later in the novel, which awards power to the grandmother figure.

11. This criticism of *Praisesong for the Widow* is not intended as a generalization about Marshall's work as a whole. Her previous novel about Barbados, *The Chosen Place, the Timeless People* (1969), exhibits an acute political awareness; there is nothing inherent in a Caribbean island location that automatically excludes sensitivity to political questions.

12. Carby's argument is presented in "The Quicksands of Representation: Rethinking Black Cultural Politics," the final chapter in her *Reconstructing Womanhood: The Emergence of the Afro-American Woman Novelist* (New York: Oxford University Press, 1987), pp. 163–75, and elaborated in "Ideologies of Black Folk: The Historical Novel of Slavery," in *Slavery and the Literary Imagination: Selected Papers from the English Institute, 1987,* ed. Deborah E. McDowell and Arnold Rampersad (Baltimore: Johns Hopkins University Press, 1989), pp. 125–43. The critical reassessment of the central folk line defined by the Alice Walker–Zora Neale Hurston connection is exemplified by Mary Helen Washington's reconsideration of *Their Eyes Were Watching God:* "'I Love the Way Janie Crawford Left Her Husbands': Zora Neale Hurston's Emergent Female Hero," in her *Invented Lives: Narratives of Black Women, 1860–1960* (Garden City: Doubleday, 1987), pp. 237–54.

13. Naylor comments in her own voice on football in the boxed inset, "Keeping Up with the Characters," accompanying the review of *Mama Day* in *The New York Times Book Review*, February 21, 1988, p. 7.

14. The survey is Alden T. Vaughn's, in his two articles "Caliban in the 'Third World': Shakespeare's Savage as Sociopolitical Sym-

bol," *Massachusetts Review* 29 (1988): 289–313 and "Shakespeare's Indian: The Americanization of Caliban," *Shakespeare Quarterly* 39 (1988): 137–53. Thomas Cartelli's "Prospero in Africa: *The Tempest* as Colonialist Text and Pretext," in *Shakespeare Reproduced*, pp. 99–115, is wholly occupied with the dynamics of the Prospero-Caliban relationship.

15. The mother is identified as an artist in Paule Marshall, "Shaping the World of My Art," *New Letters* 40, 1 (October 1973): 97–112 (subsequently incorporated in "From the Poets in the Kitchen," *New York Times Book Review*, [January 9, 1983]); Alice Walker, "In Search of Our Mothers' Gardens," *Ms.* (May 1974); and June Jordan, "Notes of a Barnard Dropout (1975)," in her *Civil Wars* (Boston: Beacon Press, 1981), pp. 96–102.

16. Just as Toni Morrison acknowledges Paule Marshall as a predecessor ("Conversation," p. 589), so Marshall names Gwendolyn Brooks as a precursor: see Marshall's contribution to "The Negro Woman in American Literature," *Freedomways* 6, 1 (Winter 1966): pp. 23–24.

17. For a detailed analysis, see my "Images of Nurturance in Toni Morrison's *Tar Baby*," *CLA Journal* 28, 1 (September 1984): 11–32.

18. In "The Woman in the Cave: Recent Feminist Fictions and the Classical Underworld," *Contemporary Literature* 29 (1988): 369–402, Margaret Homans suggests a parallel in *Linden Hills* between Willa Nedeed's relation to her husband and the quality of Naylor's recourse to Dante. Homans, moreover, praises Naylor's tacit admission of her literary containment or entrapment as an acknowledgment of "the limits of feminist revisionism" (p. 371). But two points need to be made. First, Naylor's dependence on the model of the *Inferno* is excessive and stifling; the cumbersome apparatus derived from Dante constitutes a structural weakness in the novel. Second, Naylor's situation in *Linden Hills* is not a fixed, final position. *Mama Day* reconsiders the conflict between male literary tradition and female author in very different terms, the difference being made not by the replacement of Dante by Shakespeare, who, like Dante, offers patriarchal forms that efface women, but rather by Naylor's more actively critical manner of negotiating her relations with the established tradition. *Mama Day* is the better for providing what Homans does not find in *Linden Hills*—the "countertradition of strong womanhood to oppose the destructive legacy of patriarchy" (p. 396). See Valerie Traub, "Rainbows of Darkness: Deconstructing Shakespeare in the Work of Gloria Naylor and Zora Neale Hurston," in vol. 2 of *Women's Re-Visions of Shakespeare*, ed. Marianne Novy (Urbana: University of Illinois Press, forthcoming).

19. Gloria T. Hull, "Afro-American Women Poets: A Bio-Critical Survey," in *Shakespeare's Sisters: Feminist Essays on Women Poets*, ed.

Sandra M. Gilbert and Susan Gubar (Bloomington: Indiana University Press, 1979), pp. 165–82; quotation from p. 165.

CHAPTER 8

1. The volumes of Rich's poetry cited here are, in chronological order, *A Change of World* (New Haven: Yale University Press, 1951); *The Diamond Cutters* (New York: Harper, 1955); *Snapshots of a Daughter-in-Law* (New York: Harper and Row, 1963); *Necessities of Life: Poems, 1962–1965* (New York: Norton, 1966); *Leaflets: Poems, 1965–1968* (New York: Norton, 1969); *The Will to Change: Poems, 1968–1970* (New York: Norton, 1971); *Diving into the Wreck: Poems, 1971–1972* (New York: Norton, 1973); *Poems Selected and New, 1950–1974* (New York: Norton, 1975); *The Dream of a Common Language: Poems, 1974–1977* (New York: Norton, 1978); *A Wild Patience Has Taken Me This Far: Poems, 1978–1981* (New York: Norton, 1981); *Sources* (Woodside, Calif.: Heyeck Press, 1983). Prose extracts are drawn from *On Lies, Secrets, and Silence: Selected Prose, 1966–1978* (New York: Norton, 1979); *Blood, Bread, and Poetry: Selected Prose, 1979–1985* (New York: Norton, 1986); *Of Woman Born: Motherhood as Experience and Institution*, Tenth Anniversary Edition (New York: Norton, 1986). For an extension of the present discussion to Rich's latest volume, *Time's Power: Poems, 1985–1988*, see my article in *Hurricane Alice: A Feminist Quarterly* 6, 4 (Fall/Winter 1989): 4–5.

2. In *Ariadne*, a play privately printed in 1939 when Rich was age ten, the daughter's experience of paternal constraints is clearly expressed, as is her desire for liberation from them. However, in *Not I, But Death*, Rich's second play two years later, the family motif is entirely absent, replaced by an extended meditation on suicide that may be partly inspired by Hamlet's "To be or not to be" speech.

3. The familial resonance of the term *perfection* is suggested by a later statement: "according to my father's plan," Rich was to be "the perfect daughter" (*Of Woman Born*, p. 223). In an interview with Elly Bulkin (*Conditions* 1 [April 1977]), Rich indicates that "Stepping Backward" was "addressed to a woman whom I was close to in my late 'teens,'" but notes that "it could have been written to anybody" (p. 64).

4. The convergence and doubling of father and husband implied here is explicitly indicated in the recent poem *Sources*. The difference between them turns out to be no difference:

> But there was also the other Jew. The one you most feared, the one from the *shtetl*, from Brooklyn, from the wrong part of history, the wrong accent, the wrong class. The one I left you for. The one both like and unlike you, who explained you to me for years. . . . The one who, like you, ended isolate. . . . For so many years I had thought you

and he were in opposition. I needed your unlikeness then; now it's
your likeness that stares me in the face.

This sense of repetition, of the similarity between parental figures
and the new marriage created by the departing daughter, informs
the poem "The Middle-Aged" in Rich's second volume, for it contains two discoveries: the revelation and indictment of the parents'
relationship, but also the anguished realization that the daughter
herself, in passing from youth to middle age, from innocence to
experience, has become implicated in the same terms:

> All to be understood by us, returning
> Late, in our own time—how that peace was made,
> Upon what terms, with how much left unsaid.

5. T. S. Eliot, "Ulysses, Order, and Myth," *The Dial* 75, 5 (November 1923): 480–83; quotation from p. 483.
6. On the father's role as the educator of his daughter, see
Rich's account in *Of Woman Born* (p. 222); on his specific involvement
in her poetic training, see her comment in "Split at the Root": "he
criticized my poems for faulty technique and gave me books on
rhyme and meter and form" (p. 113). In poetic distillation this becomes the image in *Sources:* "the room with the books / where the
father walks up and down / telling the child to *work, work.* . . ."
Additional details on the father's role as Rich's first teacher of poetry
are provided by the interview in *The Island* 3 (May 1966), p. 2, and
Wendy Martin's interview cited in *An American Triptych* (Chapel Hill:
University of North Carolina Press, 1984), p. 173. Arnold Rich's *New
York Times* obituary (April 19, 1968, p. 47) describes not only his
medical career but also his artistic activities, including the writing of
verse.
7. In context, the poem immediately following, "Mourning
Picture," recapitulates the attraction of the daughter's death. The
girl, as though from unbearable family pressures, predeceases her
parents, whom she envisions without her in a state of abandonment:
"my father and mother darkly sit there, in black clothes."
8. In an earlier poem about her sister's growing up, "At Majority," in *Snapshots of a Daughter-in-Law*, Rich had used Cordelia as a
positive image—"Grave as Cordelia's at the last"—signaling not
only that she acknowledged Shakespeare's preeminence but also
that her work was contained within a Shakespearean framework.
9. The complacent reference to Caliban in "At Hertford House,"
in *The Diamond Cutters*, indicates the self-critical aspect of Rich's new
perception.
10. The *New York Times* reports the suicide of Rich's husband in
an obituary notice on October 20, 1970, and "A Valediction Forbid-

ding Mourning" is dated 1970, but whether the poem refers only to the breakup of their marriage or is more specifically a response to the suicide remains uncertain. Wendy Martin in *An American Triptych* gives the sequence of events as follows: "In 1970, she left her marriage; later the same year, Alfred Conrad, her husband, committed suicide" (p. 187).

11. In a 1971 interview—"Talking with Adrienne Rich," *Ohio Review* 13 (1971): 29–46—Rich comments on

> what happens when a poet has to confront his "masters," you know, the old masters, and deal with the fact that he would really love to be doing what they were doing, but he can't, not from impotence, but just because that can't be done anymore. You know, Keats having to confront Shakespeare, having to confront Milton and say, "No. This is not what I want to do."
>
> (p. 39)

Quoting Shakespeare's Sonnet 55 as a mode she rejects (p. 41), Rich goes on to link literary revision to a more fundamental revision of the cultural construction of genders: "What it means to be a man, what it means to be a woman" becomes "the ultimate political question" that "is going to affect all the other questions" (p. 45). Shortly thereafter, the word *political* enters Rich's poetry as the last word of "Translations" in *Diving into the Wreck*.

12. *John Donne's Poetry* (Cambridge: Cambridge University Press, 1971), p. 86.

13. I owe this insight to Valerie Traub.

14. One of the new poems in *Poems Selected and New, 1950–1974* takes Freud's term *family romance* as its title in order to reconstitute it. The absence of the father which makes possible a different image of the family is literally the case for Rich's sons—"Since we had no father to bless us, we were free"—and is effectively true for Rich as daughter in that her father withheld the parental blessing.

15. For this reason there is a contradiction in Helen Vendler's recommendation, after previously acknowledging the validity of Rich's development beyond the "Hermione-statue always there when her husband chose to come back" imaged in "An Unsaid Word" in her first volume, that Rich return to Shakespeare: "Why not tell women to imitate Keats or Shakespeare? There are models for such 'thinking through the body'; that they are men does not vitiate their usefulness" (*Part of Nature, Part of Us: Modern American Poets* [Cambridge: Harvard University Press, 1980], pp. 239, 267). Vendler treats the body here as though it were ungendered and thereby she avoids the issue of Shakespeare's adequacy to the questions of gender difference and of sexual politics that Rich raises.

16. This continuing critical perspective is what makes *Sources* dif-

ferent from the ideal father-daughter union Sharon Olds imagines in "My Father's Breasts" (*The Dead and the Living* [New York: Knopf, 1984]). In Rich's refiguration, her father's suffering beneath "the face of patriarchy" is made visible. But this realization of the father's vulnerability is made possible only by her prior opposition to patriarchy. It presupposes, as she puts it in her essay on Emily Dickinson, the process of "movement from childhood to womanhood, of transcending the patriarchal condition of bearing her father's name and 'crowing—on my Father's breast—'" (*On Lies, Secrets, and Silence*, p. 172). The discovery of paternal suffering leads Rich to reaffirm rather than to abandon these premises. My feeling for Sharon Olds's poem as well as for the project of "uncovering this invisible father" is informed by Patricia Yaeger's essay "The Father's Breasts," in *Refiguring the Father: New Feminist Readings of Patriarchy*, ed. Patricia Yaeger and Beth Kowaleski-Wallace (Carbondale: Southern Illinois University Press, 1989), pp. 3–21. It is worth noting that Olds's new poems on the father in *The Gold Cell* (New York: Knopf, 1987) display far greater ambivalence.

    17. Vendler hopes for "a new generosity" in Rich's work in the final line of her review of *Diving into the Wreck* (*Part of Nature, Part of Us*, p. 262). What I most admire about Vendler is her continuing commitment to Rich as an indispensable poet. Vendler's opening statement in 1973—"Someone my age was writing down my life. . . . But here was a poet who seemed, by a miracle, a twin: I had not known till then how much I had wanted a contemporary and a woman as a speaking voice of life" (*Part of Nature, Part of Us*, p. 237)—is matched by the need expressed in her most recent review of Rich—"I have read, and not for political reasons, almost everything she has written" ("A Plain-Style Poet," review of *The Fact of a Doorframe*, *The New Republic* 192 [January 7 and 14, 1985]: 32–34). However, Vendler's sense of twinship with Rich has been marked from the outset by defensiveness. This identification means, on the one hand, that Vendler cannot stop reading and reviewing Rich and, on the other, that she cannot stop censuring Rich and wishing/advising her to be different. Vendler's praise of *Diving into the Wreck* is apologetic and guarded. The praise is summarily withdrawn in Vendler's attack on *Of Woman Born* (in *Part of Nature, Part of Us*); remains faint in "All Too Real," review of *A Wild Patience Has Taken Me This Far*, *New York Review of Books* (December 17, 1981): 32–36; then revives, but conditionally: "From a poet who believes this, all things are to be hoped" (last line of "A Plain-Style Poet"). The latter two reviews have now been collected in *The Music of What Happens: Poems, Poets, Critics* (Cambridge: Harvard University Press, 1988).

    The chief problem with Vendler's writing on Rich is that Vendler lends her considerable prestige to the absolute separation of poetry and politics and to the view that the latter can only be a hindrance to the former. But even Vendler's subtlety and elegance cannot conceal the intellectual thinness of her claim to "find Rich more often a personal poet, psychological rather than social" ("A Plain-Style Poet," p. 33). Rich's poetry unquestionably possesses a powerful psychological dimension, but this can be severed from Rich's politics only by a studied indifference to what Rich means by political and to how it enables rather than reduces her psychological perception. Vendler concedes that "all writing is ideologically motivated"—"To that remark there is no response" (*Part of Nature, Part of Us*, p. 270), but she does not write with full awareness that her own position is ideological, preferring to imply that she herself can occupy the nonideological high ground.

18. *Sources* may be seen as an answer to Helen Vendler's claim that Rich "refuses full existential reality to men" (*Part of Nature, Part of Us*, p. 265). If so, it is an answer on Rich's terms, not Vendler's: "If women cease to channel their energies toward the nurture and the consolation and the emotional feeding of men, men are going to have to start acting more humanly for themselves. . . . And then they will begin to have an existential reality which they have been hitherto denied" (Interview with Blanche M. Boyd, *Christopher Street* [January 1977], p. 11). Rich is firm in her insistence that men must change, but her perception of both their present and potential existential reality is extremely sensitive. Vendler repeats her charge—"It is hard to believe in an empathy reserved for one segment of humanity alone"—citing three examples: "Whitman tending the Civil War dead; Keats tending his dying brother; Arthur Severn tending the dying Keats" ("All Too Real," p. 34). However, Vendler's predilection for the individual and personal and her refusal to consider social context mean that she neither meets nor touches Rich's discussion of overall cultural values. Keats's care of his brother does not in itself prove that his poetic representation of genders is free of patriarchal assumptions.

19. Lamenting the betrayal of her poetic sensitivity by the crudeness of politics is a staple of negative responses to Rich's poetry. An early example is Robert Boyers's review in *Salmagundi* 22–23 (Spring–Summer, 1973): 132–48; of particular interest are his discussion of "After Dark" as a model of what is best in Rich and his use of the term *generous* to describe his approval of the sensibility he finds in this poem. A recent instance is William Logan's review in *The New York Times Book Review*, January 18, 1987, p. 13. Rich comments on Logan's opposition of poetry and politics in the final paragraph of an article by Nan Robertson—"A Poet's Political and Literary Life," *The New York Times*, June 10, 1987, p. C21.

20. One reason for the intricacy of political inquiry in Rich's po-

etry is its dramatization as a speaking voice with "all kinds of things happening in it." In the *Ohio Review* interview, Rich draws attention to "the speaking voice in the poem":

> The other thing is . . . over against that image-making, I'm very much interested in the possibilities of the 'plainest statement' at times, the kind of things that people say to each other at moments of stress. . . .
> . . . But you get started, don't you, with a kind of tone. And the tone of voice and the intonation dictate a kind of basic line length, and then they also dictate something which is like paragraphing in writing prose, that there are certain lengths of statement, lengths of voice, of monologue, if you want to call it that, that emerge, and they break up into sections. Then you begin something new—a verse paragraph . . . It's like conversation. I mean, I'm sure if we really sat and listened to this tape we could hear the conversation speeding up, slowing down, all kinds of things happening in it.
>
> (pp. 37–40)

In a more recent interview in Stanford Institute for Research on Women and Gender, *Newsletter* 11, no. 2 (Winter 1987): 1–3, Rich remarks: "I think my poetry is much more orally generated than visually" (p. 2).

21. The most striking expression of Rich's reorientation toward Marxism is her review of Raya Dunayevskaya's writing in "Living the Revolution," *The Women's Review of Books* 3, 12 (September 1986): 1, 3–4. For Spivak's work, see "Feminism and Critical Theory," in *For Alma Mater: Theory and Practice in Feminist Scholarship*, ed. Paula A. Treichler, Cheris Kramarae, and Beth Stafford (Urbana: University of Illinois Press, 1985), pp. 119–42, and reprinted in her *In Other Worlds: Essays in Cultural Politics* (New York: Methuen, 1987); and "Imperialism and Sexual Difference," *Oxford Literary Review* 8 (1986): 225–38.

22. My own critical view of the sexual politics of gender-role assignments in *King Lear* and *The Winter's Tale* is given in *Patriarchal Structures in Shakespeare's Drama* (Berkeley and Los Angeles: University of California Press, 1985), pp. 105–15 and 148–72.

23. " 'This Is and Is Not Cressid': The Characterization of Cressida," in *The (M)other Tongue: Essays in Feminist Psychoanalytic Interpretation*, ed. Shirley Nelson Garner, Claire Kahane, and Madelon Sprengnether (Ithaca: Cornell University Press, 1985), pp. 140–41.

24. I share Alan Sinfield's opposition to "appropriation—the attempt to juggle the text into acceptability" because it collapses the two separate steps that should comprise historical exploration:

> We should use these resources to recreate imaginatively an alien society and its informing ideology, and to locate the text within those structures. The scholar may wish to rest there, but the reader who demands modern relevance may use this recreated otherness as a

vantage point from which to re-examine and reassess present-day attitudes, allowing the alien perspective to stimulate and provoke.

("Against Appropriation,"
Essays in Criticism 31 [1981]: 182)

I would argue, however, that the second step is not optional and that consideration of "modern relevance" is a necessary part of the scholar's task.

25. For further commentary on Woolf's account of Shakespeare and on Rich's critique, see n. 5 (pp. 252–53) of my "Shakespeare and the 'Author-Function,'" in *Shakespeare's "Rough Magic": Renaissance Essays in Honor of C. L. Barber*, ed. Peter Erickson and Coppélia Kahn (Newark: University of Delaware Press, 1985). Chapter 4 of Alice Fox's *Virginia Woolf and the Literature of the English Renaissance* (Oxford: Oxford University Press, 1990) provides a useful survey of Woolf's references to Shakespeare.

26. The concept of androgyny figures not only in Woolf's image of Shakespeare's mind and in *Orlando*; it operates as well in *To the Lighthouse*, as Maria DiBattista signifies by using Carolyn Heilbrun's phrase "The Grace of Androgyny" for the title of the final section of the chapter on the novel in her *Virginia Woolf's Major Novels: Fables of Anon* (New Haven: Yale University Press, 1980), pp. 100, 109. The official poetic announcement of Rich's rejection of this concept occurs in "Natural Resources" in *The Dream of a Common Language*, but it is also present as a subtext in "Integrity," whose opening line provides the title *A Wild Patience Has Taken Me This Far*. Revising "The Stranger" in *Diving into the Wreck*, in which androgyny served as a vehicle for reconciling anger and mercy, Rich now associates the combination of anger and tenderness that comprises her integrity with opposition to androgyny: see Rich's note giving Janice Raymond's essay "The Illusion of Androgyny" as the context for the term *integrity*.

DiBattista's study of Woolf's androgyny depends heavily on Carolyn Heilbrun's *Toward a Recognition of Androgyny* (1973), a source that Rich has renounced in *Of Woman Born* (note, pp. 76–77). Heilbrun reviews the topic in "Androgyny and the Psychology of Sex Differences," in *The Future of Difference*, ed. Hester Eisenstein and Alice Jardine (New Brunswick, N.J.: Rutgers University Press, 1985), pp. 258–66. Rich, however, maintains her position in her comment in *Signs* 9, 4 (Summer 1984): 734. Hence this conceptual division remains in effect.

AFTERWORD

1. For purposes of this discussion, I concentrate on my location by race and gender. A complete cultural analysis would involve a

fuller specification. For example, to define white in more precise ethnic terms, my paternal grandparents both came from Sweden; since my grandmother died before I was born, my contact with this heritage centered on the person of my grandfather, who served as a state representative in Boston, all the while maintaining his barbershop in downtown Worcester, Massachusetts. The ethnic lineage I inherit from my maternal grandparents is a mixture of English, Anglo-Irish, and Irish, the Irish line derived from the working-class forebears who came to the United States during the potato famine of the 1840s. Although I am middle-class both in family of origin and in present circumstances, my education involved traveling such social distance across class gradations that Richard Hoggart's account of the working-class scholarship boy in *The Uses of Literacy* (1957) had a deep resonance. Though my faith is now secular, my religious background is Protestant. Not only am I heterosexual but my daily round is defined by my position as father in a traditional nuclear family of five. Within the boundaries of this identity constellation, my belief in literature as a medium of cultural exchange may seem to place a heavy burden on imaginative faculties. I want to affirm literature's power to fulfill this mediating role; at the same time, I would agree that literature cannot be the sole means of communicating across cultural differences.

2. The essay has been reprinted in *Alice Walker*, ed. Harold Bloom (New York: Chelsea House, 1989), pp. 5–23.

3. Gerald Graff and William E. Cain, "Peace Plan for the Canon Wars," *The Nation*, March 6, 1989, pp. 310–13, and Graff, "Teach the Conflicts," *South Atlantic Quarterly* 89 (1990): 51–67. Graff's proposed solution seems ethereal and sanguine, however, when compared to Hazel V. Carby's incisive analysis of curricular structures in "The Canon: Civil War and Reconstruction," *Michigan Quarterly Review* 28 (1989): 35–43.

4. Diane Ravitch, "Multiculturalism: E Pluribus Plures," *The American Scholar* 59, 3 (Summer 1990): 337–54. By contrast, William Bennett in *Our Children and Our Country* (New York: Simon and Schuster, 1988) simply assumes what is to be proven when he defines common culture as "the things that bind Americans together as one people" (p. 47) and effectively short-circuits serious recognition of conflict and difference.

5. Peter Shaw, "Feminist Literary Criticism: A Report from the Academy," *American Scholar* 57 (1988): 495–513; quotation from p. 508. This article is reprinted in Shaw's *The War against the Intellect: Episodes in the Decline of Discourse* (Iowa City: University of Iowa Press, 1989).

6. Rich speaks of "identity politics" in the foreword to *Blood,*

Bread, and Poetry: Selected Prose, 1979–1985 (New York: Norton, 1986), p. xii.

7. Hazel V. Carby, *Multicultural Fictions,* Occasional Stencilled Paper no. 58 (Birmingham: Centre for Contemporary Cultural Studies, 1980); "Multiculture," *Screen Education* 34 (Spring 1980): 62–70; and "Schooling in Babylon," in Centre for Contemporary Cultural Studies, *The Empire Strikes Back: Race and Racism in 70s Britain* (London: Hutchinson, 1982), pp. 183–211. Jenny Bourne, "Towards an Anti-Racist Feminism," *Race & Class* 25 (1983): 1–22, and "Homelands of the Mind: Jewish Feminism and Identity Politics," *Race & Class* 29 (1987): 1–24. Bourne's comments in the latter on Elly Bulkin, Minnie Bruce Pratt, and Barbara Smith, *Yours in Struggle: Three Feminist Perspectives on Anti-Semitism and Racism* (New York: Long Haul Press, 1984), should be compared with Adrienne Rich's review "Across the Great Divide," *The Village Voice,* May 28, 1985, pp. 57, 60. Interview with June Jordan by Pratibha Parmar, "Other Kinds of Dreams," *Spare Rib,* no. 184 (November 1987): 12–16; June Jordan, "Waiting for a Taxi," *The Progressive* 53, 6 (June 1989): 16–18; and Jordan, "Beyond Gender, Race, and Class" (manuscript).

8. Stuart Hall, "New Ethnicities," in *Black Film, Black Cinema,* ed. Kobena Mercer (London: Institute of Contemporary Arts, 1988), pp. 27–31; quotation from p. 29. Related work by Hall includes "Minimal Selves," in *Identity: The Real Me,* ed. Homi Bhabha (London: Institute of Contemporary Arts, 1987), pp. 44–46; "Images of Commonwealth," *Ten.8: Quarterly Photographic Magazine,* no. 25 (1987): 58–60; "The Mirror or the Lens" and "Prospects," in Noelle Goldman and Stuart Hall, *Pictures of Everyday Life: The People, Places and Cultures of the Commonwealth* (London: Comedia, 1987), pp. 9–15 and 148–51; the interview in *Block* 14 (1988): 11–14; "Cultural Identity and Cinematic Representation," *Framework,* no. 36 (1989): 68–81; and "The Meaning of New Times," in *New Times: The Changing Face of Politics in the 1990s,* ed. Stuart Hall and Martin Jacques (London: Lawrence and Wishart, 1989), pp. 116–34. A survey of recent British material is available in *Identity: Community, Culture, Difference,* ed. Jonathan Rutherford (London: Lawrence and Wishart, 1990). For an American equivalent, see *Out There: Marginalization and Contemporary Cultures,* ed. Russell Ferguson, Martha Gever, Trinh T. Minh-ha, and Cornel West (New York: The New Museum of Contemporary Art; Cambridge: MIT Press, 1990), especially Cornel West's "The New Cultural Politics of Difference," pp. 19–36.

9. On this point see Henry Louis Gates, Jr., "Whose Canon Is It, Anyway?" *The New York Times Book Review,* February 26, 1989, pp. 1, 44–45, and John Guillory, "Canonical and Non-Canonical: A Cri-

tique of the Current Debate," *English Literary History* 54 (1987): 483–527.

10. Alvin Kernan, "Criticism as Theodicy: The Institutional Role of Literary Criticism," *Yale Review* 77, 1 (Autumn 1987): 86–102; quotations from pp. 101 and 99. See also my review of Kernan's *The Death of Literature* in *Criticism* 33 (1991): 263–65.

Index

Compositor: Braun-Brumfield, Inc.
Text: 10/12 Palatino
Display: Palatino
Printer: Braun-Brumfield, Inc.
Binder: Braun-Brumfield, Inc.